Luminos is the Open Access monograph publishing program
from UC Press. Luminos provides a framework for preserving and
reinvigorating monograph publishing for the future and increases
the reach and visibility of important scholarly work. Titles published
in the UC Press Luminos model are published with the same high
standards for selection, peer review, production, and marketing as
those in our traditional program. www.luminosoa.org

Immunity on Trial

Immunity on Trial

Ethiopian Courts, Chinese Corporations,
and Contestations over Sovereignty

———

Miriam Driessen

UNIVERSITY OF CALIFORNIA PRESS

University of California Press
Oakland, California

Suggested citation: Driessen, M. *Immunity on Trial: Ethiopian Courts,
Chinese Corporations, and Contestations over Sovereignty*. Oakland: University
of California Press, 2026. DOI: https://doi.org/10.1525/luminos.263

Library of Congress Cataloging-in-Publication Data

Names: Driessen, Miriam, 1985–author
Title: Immunity on trial : Ethiopian courts, Chinese corporations,
    and contestations over sovereignty / Miriam Driessen.
Description: First edition. | Oakland, California : University of
    California Press, [2026] | Includes bibliographical references and index.
Identifiers: LCCN 2025034136 (print) | LCCN 2025034137 (ebook) |
    ISBN 9780520425453 cloth | ISBN 9780520421295 paperback |
    ISBN 9780520421301 ebook
Subjects: LCSH: Privileges and immunities—Ethiopia |
    Immunities of foreign states—Ethiopia | Corporations, Foreign—
    Law and legislation—Ethiopia | Corporations, Chinese—Ethiopia |
    Corporate power—Ethiopia | Courts—Ethiopia | Equality before the law—
    Ethiopia
Classification: LCC KRP3838 .D75 2026 (print) | LCC KRP3838 (ebook) |
    DDC 346.63/066—dc23/eng/20250903

LC record available at https://lccn.loc.gov/2025034136
LC ebook record available at https://lccn.loc.gov/2025034137

GPSR Authorized Representative: Easy Access System Europe,
Mustamäe tee 50, 10621 Tallinn, Estonia, gpsr.requests@easproject.com

35   34   33   32   31   30   29   28   27   26
10   9   8   7   6   5   4   3   2   1

CONTENTS

MAPS

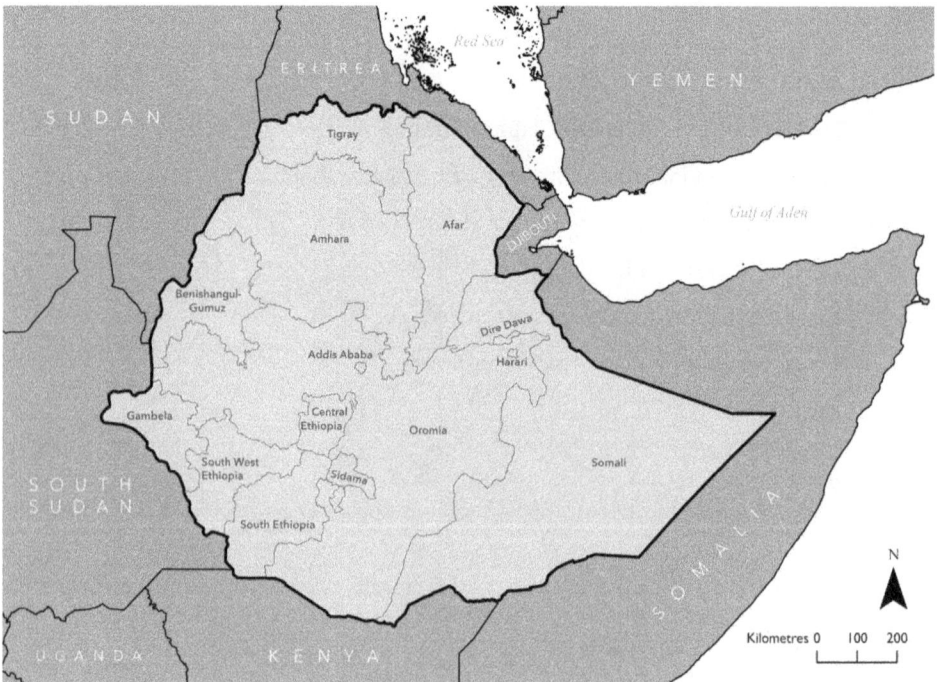

MAP 1. Map of Ethiopia. (Boundary data credit: United Nations Office for the Coordination of Humanitarian Affairs (UNOCHA), CC BY-IGO, Deed—Attribution 4.0 International—Creative Commons.)

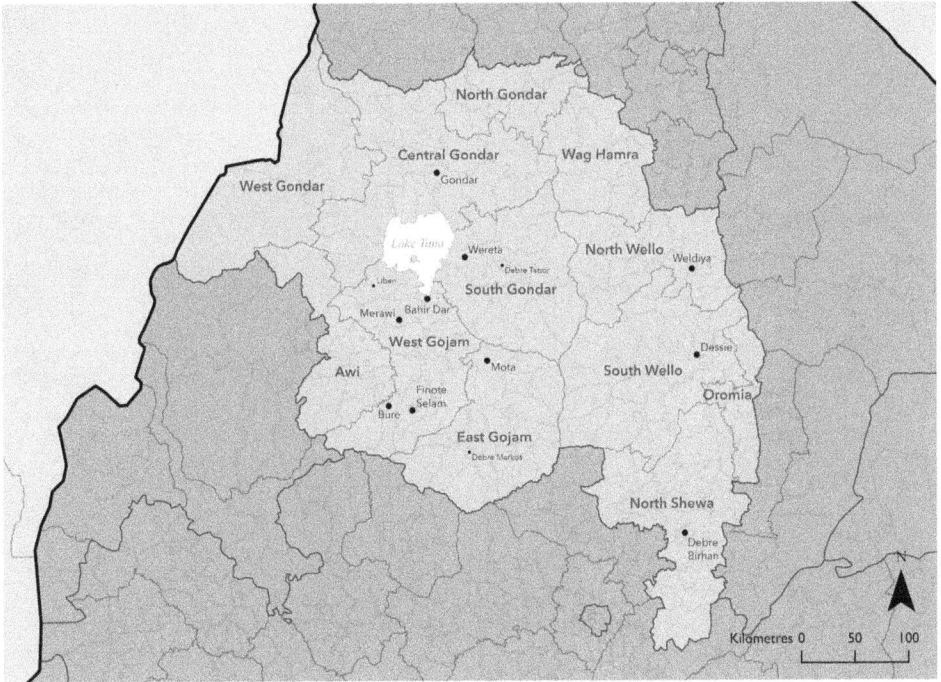

MAP 2. Map of Amhara. (Boundary data credit: UNOCHA, CC BY-IGO, Deed—Attribution 4.0 International—Creative Commons.)

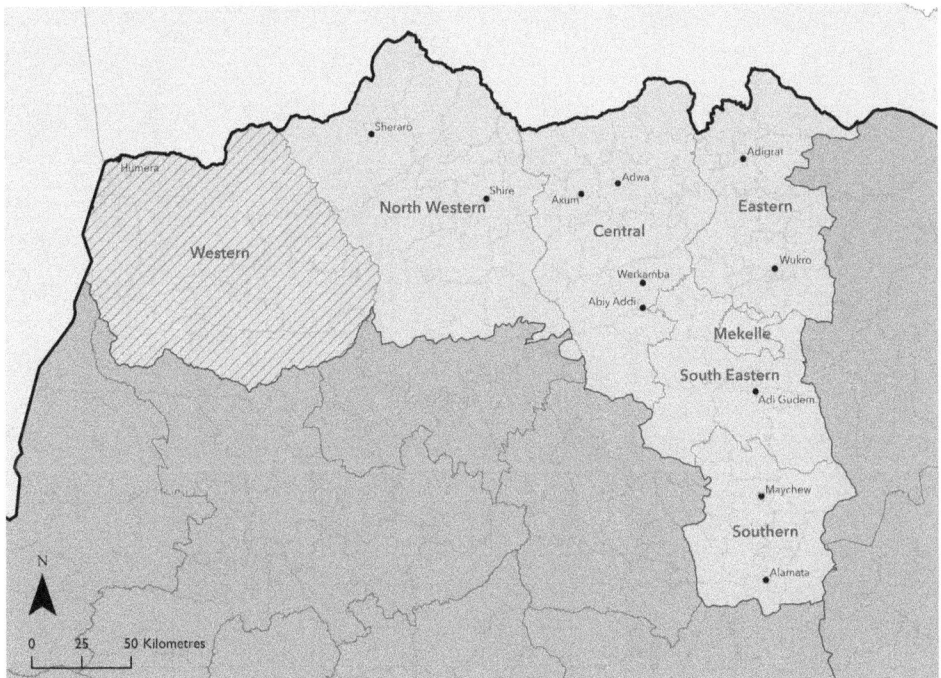

MAP 3. Map of Tigray. Note: apart from the major cities and towns, the map also shows the contested Western region of Tigray. (Boundary data credit: UNOCHA, CC BY-IGO, Deed—Attribution 4.0 International—Creative Commons.)

Introduction

Everyone had retreated to rest in the scarce shade when Benli Li mounted a loader parked on the construction site.[1] He was bantering with an Ethiopian laborer under his direction and dared him to step into the machine's bucket. The worker complied, perhaps hesitant to go against his expatriate manager's request or eager to prove his courage. The Chinese foreman ignited the engine. The machine shot forward. Within moments, the young man lost his balance and landed on the ground. Unable to bring the machine to a halt, Li drove over him.

On July 24, 2016, the Supreme Court of Amhara, Ethiopia, summonsed the twenty-six-year-old site supervisor to a hearing of its mobile bench at Debre Tabor, a mountain town in South Gondar. The state prosecutor demanded a prison sentence, charging Li with homicide caused by severe negligence.[2]

Li, however, did not appear, and the local police failed to find him.

Months went by before the court arranged a new hearing.

Yet again, the police officers of Farta Wereda, the rural county in which the incident occurred, visited the Chinese camp and returned empty-handed. They requested another adjournment. "This time," they wrote in their note to the Supreme Court, "we promise that we will bring him to court."[3]

They failed yet again.

As procedure requires, the court then turned to the national press agency. It placed a public summons in the English-language newspaper *The Ethiopian Herald* and its Amharic counterpart *Addis Zemen*, calling Li to attend court on January 27, 2017. Should he fail to turn up, the papers said, the court would conduct the proceedings in absentia.

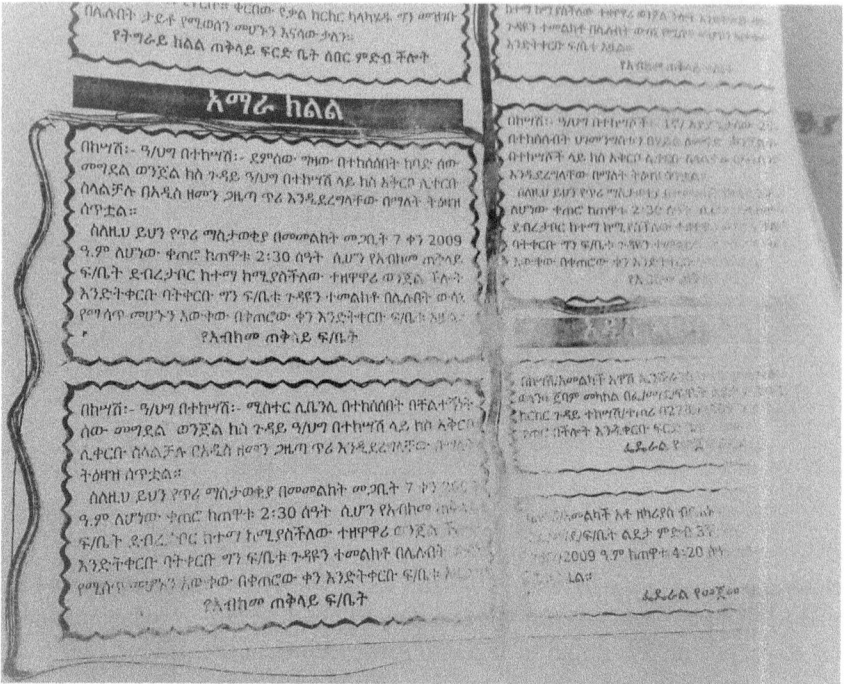

FIGURE 1. Copy of newspaper clipping of Benli Li's public summons (bottom left) in *Addis Zemen*.

Having received no word from Li or anyone who knew his whereabouts, the court went ahead with the trial. Forgoing defense, Benli Li was convicted of homicide by negligence on July 24, 2018. The bench considered the fact that he had no criminal record as a mitigating circumstance and sentenced the foreman to four years and five months in prison. It ordered the South Gondar Police Department to arrest him.

Li, however, had since disappeared. His company had stepped in, bailed him out, and put him on the first flight back to China.[4]

IMMUNITY

This case left me, as it might leave you, with many questions. Why did neither Li nor his Chinese employer cooperate with the prosecution proceedings? Why was the foreman granted bail in a situation in which the right to bail was questionable?[5] How did he subsequently manage to leave the country? Why were the police unable to arrest Li and bring him to trial? And why did the judiciary persist in seeing through the proceedings while knowing the accused had long left the country? Benli Li's fate, I found, would have been radically different were he an Ethiopian foreman. Neither he nor his company would have been able to refuse cooperation. Even if he had someone to cover the fees for a bond or could cobble these together himself, he might not have been granted bail. And where would he go, were he to take to his heels? Would he have dared to ignore the court summons or defy police orders? But Li was a Chinese national. His association with a powerful country—one that extends loans to Ethiopia, carries out infrastructure projects, and fuels the nascent manufacturing industry—put him in a radically different position.

At once surprising and expected, the episode of Benli Li leads us to the central theme of this book: immunity. Global hierarchies and the material inequalities on which they are founded create situations in which some parties enjoy exemption from legal process or can command such an exemption, as in the case of Li. Yet how do such exemptions come about? And why?

Best known as a biomedical concept, immunity describes the condition of being resistant to a particular infectious disease or pathogen—a bacterium, virus, or other microorganism that can cause a disease.[6] Immunity in the legal or political sense means being exonerated from or able to avoid legal process and prosecution.[7] Whereas the condition of immunity in biology can be developed naturally through exposure, political and legal immunity is typically either awarded by a sovereign—a national government or a supranational organization like the United Nations—or agreed upon in commercial contracts that govern cross-border economic transactions. In the former case, the 1961 *Vienna Convention on Diplomatic Relations*, for example, extends immunity to diplomats, and the 1946 *Convention on the Privileges and Immunities of the United Nations* to UN representatives and employees. In the latter case, the commercial exception to foreign sovereign immunity,[8] implemented through governing law clauses, waives the immunity of a state when it is a party to a private commercial contract, such as a loan agreement.[9] Of course, the distinction between the public and private nature of a state's transactions is rarely unambiguous, as some scholars caution and popular debates about sovereignty and its protection testify.[10]

Traditionally, immunity is justified by the assumption that certain social and political aims outweigh the value of imposing liability. The nature of these aims, however, remains undefined and can in practice be contested. To be exempt from the rules, by law and in practice, is a privilege granted to the powerful or, in the case of Li and other protagonists in this book, representatives of powerful entities. Immunity, then, is created by global inequalities. The structural disparities that underpin it can turn immunity into an unjust prerogative. Indeed, critics of immunity liken immunity to impunity—the freedom from punishment or the negative consequences of one's actions.

Carl Schmitt, German political theorist and Nazi sympathizer, once posited that the sovereign not only sets the rules but, more importantly, also determines the exemptions from these rules: the state of exception.[11] The omnipotent sovereign to which Schmitt and his predecessor enlightenment thinker Thomas Hobbes,[12] as well as subsequent political theorists and philosophers such as Giorgio Agamben, refer, however, exists mostly in theory.[13] In practice, as anthropologists have illuminated, sovereignty is compromised,[14] contested,[15] graduated,[16] divided,[17] distributed,[18] layered,[19] and nested.[20] The state of exception, then, is negotiated as much as it is imposed.

Set against the backdrop of an extraordinary wave of litigation against Chinese corporations in Ethiopia, *Immunity on Trial* probes the question of immunity in everyday encounters steeped in highly asymmetrical power relations. First, it shows how structures of inequality engender immunity. Second, it demonstrates how immunity is debated and negated or generated in the process by those who *fight, exact, grant,* or *weigh* immunity: Ethiopian plaintiffs who seek to hold their expatriate employer liable while criticizing the state for failing its citizens, Chinese defendants who justify claims to immunity, government officials who surrender part of their sovereignty with an eye to spurring development, and judges who at times resist and at other times extend requests to immunity, as they weigh arguments for and against it.

The book unearths how exceptions and exemptions from the rules are produced and questioned, justified and delegitimized, affirmed and dismantled. In Ethiopia, state courts have become critical forums in which immunity is debated, and their judges are animated commentators in national debates on immunity. The bench's determination to render a verdict and serve justice does not always pay off, as the episode of Benli Li dramatically demonstrates. In other instances, however, they have been remarkably successful.

IMMUNITY VERSUS SOVEREIGNTY

Ethiopian judges often smiled when remembering their first encounters with Chinese litigants. They recalled Chinese enterprise managers saying "We're not litigating this case,"[21] "We were invited [to Ethiopia] by the government. We should not have to go to court,"[22] and "We're investors. We deserve special treatment."[23] The Chinese parties who came to their courts were uncooperative at best. In fact, many had initially refused to attend court, binning or tearing up court summonses. In court, some Chinese litigants had walked up to the judges, interrupted them, made a scene, or walked out, accusing the court of interrupting activities that were crucial to the country's development. Over time, however, judges managed to rein in rebellious and resistant expatriate managers. Even so, establishing authority and enacting jurisdiction remained works-in-progress.

Judges described the above scenarios variously as claims to immunity, administrative complaints, displays of disrespect, or attempts to circumvent the legal system. I refer to them as claims of immunity—not in the strict legal sense[24] but, more broadly, to include informal and extralegal requests to be exempted from legal process and prosecution. Expatriate enterprise managers rarely articulated their claims in formal statements of response, aware as they were that they did not enjoy immunity by law.[25] If their claims were not accepted in the courtroom, they brought them to the court president, the mayor, the regional president, or, if the stakes were high enough, the prime minister's office.

Framing their activities as a gift for which they expected something in return, whether in the form of gratitude or legal leeway, many Chinese corporate representatives believed they ought to be exonerated from liability and felt wronged when their requests were disregarded. Gifts, as Marcel Mauss observed, demand reciprocation.[26] Development assistance, in the managers' eyes, amounted to a social value that equaled or surpassed the value of imposing liability.

In contrast, Ethiopian legal professionals, much like Mauss, pointed to the self-interest wrapped up in these supposed gifts.[27] Chinese companies earn millions of US dollars in Ethiopia, while loans boost China's geopolitical leverage. Judges saw their flat refusal to submit to national jurisdiction as more than a nuisance or an impediment to legal procedure. They put respect for the law on par with respect for the country and its people, as late Prime Minister Meles Zenawi once did when he compared a foreigner who breaks the law to a man who rapes a woman.[28] Just as a rapist inflicts severe harm on a victim, a foreign national who disrespects the law desecrates the integrity of the country. Meles likened disrespecting the law to the intrusion in a body or, in this case, a body politic.[29]

CONTESTATIONS OVER JURISDICTION

Ethiopian judges took it upon themselves to demarcate the contours of their jurisdiction—contours that were rendered unstable by disputants' subversive practices. They sought to retain authority over disputes that foreign parties hoped to see settled through informal negotiation, mediation behind the closed doors of the embassy, or international arbitration. By so doing, they expanded and solidified their jurisdiction. The jurisdictional tensions between insistent judges and contrarian litigants that emerged from contested claims of immunity thus show that jurisdictions can be indeterminate and malleable. Unsolicited claims of immunity and judges' attempts to resist them raise fundamental questions about the nature of jurisdictions and their reach.

Shaunnagh Dorsett and Shaun McVeigh describe jurisdiction as "the practice of pronouncing the law."[30] Pointing to the concept's Latin roots—*ius* (law) and *dicere* (speak)[31]—they posit that jurisdiction inaugurates the law while determining its limits. Building on this idea, Justin Richland depicts the establishment of jurisdiction as "metadiscursive moments"[32] in which the courts or other governmental institutions "pose the question of their own authority to themselves."[33] Yet speaking to itself is not enough to convey or exert authority. To effectively speak itself into being, jurisdiction and its guardians require an audience.[34] They aspire to be heard by complacent *and* non-complacent subjects to institute themselves and retain effective operation.

As this book elucidates, jurisdictions should not be taken for granted, even though they often are.[35] They emerge from jurisdictional conflicts, arising from different interests in and perceptions of local and global legal orders, and are questioned by them.[36] Few parties, I show, challenge jurisdiction's sway as much as foreign enterprises and citizens from powerful countries, whether they come from China, the United States, or elsewhere. Through their outright refusal to acknowledge and submit to national or regional jurisdictions, they can pose an existential threat to judicial and, by extension, sovereign power.

SAFEGUARDING SOVEREIGNTY, PAST AND PRESENT

Concerns about sovereignty and contestations over jurisdiction hark back to the imperial era, when Ethiopia was better known as the Abyssinian Empire. Fears about the loss of sovereignty, accompanied by a persistence to fight for it, reached a height during the Scramble for Africa between 1885 and 1914, when European colonial powers carved the continent up among themselves. In 1896, Abyssinia secured a victory over the Italian army,[37] stalling European colonial ambitions on its territory, although not for long. Threats to Ethiopian sovereignty lasted well into the twentieth century, as chapter 1 chronicles.

When Ethiopia first received foreign aid in the 1950s, it did so as a sovereign state, in contrast with its African neighbors.[38] Emperor Haile Selassie managed, by and large, to retain ownership and control of his policy agenda, arguably more so than other African leaders. So did successive Ethiopian governments.[39] Initially low, aid levels began to rise in the mid-1990s after the establishment of the Federal Democratic Republic of Ethiopia (FDRE). The formation of, first, the transitional government (1991–95) and, later, the government led by the Ethiopian People's Revolutionary Democratic Front (EPRDF; 1995–2019)[40] was overseen by Western governments and supranational institutions.[41] However, throughout the 1990s and 2000s, Western donors proved at once demanding and unreliable partners, calling for privatization and austerity and suspending aid whenever they disagreed with the course of Ethiopian domestic politics.[42]

Meles Zenawi, however, stood his ground in heated disputes with the International Monetary Fund (IMF) over aid expenditure, early loan repayment, and market liberalization.[43] He insisted on retaining state ownership in the agricultural,[44] financial, and telecommunications sectors,[45] his confidence undoubtedly boosted by Ethiopia's close diplomatic partner, China. Facing comparable pressures, China, too, had opted for partial liberalization when it transitioned from a planned to a market economy in the 1980s and 1990s, deftly defying Bretton Woods's directives. China's moral, political, and financial support bolstered Ethiopia's leverage against paternalizing and, at times, patronizing Western institutions and countries.[46]

All the while, from the late 1990s through to the 2010s, China upturned Ethiopia's aid and development landscape. Its building contractors constructed a large share of federal infrastructure,[47] from roads to fiber-optic cables;[48] its intrepid investors became frontrunners in a budding manufacturing industry;[49] and its entrepreneurs in trade and hospitality increasingly found profitable niches[50] despite restrictive government policies.

Although welcomed, the growing Chinese presence also raised renewed concerns about dependence—concerns that were taken into the courtroom. This unease was, however, not about the recognition of sovereignty per se. Few, if any, would deny that Ethiopia is a sovereign state. If sovereignty is at stake, it is the country's *internal* sovereignty, which is challenged by ethnic strife and fragmentation. Instead, at issue is the acknowledgment of external sovereignty in *deeds* apart from *words*, entailing respect for national jurisdiction, local laws, and state authorities.

Words were often empty, not just those of Chinese actors but also those of their Western counterparts. Indeed, more recently, US sanctions in response to the atrocities committed in the Tigray War gave rise to popular disquiet and distress about sovereignty. In 2021, thousands of Addis Ababans took to the streets, chanting slogans and carrying billboards with phrases like "Ethiopia doesn't need a babysitter." While most news outlets referred to the generic "foreign forces" infringing on Ethiopian sovereignty, the protesters were more explicit, comparing the chokehold that led to George Floyd's death at the hands of US police with the pressure imposed on Ethiopia by Western countries. Through a rally called "Voices of Freedom and Sovereignty" and a social media campaign with the hashtag #HandsOffEthiopia—an explicit reference to the global movement galvanized by the slogan "Hands Off Ethiopia" in response to the brutal Italian invasion of 1936[51]—the organizers spurred popular sentiment against foreign interventions in Ethiopia's internal affairs.[52]

The Chinese government, meanwhile, pursued a noninterventionist approach, upholding its long-standing commitment to refrain from interfering in the internal affairs of other countries.[53] At the time, diplomatic relations between China and Ethiopia—which had been strained after Abiy Ahmed took office in 2018, denouncing not only the EPRDF establishment but also its Chinese allies—were improving. The opposition had long accused EPRDF officials of engaging in nefarious alliances with local state firms and Chinese enterprises. The attitudes of ordinary Ethiopians toward China during the twenty-seven years of EPRDF rule had been ambiguous. Those to whom I spoke during fieldwork in 2011, 2012, and 2017 were grateful for China's contribution to developing the country's infrastructure network and bolstering its manufacturing industry. Yet they were equally aware of the new dependencies the Chinese presence generated.[54] During this period, the foreign force to be reckoned with was China.

To be sure, I do not wish to make a case for Chinese exceptionalism. American, British, German, Turkish, and Indian companies, along with their managers, also test the boundaries of jurisdiction as they seek exemptions from legal processes and prosecution. The strategies they employ and the attitudes they exhibit are comparable. The dynamics described in the book, then, apply to all corporate actors. However, given the unprecedented involvement of Chinese actors in Ethiopia, it was they who frequented the court and raised the question of immunity most often.

RIGHTS OR DIGNITY?

"If a foreign company beats us when giving us bread, we rather lose our bread than lose our dignity," late Ethiopian Prime Minister Meles Zenawi allegedly remarked in the aftermath of a dispute on a Chinese-run construction site.[55] The incident began as a quarrel between a Chinese supervisor and an Ethiopian laborer and escalated when the former beat the latter, evolving into a fistfight between the parties and bystanders, eventually causing a nationwide outcry. Meles, an advocate of closer ties with China when he was in office,[56] was well aware of the country's growing dependence on Chinese capital. In his statement, he deployed the metaphor of bread as a source of livelihood to allude to the indispensability of its contribution to the Ethiopian economy. Yet an assault on a worker's dignity was the red line. The prime minister ordered the project be suspended until the Chinese company's representatives issued an apology.

The seasoned Ethiopian leader drew a parallel between the humiliation of an individual worker and the humiliation of a country. Note his use of the pronoun "us." His interpretation of dignity as a *collective* good resonates with grievances expressed by Ethiopian plaintiffs who brought cases against Chinese corporations. Many went to court to restore not just their self-worth but also the worth of a collective, be it their colleagues, the community, or the country.

Dignity, a delicate subject, was intricately linked to self-determination.[57] Many Ethiopians I talked to likened and linked threats to collective dignity to past instances of national humiliation and spoke to a collective sense of being Ethiopian, which is intimately connected to profound yet precarious pride in the country's sovereign past.[58] Aware of popular sentiments, Meles's decision to suspend the Chinese project and, more importantly, announce it in public was a performative strategy. It showed that the government cared about its people.[59] Ironically, however, it was the EPRDF, the ruling coalition between 1991 and 2018, and its leading party, the Tigray People's Liberation Front (TPLF), that were criticized for selling Ethiopia out to foreign investors at the cost of their own citizens. More recently, the administration of Abiy Ahmed has also come under fire for failing its citizens. State and corporate interests and visions continue to converge, requiring citizens to pay the price for development—a price paid not just in labor but also in dignity.[60]

Ethiopian workers described assaults on dignity as the denial of voice, the denial of face, and the denial of humanity (see chapter 2). In portraying the relationship between expatriate employers and themselves as akin to that between master and servant or jailor and prisoner, they exposed the stark power imbalances, deepened by racial inequality that enabled expatriate managers to make their own laws, disregarding both the sovereignty of the host country and the dignity of its people. The imagery of the servant or prisoner evokes this loss of human worth: The slave and the inmate are stripped of agency, their voice and will silenced. "They want you to wash their feet," a mechanic who had sued his former Chinese employer for unlawful dismissal remarked,[61] alluding to the traditional Ethiopian practice of foot-washing, in which women, children, or servants washed the feet of senior family members and guests. More than a gesture of conviviality and hospitality, the practice symbolizes steep hierarchical relations.[62] For him, washing the feet of a foreign employer was not merely demeaning. It was an affront to his dignity and that of his Ethiopian coworkers.

Plaintiffs' understandings of dignity defy the individualist foundation given to it by Greek philosopher Cicero and German enlightenment thinker Immanuel Kant. The former contended that all humans are endowed with *dignitas* and worthy of respect for the sole fact of their existence,[63] the latter that humanity is an end in itself and bears no price. Like Cicero, Kant associated his anti-utilitarian and anti-authoritarian interpretation of dignity with the idea of human capacity, rooted in the faculty of reason to act morally.[64] My interlocutors and I, however, show that dignity is intrinsically collective and affective rather than individual and rational.[65] The worth of a person or group requires an audience that acknowledges it. Furthermore, as black writers from Frantz Fanon to James Baldwin have poignantly emphasized,[66] dignity is transactional: Those who infringe on the dignity of others elevate their own status at the expense of others.

By demanding dignity, as Miguel Pérez intimates, people seek to "reframe the terms of their participation in society as ethical-political subjects."[67] If contentions over dignity and its assertion concern at least two parties—those who give and who receive dignity, and those who deny and are denied dignity—they reframe the subjectivities of both. By going to court, Ethiopian plaintiffs seek justice by negotiating the terms not just of their own participation in society but also of their opponent: foreign corporations. Through legal action, they question the privileges enterprises enjoy and the injustices to which these give birth. They moreover propose the obligations for which Chinese multinationals ought to be liable and condemn the state for failing to hold them to account. By so doing, they redefine not just their own subject position but also that of the counterparty and the state.

OF INTERVENTIONS, INVITATIONS, AND EVERYTHING IN BETWEEN

Powerful states, Stephen Krasner propounds in his critique of sovereignty, can coerce weaker states into accepting the intervention of external authority structures,[68] while the governments of weaker states may choose to issue invitations by making strategic concessions to sovereignty in return for financial benefits or political leverage.[69] Ethiopia's dependence on international creditors renders it vulnerable to interventions. It also puts the country in a position in which it is more likely to extend invitations with an eye to opening opportunities for foreign funding that can be used for nation-building activities that,[70] paradoxically, bolster its sovereignty.[71] Through both *intervention* and *invitation*, powerful states can obtain immunity, even if, as I show, the two often overlap.

The dynamics of intervention and invitation do not merely play out in the higher echelons of power. They equally crystallize in disputes on the ground, perhaps more acutely so. Whenever the stakes are high, such as in criminal cases that threaten to tarnish the reputation of the Chinese community and in civil cases concerning considerable claims, interventions are common. As I discuss in chapters 1 and 4, interventions take the form of unannounced visits to the court president or presiding judge by Chinese managers or letters penned by their embassy. Concurring with expatriate managers that the law ought not stand in the way of development, Ethiopian government officials regularly turn interventions into invitations through a phone call to the court, demanding the case be suspended or closed. This is not to say that judges give in to state functionaries. On the contrary, they collectively and effectively resist claims of immunity, whether requested by Chinese corporate managers or granted by the state—not to mention the fact that the sheer number of lawsuits against Chinese corporations has made interventions in each case, or even a small percentage of them, impossible.[72]

Inspired by anthropologists of sovereignty, I approach immunity as a relational concept.[73] Sovereignty, in the words of Jean Dennison, is "an inescapable web of negotiation, contention, and concession that leads to further entanglement."[74] Immunity, too, emerges from constant bargaining. What is more, states are fragmented and their representatives divided. As Daniel Mulugeta illustrates in his work on the everyday state in Africa, state functionaries pursue diverse aims, given their distinct positions within the government apparatus on top of their personal views, social backgrounds, and career trajectories.[75] Even if most judges sought to resist requests for immunity and enact their jurisdiction, thus displaying a collective goal or consciousness, they expressed contrasting perspectives on the regulation of Chinese capital and its adverse effects. As I discuss in chapter 6, left-leaning judges tended to rule in favor of Ethiopian plaintiffs, whereas their right-leaning colleagues were more sympathetic toward Chinese defendants. Furthermore, negotiating immunity inside and outside the courtroom was, like enacting sovereignty, an unfinished project.[76] The arrival of new Chinese enterprises and uninformed managers forced judges to continuously assert their authority and jurisdiction anew.

LOCAL COURTS AS GLOBAL ACTORS

By exploring how geopolitics enters the courtroom, this book picks up on two calls. The first is Eve Darian-Smith's suggestion to connect local and international legal arenas and scrutinize their dynamic interactions;[77] the second is Sara Dezalay and Sharon Weill's proposal to study lower courts as global actors.[78] Nation-states are never discrete legal units operating within international and transnational domains. Rather, as Darian-Smith argues, they are enmeshed in myriad subnational and supranational legal relationships that cut across geographical borders.[79] To grasp the interplay between legal arenas at various scales, she suggests adopting a global socio-legal perspective of method and analysis.[80] I seek to decenter the nation-state by examining how global legal, financial, and political forces destabilize national sovereignty through contestations over immunity.

National courts have emerged as brokers of sovereignty. Lower courts, Weill shows in her study of French criminal courts, increasingly hear transnational disputes on issues such as international terrorism.[81] Operating in a space that is more independent from the higher echelons of executive power, lower courts are better positioned to promote certain political views and resist state policies. As such, they can influence international processes and the regulations that govern them. Ethiopian disputants who, en masse, sue Chinese corporations have similarly transformed Ethiopian lower courts into global actors. Thanks to thousands of petitioners, judges have become public commentators on local *and* global matters. Indeed, without disputes to adjudicate, judges remain mute.

Scholarship on conflict resolution in Chinese engagement with Africa and beyond has thus far fixated on international and transnational law.[82] However, few disputes are resolved through diplomatic negotiation.[83] Even fewer end up in international arbitration.[84] Domestic arbitration is gaining popularity, but the number of cases brought to the Chamber of Commerce in Addis Ababa[85] or solved in ad hoc arbitration tribunals is negligible compared with the number of court cases.[86] Keen to attract foreign investment, the Abiy administration has strengthened the regulation of domestic and international commercial arbitration. Following the country's 2020 ratification of the *New York Arbitration Convention*,[87] Ethiopian legislators developed a legal framework governing the conduct of arbitral proceedings and the enforcement of arbitral awards.[88] However, the promotion of arbitration by the government and its embrace by elite lawyers as "the best option"[89] deflect attention from the fact that most legal complaints are brought to national courts and pertain to state law. If fast and effective, as lawyers insist, arbitration is also costly. Few Ethiopian claimants can or want to bear the cost of arbitration, especially when there is a viable alternative: litigation. Few contracts between Chinese and Ethiopian parties contain an arbitration clause. If they do, the parties sometimes ignore the clause and take legal action instead, or they turn to court when dissatisfied with an arbitral award. In recent years, however, Chinese companies have begun to embrace arbitration. What the effect of this will be remains to be seen.

In sum, a broad spectrum of cases ends up in state courts, from labor disputes to family cases, and from land-based conflicts to contractual disputes. Yet, how does geopolitics enter the courtroom alongside petitioners?[90] As local manifestations of geopolitical tensions, disputes in Ethiopian–Chinese encounters seldom concern only the Ethiopian plaintiff and the Chinese respondent or, more rarely, the Chinese plaintiff and the Ethiopian respondent. The disputants do not present just their side of the story to pursue individual claims. Their side of the story represents a political position in the relationship of the two countries and addresses the structural inequalities between them. Put differently, they embody abstract concepts, such as the nation, and their conflicts are taken to signal geopolitical friction.

The plaintiffs I talked to experienced grievances collectively, even when they filed legal complaints individually. The individual and the collective prevalent in narratives of litigation and courtroom conversations is perhaps epitomized by the frequent confusion about the foreign opponent's name and status. Some Ethiopian plaintiffs wrote "China" as the respondent, directed their claim to "CC" or "CCC" instead of "CCCC" (China Communications Construction Company), or sued the wrong Chinese corporation. Rather than dismissing these slippages as mere ignorance, I see them as symptomatic of how Ethiopian disputants perceive the counterparty.

By going to court, petitioners sought to warn, critique, condemn, challenge, and occasionally vilify not just a single company but also a phenomenon—structural injustice derived from structural inequality—or a larger entity: the Chinese community or foreign capital more broadly. The homogenization of Chinese actors was most pronounced among those who did not directly interact with Chinese managers, such as plaintiffs in extracontractual cases. Those who were in close contact with Chinese individuals, of course, could pinpoint differences among enterprise managers and companies. Even so, they, too, often addressed "the Chinese" as an aggregate, a single actor.[91]

Derek Sheridan proposes that we draw a metaphorical connection between interpersonal and international relations to understand the ethics of everyday interactions in which global inequalities are negotiated. Material disparities, he argues, both precede and shape the experience of interpersonal relationships: "'China' does not 'meet' 'Africa,' in other words, because Chinese and Africans have already been interconnected, even if indirectly, through mutual participation in the global economy."[92] This global economy has tied Ethiopia to China and Ethiopians to Chinese in relations of debt (or credit), shaping expectations of the other and views about them. Global inequalities also underwrite conflicts and can have a constraining effect, as Cheryl Mei-ting Schmitz shows in her discussion of a labor dispute between an Angolan worker and his Chinese managers.[93] The material inequalities imbued in Afro–Chinese encounters stand in the way of compassion, impeding the resolution of tensions among actors, even if they are prepared to tackle them.

Tensions that lingered under the surface at the workplace or in business transactions were spelled out at trial, rendering the courtroom a contentious and confrontational space. Lawsuits brought global inequalities into plain sight.

Meanwhile, the judges charged with adjudicating Ethiopian–Chinese disputes became arbitrators not just of the conflicts between the disputants in front of them but also of political and social dynamics outside the courtroom. Litigants and animated observers viewed their judgments as commentaries on the position of Chinese corporations—or "China"—in Ethiopian society.

As I will explain in chapter 4, judges enjoy vast discretion in cross-cultural dispute resolution. When disputing parties do not have a language in common and are unfamiliar with one another's social practices and cultural codes, the court provides a critical avenue for communication and interpretation. It facilitates and, at times, establishes communication between parties that rarely talk to one another or are hesitant to do so due to structural barriers of power and inequality. Their discretion to fill communication gaps further solidifies their role as mediators and commentators who tie local to global issues. Their discretionary power, moreover, enables them to shape the subject positions of disputing parties and the power dynamics between them—provided, of course, they prevent them from being taken out of court.

Like other multinational corporations,[94] Chinese firms seek to "lift" disputes out of the context in which they originate to reach a settlement behind the closed doors of the embassy or international arbitration chambers. It is feared that public trials fuel social discontent and "cause trouble," as Chinese managers euphemistically put it. Creating a distance between the location of a dispute and its resolution is part of a broader strategy that Hannah Appel powerfully describes in her work on the oil and gas industry in Equatorial Guinea to disentangle the corporation from the social environment in which it is embedded.[95] By so doing, corporations seek to minimize regulation, manage risk, disperse liability, and, ultimately, protect profit.[96] Chinese firms also use other practices that generate the same effect, such as founding multiple subsidiary companies and separating headquarters from the operation and finance locations.[97] The multilayered contracts that order these arrangements complicate the calculus of obligation, risk, and responsibility, as Suzana Sawyer shows in her discussion of a lawsuit initiated by Ecuadorian plaintiffs against the US oil giant Chevron.[98]

An added complexity in the context of Chinese firms' involvement in the Ethiopian infrastructure sector is the illicit nature of certain corporate relations. Some contracts signed between Chinese contractors and Chinese subcontracting firms are not endorsed by the Ethiopian client (for example, the Ethiopian Roads Authority and Ethiopian Railway Corporation)—which is a contractual requirement—and are effectively void.[99] These arrangements further obfuscate the corporate form. Unknowingly, Ethiopian claimants consistently sued Chinese subcontracting firms that lacked legal personality. However, the courts did not require the submission of a business license unless the issue was brought up as a preliminary objection. It rarely was, as the Chinese subcontractor did not want its unlawful practices to come to light or to jeopardize its relationship with the contractor. As a result, Ethiopian claimants could obtain a court victory even against paperless Chinese enterprises.

The opportunities for jurisdictional jockeying that multilayered contracts, whether legal or illegal, create often play to the advantage of wealthy corporations with the resources to hire large legal teams. However, due to social, cultural, and linguistic barriers, the corporate "haves" did not necessarily come out ahead in Ethiopia against local "have-nots," as I will elaborate on in chapter 2.[100] Indeed, the court cases relayed in the book reveal the limits of "offshoring"—if the offshore is taken as a metaphor, a set of corporate strategies instead of a spatial configuration.[101] While Chinese firms seek to "thin out" liability, communities in Ethiopia effectively "thicken" liability by preventing disputes from being lifted out of the country and holding enterprises responsible for corporate practices, including labor management, public relations, and environmental practices. Put differently, litigants and judges alike "onshore" the corporation. They resist corporate strategies of distancing and disentangling by re-embedding the corporation in the local community. Combined, the processes of offshoring and onshoring illustrate the dynamic interactions between local and global forces and legal arenas.

FROM THE BOARDROOM TO THE COURTROOM

On January 25, 2020, the day before I set off north from Addis Ababa to visit a Chinese camp in southern Tigray, I received a phone call. China was engrossed by an unknown virus, and Chinese state firms had received firm directions from Beijing. My host could no longer welcome me. Unaware of what this virus was or how deadly it would be, I decided to travel anyway and disembarked not in Raya, as planned, but at the final bus stop in Mekelle. I spent the subsequent seven months there as the global Covid-19 crisis unfolded.[102] The coronavirus reached Addis Ababa in March. The first case in Mekelle was detected only in May 2020, when the city had eased what was popularly known as its "Chinese-style" lockdown. Fear had long since abated.

In Ethiopia, as in many other sub-Saharan African countries, the virus would not have the devastating effect it had in other parts of the world. A running joke had it that China, as always, sent a low-quality variant to Africa, while Europe and North America received the high-quality virus. The punchline referred to the shoddy made-in-China commodities sent to Africa and sold across the continent.[103] As early as August 2020, people to whom I spoke averred that Ethiopia had dodged the virus. Life returned to normal.

Around this time, political tensions in Mekelle escalated in the run-up to the controversial Tigray elections. While national elections scheduled for August had been called off due to the coronavirus, the Tigray government insisted on allowing people a vote, citing respect for the constitution.[104] The defiant region went ahead with elections. Fearing unrest in the northernmost region, I relocated to Bahir Dar, where I witnessed the war erupt in early November 2020.[105]

I collected most of the material for this book during this turbulent eleven-month period. In addition, I draw on earlier stints of field research in 2017, when I spent the summer in the homeland of the Nyangatom in southern Ethiopia, and in 2019, when I was based in Dire Dawa and Addis Ababa for more than two months. Occasionally, I refer to my earlier research in 2011 and 2012, when I lived in workers' camps along project roads and spent most of my time on building sites or in the contractor's and consultant's offices, witnessing the wave of litigation and the sentiments that fueled it.

In contrast to my previous research, documented in *Tales of Hope, Tastes of Bitterness: Chinese Road Builders in Ethiopia* and earlier work,[106] this time I chose to focus on the Ethiopian perspective. Hitherto, I had carried out field research alone. In 2020, I decided to work closely with two Ethiopian colleagues—a decision I never regretted. Bereket Asmelash and Zewdu Mengesha, both legal scholars, provided indispensable professional guidance, practical assistance, and moral support. Without them, this study could not have begun or taken shape in the way it has. Their contribution can be felt in all parts of the book.[107] If I use the pronouns "we" and "us," I am referring to Bereket and myself in Tigray or Zewdu and myself in Amhara. In 2011, 2012, 2017, and 2019, I was alone, and when I refer to this work, I stick with the singular pronoun "I" more common in anthropology and law.

The pages of this book reflect on observations in the courthouse and beyond, interviews with judges, lawyers (many of whom were former judges), prosecutors, court support staff, police officers, liaison officers cum facilitators who dealt with court cases and had acquainted themselves to various degrees with the law, and Ethiopian and Chinese litigants.[108] Scholars tend to separate judges from litigants and legal professionals from laypeople to focus on one or the other group. In Ethiopia today, however, judges and litigants alike are participants in national debates about global capital, raising questions of immunity and sovereignty inside and outside the courtroom. Hence, I consider the two groups together. Of course, this is not to say that they were in a similar position or harbored similar ideas.

In addition to interviews and casual conversations, I analyzed court dockets and hundreds of case files. Most court dockets and case files were handwritten and not yet uploaded to digital databases, making a quantitative analysis challenging. Things are different in neighboring Kenya. In 2022, I mined the online Kenya Law Cases Database for lawsuits against Chinese parties to enable comparison (see the conclusion). Throughout, I consider the broadest range possible of lawsuits involving Chinese parties, from land disputes to family cases, contractual disputes to criminal suits, and extracontractual claims (tort cases in common law) to labor suits, entertained by courts at all levels of jurisdiction in the state and federal court system—a system that is built on a civil legal tradition but has borrowed elements from common law (see chapter 6). While the lower courts, known as *wereda*

Federal Supreme Court cassation bench	
Cassation bench	Federal Supreme Court
State Supreme Court	
State High Court	Federal High Court
State First Instance Court (*wereda* court)	Federal First Instance Court

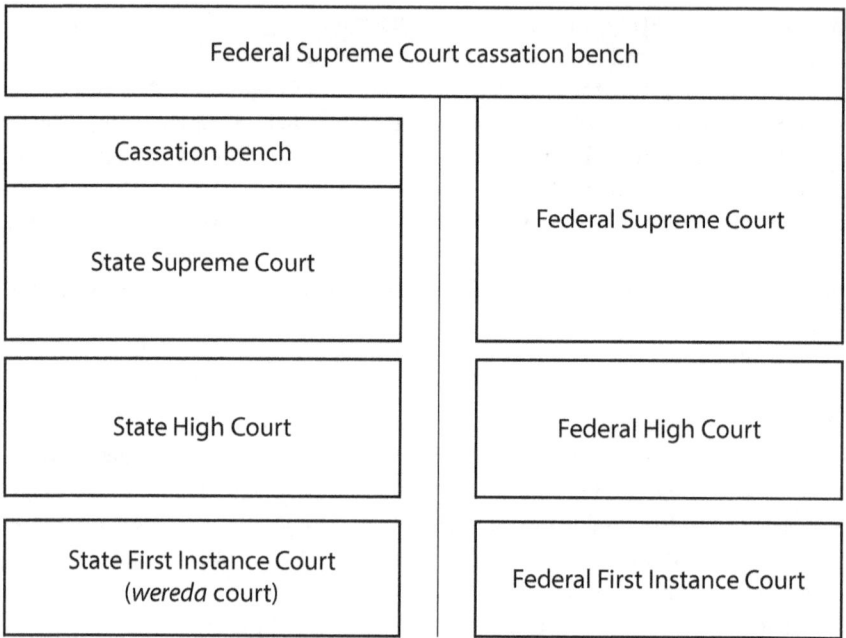

FIGURE 2. Ethiopia's two-tier court system.

courts, hear labor cases, high courts have first-instance jurisdiction over most contractual and extracontractual disputes. Substantial claims involving more than five
hundred thousand Ethiopian birr (14,350 US dollars) fall under the jurisdiction of
the Supreme Court of the respective state.

Although lawsuits involving a foreign party concern federal law,[109] the federal
courts can delegate their mandate to the regional courts. State-tier courts handle
most cases involving foreign parties as a result. The final court of appeal is the cassation bench of the Federal Supreme Court in Addis Ababa, which sits atop the
two tiers and can revise decisions given by both state and federal courts.[110] Appeals
are common, as Chinese managers have learned they stand a better chance in the
higher courts.[111]

Registrars, the gatekeepers of court dockets and case files, were often occupied
with assisting litigants. Reluctant to impinge on their activities, especially during
a period in which Covid-19 measures disrupted everyday operations, I saw only a
fraction of cases concerning Chinese corporations in each court—332 in total,
heard in various courts in Addis Ababa, Amhara, and Tigray. Many other lawsuits were relayed to us by the legal professionals who had entertained them, the
litigants who had been party to them, or both. Tracing disputes to their source
led Bereket and me to central and southern Tigray and Zewdu and me to East
and West Gojjam in Amhara, where Chinese projects had sparked litigation

waves. Alone or with Bereket and Zewdu, I visited two dozen courts at all levels of jurisdiction in the state and federal systems.

In Mekelle, Bereket and I spent the most time in Kebele 16. Dotted with bars, nightclubs, copy shops, and lawyers' offices, this historical neighborhood is home to two courts, the Tigray Supreme Court being one of them. Attracting people from all walks of life, Kebele 16 is a place where people meet over a coffee along the cobblestoned alleys or a beer in one of the bars "the size of a small lift or a large refrigerator," as Tigrayan writer Abel Guesh put it:[112] "If you scratch your hair, you risk scratching the hair of the person sitting behind you."[113] The only tarmac road that crosses the neighborhood is lined with jacaranda trees, its sides filled with people playing games or chewing over the latest news. Guesh famously painted Kebele 16 as a place where "the party [the TPLF] is gossiped about as if it were a person" and where ideas emerge that can both make and break the country.[114] Feared to be a hotbed of political mobilization, Kebele 16 was the first place to which the Ethiopian National Defense Force turned after its capture of Mekelle on November 28, 2020, rounding up youths.[115] Except for two months of lockdown, Kebele 16 was bursting with life before I left, two months before the start of the war.

In Bahir Dar, the Amhara Supreme Court sits on one of the city's main arteries that follows the shoreline of Lake Tana. The High Court of Bahir Dar can be found next door. Zewdu and I spent much time in a café across the road, going through scanned cases or transcribing interviews after interviewing legal professionals and litigants in the courtyard of my guesthouse. The city remained, by and large, unaffected by the war, as did the courts, whose premises remained filled. The deafening and threatening sound of warplanes that set off from the city and a series of missile attacks targeting its airport were the only reminders of what was going on further north. While the situation in Tigray has calmed since the peace accord signed in November 2022, two years after the start of the war, parts of Amhara have been engulfed in fighting between local militia and the federal army since 2023.

Ethiopia is a country of deep political rifts. Bereket declined my invitation to join me in Bahir Dar out of fear. Anti-Tigrayan sentiments in Amhara, having flared up years earlier, were on the rise. Had I invited Zewdu to join me in Tigray or Oromia, he also would have turned down the offer. Being foreign, white, and female, I enjoyed the unearned privilege of unrestricted mobility. Moving between restive regions, I was struck by the fact that legal professionals and litigants of different ethnic groups stood up for and behind their country. They sought to protect the sovereignty of the Ethiopian people rather than that of Tigray or Amhara. (I met only one person, a Tigrayan court reporter, who entertained secessionist ideas, yet even he admitted that secession was unrealistic.) Most importantly, my findings in Addis Ababa, Dire Dawa, South Ethiopia Regional State, Tigray, and Amhara were strikingly similar. For this reason, I refer to national rather than regional sovereignty and frame immunity as a national, not a regional, concern.

The seismic shifts Ethiopia has undergone at both the national and local levels since my main stint of field research in 2020 make this book a historical account, covering the EPRDF era and the subsequent transition years. Yet Chinese involvement in Ethiopia shows few signs of abating. As this manuscript goes to press, Ethiopian–Chinese diplomatic relations seem as robust as they were before. Chinese construction firms continue to build roads and real estate, foreign direct investment from China even increased after Covid-19,[116] and Ethiopia remains a port of call for intrepid entrepreneurs seeking opportunities overseas, especially in the face of China's economic downturn.[117] Importantly, lawsuits involving Chinese parties continue to fill court dockets. The question of immunity, raised throughout Ethiopia's past, retains pertinence.

ROADMAP

Foregrounding the contrasting and, occasionally, converging standpoints of those who fight, exact, grant, or weigh immunity, while being attentive to the interactions between them, the book unfolds across six chapters that probe how immunity is produced, reproduced, and deconstructed in encounters. But before I turn to the book's protagonists, I travel back in time. It has become something of a mantra in Ethiopia that if you want to understand what is happening in the country today, you must look at its contested history. Ethnic violence, rural–urban inequalities, and political rifts all have firm roots in the imperial and more recent past, as has the country's dependence on foreign capital and international development interventions. Connecting past to present threats to sovereignty posed by various foreign actors—from European concession hunters and Bretton Woods dogmatists to Chinese enterprise managers—chapter 1 explains contemporary popular responses to infringements of national sovereignty and dignity. While peeling back historical layers, the chapter reveals how Chinese corporations build on existing internal and external structures of inequality and dependence.

Chapter 2 unpacks the experiences of those who *fight* immunity or what they perceive as impunity: Ethiopian plaintiffs. Following local employees of Chinese construction firms from the building site to the local courts, the chapter throws light on why local plaintiffs choose legal action. They often do so, I demonstrate, to address grievances that concern not just themselves but also a collective, be it the workforce, the local community, or the country at large. Reflecting growing pan-African sentiments in Ethiopia and beyond, some claimants mentioned seeking to protect the dignity of (black) Africans. Local plaintiffs typically jumped scales as they assessed their personal experiences with Chinese corporations against those of Ethiopia in the international arena. Stated otherwise, at stake was not so much the assertion of individual rights as the restoration of collective dignity. By taking their disputes to court, local plaintiffs moreover addressed a state that had, in their eyes, abdicated sovereignty to foreign corporate capital.

Chapter 3 shifts perspectives to those who *exact* immunity: Chinese enterprise managers. Drawing on interviews with Chinese managers and their Ethiopian lawyers, it charts the experiences of Chinese corporations and how their expatriate professionals have coped with and responded to litigation. Being summonsed to court initially came as a surprise to many of them. Construing their work as a gift to the nation, they expected gratitude for their contribution to the Ethiopian economy. To them, being subjected to legal action was the ultimate sign of ingratitude among the Ethiopians. The managers' attitude in court, characterized by disrespect and despair, played a significant role in judges' decisions against them. Their repeated requests for immunity were often brushed aside, as were the justifications they provided in favor of it. The chapter furthermore traces Chinese managers' learning processes, as it chronicles a shift from withdrawal to active involvement and from disdain to performed deference, and sheds light on the factors contributing to this change.

Homing in on the interactions between those who *fight* and *exact* immunity and the role of those who *mediate* immunity, chapter 4 draws on *Milano Hotel v. Huawei Technologies*, a leasehold dispute decided by the Tigray Supreme Court in 2019, to illustrate how opportunities of immunity emerge and how they are exploited in relations marked by structural inequalities. Tracing the evolution of the conflict between an Ethiopian tourist hotel and a Chinese telecommunications giant from the time of the signing of their lease agreement to the court ruling, it also shows what the courts do for Ethiopian and Chinese disputants and how they shape their relationship. Putting a single dispute under the microscope helps reveal the structural inequalities entrenched in the disputants' relationship and the myriad ways these inequalities frustrate the disputing process.

It further shows the centrality of communication. Its absence quickly leads disputes to escalate into lawsuits. The court plays a critical role in this regard. It restores communication by filling silences, forcing the parties to voice what they want to leave unsaid, and giving decisive interpretations of misunderstandings between them. While establishing its authority and asserting its jurisdiction, the judiciary solves linguistic bottlenecks and structural impasses. The court's communicative function is essential to shaping the relationship between Ethiopian and Chinese parties. As a communicator *and* translator, it at once lays bare and challenges the power disparities between them. In sum, this chapter shows how the court distributes responsibility and how, by so doing, it reshapes the relationship between the parties from the ground up.

Entering the courtroom, chapter 5 turns to the vantage point of those who *arbitrate* immunity, the judges, and their interactions with those who exact and support immunity. How did judges cope with resistant and rebellious expatriate managers? How did they respond to their claims of immunity? Sketching courtroom scenes recalled by these judges, this chapter charts the discursive and bodily disciplinary practices on which judges drew to rein in unwilling litigants.

Outside the courtroom, judges also dealt with interventions by government officials who supported claims of immunity and demanded cases be suspended or closed. The latter often became the bench's main nemesis. Most judges were, however, resolute in resisting demands for immunity, whether from Chinese corporations or state functionaries, and defended their jurisdiction. By so doing, they rendered the courtroom a space where they, together with local plaintiffs, could reclaim sovereignty.

The bench settled the question of immunity once and for all by asserting jurisdiction and compelling Chinese litigants to respect Ethiopian legal procedure and courtroom etiquette. Proceeding with adjudication of the dispute at hand, they facilitated communication between parties who often talked past rather than with one another. Importantly, they forced corporate actors to listen. Adjudication is, however, heavily mediated by the judge, and judges are never neutral. They amplify some voices while dimming others.

Chapter 6 shows how judges' ideological leanings and experiences with Chinese disputants in the courtroom and beyond filter into their decisions. The ambiguous status of precedent in the Ethiopian legal system allowed these judges to define the relationship between Ethiopian and Chinese parties as they saw fit by drawing on either codified law or case law. Their rulings reflect divergent positions in national debates about Chinese capital and how much leeway financial considerations should be given concerning labor practices, property, environmental concerns, and taxation. Notwithstanding their varying personal and political outlooks, all judges sought to enforce their jurisdiction and protect sovereignty.

Before revisiting and reflecting on the role of courts in negotiating immunity and restoring sovereignty, the conclusion offers a comparative perspective. Neighboring Kenya, too, has witnessed a wave of litigation against Chinese corporations. The disputes brought to courts there and their outcomes are remarkably similar to those in Ethiopia. A brief discussion of the place of state courts in Kenyan–Chinese encounters and of the centrality of the question of sovereignty across Africa gestures at the book's broader significance. It is followed by counterexamples from African countries where the courts are too weak and compromised to adopt the position they do in Ethiopia and Kenya or where other state institutions mitigate or suppress disputes. A comparison points to the moments when local courts become global actors, when they transform into nodes connecting local to global legal orders and become arenas where geopolitical contestations come to pass.

1

Sovereignty and Contested Claims of Immunity

On November 30, 2009, the prosecutor's office in West Gojjam, Amhara, sent a letter to the police notifying them that charges against Binzheng Zhang, a Chinese machine operator accused of homicide, had been dismissed "for the benefit of maintaining good relations between the two countries."[1] Seven years later, opposition leader Yilkal Getnet mentioned the letter in the media to condemn the Ethiopian People's Revolutionary Democratic Front (EPRDF), the country's ruling coalition at the time, for ceding sovereignty to Chinese corporations.[2] As chair of the Semayawi (Blue) Party,[3] Yilkal referred to the letter in a discussion on Ethiopian Satellite Television, a channel broadcast from Washington, DC, and run by opposition members in exile.[4] He presented it as evidence of the government's nepotism and nefarious alliances with foreign investors such as the Chinese. Beijing, and specifically the Chinese Communist Party, was the ruling coalition's closest ally at the time.[5]

Yilkal brought the letter to light while Ethiopia was reeling from civil unrest. Anti-government protests had started in Oromia in 2015 and spread to Amhara in 2016.[6] Targeting the Tigray People's Liberation Front (TPLF)—the dominant party in the ruling coalition—the protestors' anger was fueled by resentment over discrimination against Amharas over more than two decades of EPRDF rule. At rallies, protestors castigated TPLF elites for abusing power to enrich themselves,[7] chanting "Thief! Thief! Woyane!"[8] They blocked roads, destroyed government property, and dismantled foreign enterprises around Bahir Dar.[9] Indeed, "thief" also alluded to the land and resources the government had taken from Amharas to give to foreign investors.

The government attempted to quash the protests.[10] When disaffection and discontent intensified in 2017, it opted for reform,[11] followed by the release of political prisoners, the resignation of Prime Minister Hailemariam Desalegn, and, shortly after, the ascendance of current Prime Minister Abiy Ahmed. The outcry over the letter, then, was directed at the government as much as its Chinese allies.[12] To the public, the immunity granted to Binzheng Zhang amounted to impunity and blatant disregard for the victim's rights. The state had failed to protect and serve justice to its people. Ethiopian critics construed the exemption from prosecution granted to foreign nationals like Zhang—often at their request or that of their embassy—as a threat to popular sovereignty and national dignity. In this chapter, I explain *why* by reflecting on instances in which immunity became a topic of debate.[13]

To fully appreciate the question of immunity and the ceding of sovereignty that stirred public outrage like this, we must look to Ethiopia's past. The history of European and US incursions on sovereignty explains the emotional responses to the letter. Throughout history, the judiciary has figured prominently in debates about Ethiopian sovereignty.[14] While the judiciary's authority confirmed sovereign control, its lack signaled a loss of sovereignty. Questions about the immunity of foreign nationals and organizations were raised in various periods, especially during the imperial era and in the decades after the establishment of the Federal Democratic Republic of Ethiopia in 1991, which witnessed an influx of Chinese contractors and investors. This chapter, therefore, turns first to the past to understand present concerns about sovereignty. In the second part, I revisit the case of Binzheng Zhang and its reconstruction by a judge who had been posted in Liben, North Achefer, at the time. His reflections on the case and its political aftermath echo public sentiments, including those of the litigants and judges introduced later in the book.

THE EXTRALEGAL STATUS OF FOREIGNERS IN ETHIOPIA'S IMPERIAL PAST

Yilkal Getnet's accusation that the EPRDF government unfairly favored foreigners was reminiscent of criticism faced by Emperors Menelik II and Haile Selassie I for their leniency toward European nationals in imperial Ethiopia (until 1974). Debates about immunity feed on the ambiguous status granted to foreigners in the past as much as in the present.[15] Continuing a tradition started by Emperor Tewodros II (1855–68), Emperor Menelik II, who ruled over Abyssinia—as the empire was known at the time—during the height of the European "Scramble for Africa," took advantage of foreign skills to expand and modernize the empire.[16] During his reign, the number of foreigners increased, as did their involvement and influence at the Imperial Court. The court established health care facilities, a postal service, and water supply and transportation infrastructure with their assistance. At the same time, foreign industrialists and traders were busy setting up businesses on their own account throughout the late nineteenth and early twentieth centuries.[17]

Nevertheless, although they were admired and required for their expertise and skills, foreigners in Ethiopia had a different status from their counterparts in colonial Africa.[18] They were not permitted to hold administrative roles and enjoyed less prestige. Many undertook crafts traditionally held in low esteem in Ethiopia, such as woodwork and ironwork. The status of foreigners deteriorated further after Ethiopia's victory over Italy at the Battle of Adwa (1896) and the subsequent arrival in the capital of a large number of Italian prisoners, who were put to work as manual laborers building roads.[19] On the streets, Europeans came to be addressed using the derogatory name "Ali"—a term the Italians had themselves used when addressing their servants and soldiers in Eritrea.[20] The emperor, however, continued to treat foreigners with respect, as he was conscious that their skills and expertise were indispensable. He is said to have ordered his subjects to dismount from their mules on seeing a foreigner in a gesture of reverence that citizens were generally expected to show toward the Ethiopian nobility.[21]

By 1905, there were so many foreigners in the capital that, according to British envoy Thomas Hohler, Emperor Menelik "sent orders that no passes to come to Addis Ababa should be delivered except on application of the consular authorities, and these were instructed, per His Majesty's request, not to apply for permits for individuals who appeared to be of an undesirable or useless character."[22] According to this diplomat, the emperor's decree was prompted by public resentment of incidents in which foreigners were found guilty of crimes yet were subjected to much lighter punishment than locals. In their correspondence with the UK Foreign Office, Hohler and his colleague Captain John Lane Harrington described several such criminal cases.

One was an incident involving an Italian foreman who was supervising the construction of a bridge. Displeased with his Ethiopian assistants, he threw a stone at them, fatally wounding one. Menelik insisted that the Italian pay 160 US dollars in compensation—referred to as "blood money"—but refrained from having him prosecuted, to the dismay of the victim's relatives. In another case, a drunken Russian shot an Ethiopian and defended himself with the unacceptable remark that he thought he had hit a hyena. In this case, the emperor himself paid the compensation due to the victim's family and expelled the perpetrator from the country.[23] It was not unknown for the emperor to pay the fines of foreigners who were guilty of crimes—an act on which the public frowned. Thus, the fate of foreign citizens in the cases described by the two diplomats resembles that of their contemporary counterparts, such as Binzheng Zhang.

Emperor Haile Selassie, Menelik's successor, continued this preferential treatment of foreigners and more than once reached into his own pocket to settle a dispute between a foreign perpetrator and an Ethiopian victim.[24] Notwithstanding the emperor's magnanimity, European powers continued to voice concerns about the status of their nationals in Ethiopia's judicial system. The first of these to negotiate immunity under Ethiopian law were the French.

HOLDING ON TO SOVEREIGNTY:
THE KLOBUKOWSKI TREATY

The Franco-Ethiopian Treaty of Friendship and Commerce of 1908, better known as the Klobukowski Treaty after the French envoy who negotiated it with Emperor Menelik II, subjected Ethiopia to partial extraterritoriality—that is, immunity from the jurisdiction of the country. Article 7 of the treaty provides that French citizens and colonial subjects (*protégés*) remain under French jurisdiction until "the legislation of Ethiopia has aligned with the legislations of Europe." The treaty precipitated similar requests by other foreigners, most notably British and Italians, for similar treatment based on the most-favored nation clause in their respective bilateral treaties with the Abyssinian Empire. As a result, the privileges and immunities granted to French citizens and subjects were soon extended to those of Italy, the United Kingdom, and other nations.[25] However, the treaty protected the long-standing sovereign prerogative of the "Tribunal of the King of Kings," or the Emperor's Bench. The monarch preserved his right to a final say in instances where judges disagreed with each other.[26] Alarmed by the terms and spirit of the Tripartite Treaty signed by Italy, the United Kingdom, and France in the absence of the monarch in 1906, by which the European empires intended to forestall the possibility of a conflict over Ethiopia on the death of the emperor, Menelik was reluctant to relinquish all judicial authority.[27]

Article 7 of the Klobukowski Treaty remained a topic of heated debate in the decades after Menelik's death. Disturbed by the sovereign prerogative and the fact that Ethiopian judges ruled over lawsuits in which one of the parties was foreign and the other Ethiopian, Italy and the United Kingdom tried to convince Menelik to hire a European judge to try cases that involved foreign nationals. Their requests were disregarded. Antony Klobukowski was more realistic. "Ethiopia is not Egypt, or at least not yet," he said in dismissal of the claims of Italian envoy Count Colli di Felizzano.[28] The seasoned French diplomat was referencing Egyptian mixed courts that were staffed by British judges. These courts would later come under fire for being a blatant impingement on Egypt's sovereignty.[29]

Regent Ras Tafari, who later became Emperor Haile Selassie, institutionalized the system set out in Article 7 of the Klobukowski Treaty by establishing the Special Court (to avoid confusion and deny any resemblance between it and the Mixed Courts in Egypt) only in 1922.[30] The Special Court was created to entertain cases between foreigners and Ethiopians, while disputes between two foreign parties fell under consular jurisdiction. All the judges who staffed the Special Court were Ethiopian. This arrangement posed significant challenges to the judiciary, who had to be versed in Ethiopian criminal and civil law and were also expected to know foreign laws, especially those of France, the United Kingdom, and Italy. An added complication was that the foreign consuls who decided on cases alongside them were by no means familiar with their own laws. Other challenges were related to unclear procedures in the Ethiopian court and discrepancies between Ethiopian and foreign laws. Throughout the life of the Special Court (1922–35), Haile Selassie upheld his sovereign prerogative.

Dissatisfied with this judicial system, foreign missionaries like the British tried to obstruct the Special Court from hearing cases involving their citizens and subjects.[31] The following case illustrates the lengths to which they went.[32] It concerned Thakur Singh, a member of the Indian escort employed by the British mission in Ethiopia, who was accused of murdering an Ethiopian woman of undisclosed identity in June 1924. He had been in a romantic relationship with the victim, and it was said that she occasionally visited him. Singh confessed to the crime, claiming he found letters from another suitor in the victim's possession; what is more, she had refused to accompany him to India.

Before the trial, the British consul argued that the case ought not be tried by the Special Court. He contended that the suspect was a British soldier rather than a British subject, referring to Article 35 of the Abyssinia Order in Council 1913, which provided that the courts could try civilians but not soldiers. Furthermore, he drew on international law to argue that cases involving members of the armed forces on duty in the territory of another state must be tried by a military tribunal of the state to which the soldier belonged. In other words, Singh ought to be tried by the British consul or sent for trial to Aden, a British crown colony (1937–63) in the southern part of modern-day Yemen. The Ethiopian government rejected this argument, saying it had never consented to such an agreement and reiterating the terms of the agreement of the Special Court. The emperor eventually gave in to British demands but insisted on a payment of forty British pounds in reparation to the relatives of the murdered woman. The British mission subsequently sent Thakur Singh to Aden.

In their attempts to justify demanding immunity from Ethiopian legal process for their nationals, European diplomats presented cases to demonstrate the "uncivilized" nature of the court, especially the harsh punishments it meted out to convicts.[33] Juxtaposing physical punishments such as flogging, mutilation, and execution with the more "civilized" prison sentences imposed in Europe, they placed the different criminal justice systems on a temporal scale, which is a hallmark of legal orientalism.[34]

Regent Ras Tafari also faced criticism from the public. The foreign diplomatic corps observed that there was widespread Ethiopian antipathy to the extraterritoriality extended by the Special Court. Addison E. Southard, an American diplomat who played an important role in reestablishing relations between the United States and Ethiopia in the 1920s, noted in 1931 that "even the present special court privileges enjoyed by foreigners are distinctly resented by the Ethiopians, and I doubt whether they would yield in any substantial way to a request for revision in the direction of foreign favor or convenience."[35] He pointed to this local resentment to explain that he and other members of the diplomatic corps had provisionally abandoned discussions on the revision of Articles 3 and 7, in which they had tried to strengthen further extraterritoriality in exchange for recognizing the empire's fiscal sovereignty and its new tax legislation, which was restricted by Article 3. However, Emperor Haile Selassie stood firm and refused to allow foreign judges to practice on Ethiopian benches until Ethiopia was liberated from Italian occupation in 1941.

SURRENDERING SOVEREIGNTY: THE ANGLO-ETHIOPIAN AGREEMENTS

The Anglo-Ethiopian Agreements of 1942 and 1944, concluded after the liberation of Ethiopia from Mussolini's Italy, effectively extended extraterritoriality by introducing what the British government had long called for: European judges.[36] The 1942 agreement shaped a new legal system that was no less controversial than the Special Court had been before Ethiopia's five years under Italian rule.[37]

Even though the British war cabinet recognized Ethiopia as an independent state and supported "the Emperor's claim to the throne, as soon as the Emperor had crossed the frontier into Abyssinia"—referring to Haile Selassie's return from the United Kingdom to Ethiopia after it was freed with the help of British troops—it would "for many years need some form of international guidance in political and economic affairs."[38] Under this paternalistic pretext, the British pressed Emperor Haile Selassie to accept their advice "in all important matters, internal and external," as they expanded their influence in all spheres of government.

The agreements signed with the United Kingdom came under fire from Ethiopian nationalists who had been part of the resistance movement. Prominent Ethiopian intellectual Hakim Workneh, for instance, called the 1942 agreement "a scheme of an undying sinister imperialism."[39] Ethiopians, freed from the thrall of another European colonial power, resented and mistrusted the British. The latter's influence, formalized in the agreements, was seen as yet another attack on Ethiopia's regained sovereignty. The British government was aware of these popular concerns in Ethiopia. In cabinet discussions, "the importance was stressed of avoiding giving colour to any idea that we were treating Ethiopia as part of the British Empire." This rhetorical caution notwithstanding, post-liberation Ethiopia has often been described as a de facto British protectorate or even a semi-colony.[40]

Legal scholar Hailegabriel G. Feyissa does not mince his words in his depiction of the High Court and Supreme Imperial Court,[41] which were established on the model that the British had presented in the annex to the 1942 Anglo-Ethiopian Agreement as instruments of European extraterritoriality. Criticizing earlier accounts that praise the courts as a step toward the restoration of Ethiopian sovereignty, he postulates that the signing away of jurisdiction meant cession of national sovereignty. Semi-colonialism was thus at its height during the heyday of the Imperial High Court.

The courts were administered and staffed by British legal professionals drawn from the legal service of the Colonial Office. One of the three judges was required to be of British nationality or, according to a new provision in the 1944 Anglo-Ethiopian Agreement, a judge "of proven judicial experience in other lands," irrespective of nationality.[42] The Imperial High Court and its appellate court, the Imperial Supreme Court, reverted to existing Ethiopian laws, such as the use of the 1930 penal code for Ethiopian litigants and Italian codes for foreign citizens. In practice, judges also began applying common-law principles of equity and fairness and used existing precedents from British common law. Unlike Feyissa, however, historian Esubalew Belay Fanta, echoing earlier British scholars such as Margery Perham,[43] is more positive in his evaluation of the court in his historical account of British judges on the Ethiopian bench.[44] Despite widespread skepticism of British influence, he maintains that the Imperial High Court and the Supreme Court enjoyed considerable acceptance and public trust.

These contrasting views demonstrate that the Imperial High Court and its jurisdiction were a subject of controversy—or "unique, popular, controversial, influential and full of challenges, glories, and anomalies," in Fanta's depiction.[45] This was precisely because they were seen as a partial, if not wholesale, capitulation of jurisdiction. The introduction of foreign judges threw the question of sovereignty into new relief. However, British influence gradually waned in the following two decades. While Haile Selassie kept British judges on the Ethiopian bench, he replaced the British experts and advisers in the public prosecutor's office and the executive branches of government. Eventually, the decline of extraterritoriality went hand in hand with the modernization of Ethiopian law through codification and the institutionalization of legal education in the 1960s.[46]

During the Derg period, following the Ethiopian revolution of 1974 that ended Haile Selassie's reign and empire, senior judges were accused of being accomplices of the old regime and were dismissed.[47] Special military tribunals usurped most of the powers of the judiciary, and former courts were left to try petty cases of no interest to the administration. Legal practice ceased to be an attractive calling for lawyers, and foreigners active in the judiciary, the prosecution, and the legal services market were expelled from the country.[48] Ethiopia's justice system became increasingly isolated.

In the decades following the establishment of the Federal Democratic Republic of Ethiopia in 1991, participation in the justice sector was restricted to Ethiopian nationals.[49] This changed only in 2021 with the promulgation of the *Federal Advocacy Service Licensing and Administration Proclamation 1249/2021*, which extends the right to act as a lawyer to foreign nationals of Ethiopian origin and allows foreign lawyers to practice in cases that concern foreign law, provided they possess a license from their home country and enter a partnership with a local or foreign-born Ethiopian lawyer or firm certified under the proclamation.[50] The limited engagement of foreign professionals in the justice sector from the 1990s through the 2010s, however, did not preclude infringements of judicial sovereignty. On the contrary, the entry of a wave of contractors and investors from China and other countries since the late 1990s has catapulted the question of immunity into the center of public debate.

SOVEREIGNTY RECONSIDERED: THE CHINESE PRESENCE

Over the past two decades, a growing Chinese presence in Ethiopia has rekindled debates about sovereignty.[51] Chinese companies have been active across various sectors.[52] Road, railway, electricity, telecommunications, and water supply projects have conveyed Chinese engineers and builders to the remotest corners of the country.[53] Chinese construction firms are also sculpting the skyline of Addis Ababa, posing a threat to Ethiopian contractors in the real estate sector.[54] Furthermore, there is significant Chinese investment in the nascent manufacturing sector, in which primarily private firms from China produce everything from plywood to shoes, cement to pharmaceuticals, and ceramics to apparel.[55] To be sure, Chinese contractors and investors differ little from their Turkish, Korean, Indian, Arab, and European counterparts when it comes to interests and attitudes. Yet the sheer scope of Chinese involvement has made their place in society more visible and, at times, threatening.

Ethiopians to whom I spoke were quick to acknowledge the contribution of Chinese contractors and investors to the country and its economy.[56] In the words of an Ethiopian trader who had worked for a Chinese shoe manufacturer, "The Chinese feed the wood that lights up the fire."[57] He added a cautionary note, however, alluding to the ultimate responsibility of Ethiopians to stand on their own feet: "The question is how strong the fire is and whether we can keep it burning." People are aware of the new dependency the Chinese presence has produced. Ethiopia owes China about 14.5 billion US dollars and relies heavily on Chinese commercial loans to finance its infrastructure.[58] Furthermore, Chinese direct investment has been central to the growth of the manufacturing industry.

During the EPRDF years, the alliance between the state and Chinese corporations—and between Ethiopia and China more generally—was both pragmatic and ideological. The economic model espoused by the Ethiopian government at the time was inspired by the developmental state model of the Asian Tigers and, most importantly, China.[59] After rising to power in 1991, the TPLF sought to extend its political base.[60] It created a broad coalition, the EPRDF, and a federal system based on ethnicity, dividing the country into ethnolinguistic regions and granting ethnic groups self-determination and, ultimately, the right to secession.[61] To proponents, the system gave long-suppressed ethnic groups a voice.[62] To opponents, what some have sarcastically called the "Scramble for Ethiopia" led to the loss of Ethiopian unity and shared identity.[63] In their eyes, the government imposed the ethnic-federalist system on them, in much the same way that conniving colonial powers once carved up the African continent.

The new EPRDF-led government sought to secure legitimacy by enabling economic growth through state-driven development.[64] Rejecting the Washington Consensus model of development, late Prime Minister Meles Zenawi advocated for a strong state with a purposive development agenda. The country's distinctive development path proved successful. Ethiopia achieved double-digit growth over a sustained period, leading some to suggest that Ethiopia would become one of the "lion economies" in a rising Africa.[65] In China, Ethiopia became known as "Africa's little China."

However, the rise of Abiy Ahmed and the Prosperity Party heralded the demise of the developmental state.[66] Stiff at first, the relationship between the new prime minister and China warmed up quickly despite the new administration's sharp neoliberal turn in economy policy. China continues to be one of the largest investors in Ethiopia, together with Saudi Arabia, the United States, India, and Turkey. In 2021 alone, Chinese investment tripled, accounting for 60 percent of foreign direct investment.[67] This growth in involvement has accompanied an increase in the leverage of the Chinese government and state firms vis-à-vis the Ethiopian government.

Across Africa, Chinese actors have sought to forge sovereign exceptions through the formation of special economic zones (SEZs),[68] the extraterritorial ordering of market activities (e.g., the securitization of projects by Chinese security personnel),[69] the extension of Chinese jurisdiction beyond national borders,[70] and the creation of subsidiaries to bypass tax burdens, overcome financial insecurities, and escape liability for externalities.[71] Enabled by power imbalances, these quasi-negotiated arrangements are inspired by past forms of extraterritoriality that have, as I have shown, firm roots in the (semi-)colonial era.[72] The sovereignty regimes they produce are equally modeled on China's domestic experiments since the 1980s in shaping spaces of exception to normalized rule.[73] Ethiopia has successfully pushed back on some of these unequal arrangements while giving in to others.

Like their Western counterparts, Chinese corporations endeavor to insulate themselves from host countries' regulatory environments and, whenever possible, lift disputes out of the countries.[74] One example of jurisdictional displacement is the numerous Chinese-initiated SEZs and free-trade zones (FTZs) that have mushroomed across the African landscape—from Egypt, Zambia, and Mauritius to Nigeria, Algeria, and Ethiopia.[75] In these zones, host states selectively cede sovereignty to corporations to spur investment and smooth operations. As Omolade Adunbi elucidates, SEZs and FTZs disrupt traditional power structures and challenge local forms of sovereignty.[76] They are founded on displacement and feed on dispossession. In Ethiopia and Nigeria alike, sovereignty has become, in Adunbi's pointed words, "a highly contested terrain that pitches the communities of extraction against the state and its corporate partners."[77] As we will see, many of these contestations unfold in the courtroom.

Another way in which Chinese actors sidestep local jurisdiction and extend Chinese jurisdiction is through governing law clauses.[78] Used to determine the jurisdiction under which contracts fall, governing law clauses are common in cross-border and multijurisdictional transactions.[79] The loan agreements for the Mombasa–Nairobi Railway Project, signed between the Export–Import Bank of China and the Kenyan government, are a case in point.[80] Explicitly cast as private rather than public,[81] both agreements are governed by Chinese law, and the China International Economic and Trade Arbitration Commission in Beijing has final jurisdiction over disputes arising from them.[82] Blatantly waiving the host country's sovereign immunity,[83] the leaked agreements sent a shockwave through Kenyan society, fueling fears that the Chinese government would confiscate the railway if Kenya were to default on the loans, or, worse, that it would seize Mombasa Port, which was rumored to serve as collateral for the railway.[84] Concerned critics accused the Kenyan government of signing away its sovereignty—accusations that echo disconcerted voices in Ethiopia.[85] For one, the extension of Chinese judicial reach is cementing China's increasingly dominant position in the geopolitical arena.

Encouraged by the possibility of immunity from law instantiated by sovereign exceptions in Ethiopia and elsewhere, Chinese enterprise managers have repeatedly requested immunity in situations in which they do not enjoy it by law. Meanwhile, the state's dependence on Chinese contracting and investment has led it to extend invitations to corporations through exemptions and permit interventions by them. Far from unique, the infamous case of Binzheng Zhang testifies to this.[86]

THE CASE OF BINZHENG ZHANG

Judge Temesgen first heard that the charges against Binzheng Zhang had been waived shortly before Temesgen left Liben, North Achefer. Disturbed by the news, he decided to get to the bottom of the case. "This is not a crime brought upon complaint," he told me. "As you know, the very purpose of our criminal law is to maintain peace and order in society." He held that the Chinese man ought to be held liable in the same way as any Ethiopian citizen. "The life of a person has been lost. Solving this issue by administrative fiat and with a letter like this is inappropriate."[87]

Temesgen was the first judge assigned to Liben. In the mid-2000s, the construction of Beles, a run-of-the-river hydroelectric power plant that taps water from Ethiopia's largest lake, Tana, led to the arrival of engineers, builders, and service workers along with traders and investors lured to the region by the influx of capital.[88] The sharp population increase put pressure on the capacity of Durbete, a small town on the road from Bahir Dar to Addis Ababa and the administrative center of Achefer, leading to a decision to divide the region. As a result, Liben became the administrative center of North Achefer. Temesgen's assignment in Liben between 2007 and 2009 coincided with the peak of construction work at Tana Beles.[89] The project was nearing completion when he was transferred to another court.

The young judge was tasked with founding the court in Liben. As the office he had been allocated was too small to serve as a courtroom, Temesgen began hearing cases outdoors, seated on a stone with the litigants gathered around him. Occasionally, he went to the project site, which was a short day's walk from Liben, to hear cases. The project camps were near a place popularly known as Ahiya Chanqa ("Donkey's Shoulder"). The camp of Salini Costruttori, the Italian contractor for the project, was distinguished from another camp, nicknamed "Darfur" because of the low wages its workers earned and the abominable conditions in which they lived. The expatriate compounds of subcontractors, including the Chinese, could be found near "Darfur."

A first instance court, the North Achefer Wereda Court, heard mostly labor cases. This notorious homicide case did not fall under its jurisdiction; however, the case had been investigated by police officers working alongside Judge Temesgen in Liben, from whom he had learned the details of the case.

The homicide concerned a regrettable, if inconspicuous, work accident. Tunnel construction can be hazardous. Underground work accidents are common, especially when workers lack experience and skills. This incident, however, involved an able and respected mechanic from Debre Markos, East Gojjam. On the afternoon of the tragedy, the young man had been lining the tunnel with steel—a job requiring him to stand on an automated lifting platform. He had placed the machine in the correct position to work on the tunnel ceiling when Binzheng Zhang, a Chinese operator and foreman, arrived on-site and touched a button to raise the platform, trapping the worker against the tunnel ceiling. The mechanic died on the spot, and his body was severely deformed.

In the weeks and months after the incident, diverging stories about the intentions of the Chinese operator did the rounds in North Achefer and beyond. Some said the operator had pushed the button deliberately out of envy for his superior skills and the respect the mechanic enjoyed among colleagues. Others believed he had not noticed the mechanic standing on the platform and was innocent. Over the years, Temesgen attempted to trace the mechanic's family each time he was in Debre Markos for work. His desire to unravel this case and ensure that the family received proper compensation stemmed partially from a personal experience that had left a bitter taste.

In late 2009, around the time of the Binzheng Zhang incident, Temesgen was transferred from Liben to another court without prior notice. He suspects the unexpected transfer was related to a ruling he gave in favor of a worker against their foreign employer. In that case, the Ethiopian welder, who worked underground at the Tana Beles project, was ordered to carry out a particular task by an Ethiopian supervisor. At the same time, the Egyptian manager demanded he do something else. It was close to the end of the working day. The welder complained, after which the expatriate supervisor fired him. At the trial, Temesgen found that the welder had carried out his work appropriately. The tasks he had been assigned could not be finished that day, let alone within regular working hours. A mere informal verbal complaint against an instruction did not warrant dismissal. Judge Temesgen decided that the worker should be either reinstated or compensated for unlawful termination.

"I gave the decision on Friday morning and was requested to transfer to another place on Monday. Starting from then, I have never been back to the area," remarked Judge Temesgen, who could not think of a reason for this unanticipated transfer apart from his ruling against the foreign company. Foreign firms enjoyed certain kinds of protection from which locals—companies and individuals alike—were excluded. He had tried to balance these injustices and was punished for it. The administrative decision stung.

When asked what he made of the letter about the cleared charges against Binzheng Zhang, he replied:

> Are you asking me this as a legal expert or an ordinary citizen? If you ask me as a legal expert, I am ashamed of the letter. It would have been better to issue an administrative decision instead of writing a note under the pretext of the countries' good relationship. It is not advisable to opt for such a way out as a legal expert. If you ask me as a legal expert, I am genuinely embarrassed by this letter. We are shielding an individual responsible for another individual's death. They take advantage of the countries' positive relationship. They use it as a shield to shun responsibility. This results in impunity. Despite the different versions of the events, the charges should not have been dropped.

Temesgen's shame derives from his sense of responsibility for a system of which he is part, first as a judge and, more recently, as a lawyer. Using the pronouns "we" and "they" alternately, he at once takes responsibility for and distances himself from the events and the regrettable decision of the prosecutor. In his eyes, the incident caused reputational damage to the justice system and affected people's trust in it. He was, however, convinced that the ultimate responsibility for the decision was held by a few rotten apples in the system—"corrupt individuals," as he classified them—rather than the federal government itself. "I am sure that the decision does not reflect that of the government or that the federal government had an interest in the matter." Note that Temesgen's interpretation differs from that of Blue Party chair Yilkal and his supporters, who construed the decision as built into what they believed to be a corrupt regime.

Temesgen could not determine who was behind the decision to discontinue the case. Although he had come to know the criminal case coordinator who was asked to draft the letter and put his signature underneath it, he urged Zewdu and me not to contact him. The case and the political aftermath had left him deeply distressed. Temesgen regretted the politicization of the case seven years later, when

Yilkal Getnet directed the public's attention to the letter, saying: "This is a human rights issue, not a political matter." The fate of the victim and the injustice done to them had been lost amid this political finger-pointing.

As an ordinary citizen, Temesgen was angry about the injustice done to the victim and Ethiopians in general. His anger was directed at the system that granted foreigners immunity and impunity. Had Zhang been an Ethiopian citizen, the case would have arrived on the desk of the zonal prosecutor, who would have prosecuted the case, especially as some of the witnesses intimated that foul intent was at play. According to Ethiopia's criminal code, homicide by negligence can be punished with imprisonment of six months to three years, on top of a fine of two to four thousand Ethiopian birr.[90] The punishment would be more severe if it could be established that the operator had pressed the button intentionally, in which case the crime would be dealt with as ordinary or aggravated homicide.

Temesgen, however, was not concerned with the question of intent. What bothered him was the immunity granted to the suspect. "This man was not an ambassador or a diplomat. . . . It was a simple crime that did not involve the country's interests." Indeed, had Zhang been a member of the diplomatic community, he would have enjoyed immunity under the 1961 Vienna Convention on Diplomatic Relations. Temesgen's position as a legal expert and an ordinary citizen is reminiscent of many other legal professionals and critical observers. In this respect, it did not differ much from that of the opposition leader who brought the case to the attention of an already enraged public in Amhara and beyond. Both men raised the question of immunity and linked it to national sovereignty, the law's supreme power over a body politic, and its necessary freedom from foreign control or influence. In ceding jurisdiction, this action signaled that the nation's power was neither supreme nor free from foreign influence.

Immunity, in Temesgen's eyes, was non-transactional. It cannot be acquired or given away in return for economic development. In his reflections on the case and the broader issue of immunity, Temesgen refers to foreign nationals as a single group. On a few occasions during our lengthy interview, however, he distinguished between European and Chinese contractors. For example, he claimed that the Italian construction firm Salini Costruttori and the contractor of the Beles project had maintained a good reputation in Ethiopia since entering the country during the era of Emperor Haile Selassie:

> I heard from others that when Salini started construction work in Ethiopia, they were supposed to give a performance guarantee to the project owner, but they failed to do so. They told the emperor they had no performance guarantee but promised to complete the construction works. "We want you, Emperor, to give us your blessing." The emperor gave [them] his word and allowed them to proceed. They were able to build and complete the work. Since that period onwards, Salini has worked in Ethiopia. . . . Salini has a good reputation in Ethiopia. They have gained the trust of Ethiopians. You cannot compare Salini with the Chinese.

Part of the reason Salini enjoyed acceptance was the contribution it made—or was seen to make—to society. Indeed, the police station and courthouse in Liben had been constructed with building materials donated by the company after appeals to them by, among others, Judge Temesgen. The yellow-plastered building still features a white plastic plaque reading "DONATED BY SALINI COSTRUTTORI S.P.A. SEP. 2008" next to the office of the chief of police. It is hidden behind a curtain (whether this is to conceal the foreign origin of the building, to avoid confusing the police station for Salini's office, or to protect the plaque from damage is unclear).

This is not to say that Salini has never faced criticism from Ethiopians or that Chinese contractors do not make similar donations.[91] They do. Temesgen was, however, more critical of the Chinese than of the Europeans. "Whenever you establish a big company, you have to consider the goodwill of the company," he explained. "Goodwill is not only for today but also for tomorrow and the day after tomorrow. . . . What the Chinese do is they work today, grab the money, and disappear." Temesgen, similarly to many other legal professionals and litigants, touches here on the issue of giving and taking in relation to development assistance and foreign direct investment. Of course, notions of goodwill and reciprocity were also a subject of dispute between Ethiopians and Chinese. Chinese enterprise managers argue that, by carrying out infrastructural projects in Ethiopia, they bring urgently needed development. They *give* development to the country, be it in terms of physical infrastructure, job opportunities, or business prospects for local suppliers and subcontractors. But, in the eyes of Temesgen and many like him, Chinese companies *take* rather than give.

IMMUNITY IN EXCHANGE FOR DEVELOPMENT

In December 2020, I traveled to Liben, hoping to find the twenty-page police report about the Zhang case mentioned in the prosecutor's letter. Unfortunately, none of the pink files piled in the corner of the North Achefer Police Station archive, dating from before and after 2009, contained a police investigation report that could have revealed in greater detail what had happened. However, during my visit, I did hear stories about the case. The chief of police, Commander Abebe, connected the infamous letter to a traffic accident in which the Chinese manager of a company that installed transmission lines for the hydropower project drove off the main road in Liben town and killed a little girl, Selam.[92] This incident raised similar questions about the status of foreign nationals in Ethiopia and left the local community equally outraged.

The chief of police summoned the child's mother and grandfather to the police station to sit with us.[93] While the bereaved mother wept, using the corner of the *net'ela* shawl draped around her head to dry her tears, the grandfather recounted the story. The Chinese driver had been headed for Bahir Dar that day. According to the grandfather, Selam had been playing on the road verge and the driver's negligence caused the accident. Shortly after the accident, the driver was taken into custody while the family prepared for the funeral, which was scheduled to take place on the same day, according to Ethiopian custom. The following morning, police officer Negus, who was then based in Liben, accompanied Selam's mother and grandfather to the High Court in Bahir Dar, where they encountered a furious Chinese senior manager.

Negotiations over compensation were terse. The Chinese manager, who had rushed from Addis Ababa after learning that one of his staff had been taken into custody, offered the family fifteen thousand Ethiopian birr (approximately 1,600 US dollars at the time) in compensation. The grandfather took this offer as an insult but swallowed his anger. Eventually, the parties settled on 27,000 birr. "We felt forced into accepting this meager compensation," the grandfather said. Had the community elders settled the matter, as was normal practice, the family could have received eighty thousand or perhaps even one hundred thousand birr.

"The Chinese man said that they contribute to the development of our country," Selam's mother said through tears. "'We came here to work. Our work must not be interrupted,' they said." Pressure to accept the amount offered came at them from all sides. Finally, the court registrar strongly encouraged the parties to reconcile, as a lawsuit would take years. Police officer Negus warned the family that the Chinese engineers might soon leave the area, potentially leaving them with no compensation, and encouraged them to take the amount offered by the manager.

What struck me about the grandfather's recollections was the ambiguity surrounding the status of the Chinese driver. "The driver was a foreign national. These cases are different," the chief of police, who had thus far listened quietly to our conversation, chimed in. The confusion about the status of the driver and his liability was captured, too, by a remark from Selam's mother: "They said that even if he harms Ethiopia, he cannot be held liable." In the mother's eyes, the driver could escape liability not just for killing an Ethiopian child but also for damaging the whole country. She, too, consciously or not, connected the incident to something more significant: a matter that concerned not only her family and the local community but also Ethiopia at large.

"They told us," the grandfather continued, "that if we want to sue this man, we have to go to Addis [Ababa] because he is a foreigner." Both statements are unclear about who "they" are and whether "they" deployed this argument to discourage the family from bringing a suit or asking for more compensation. An extracontractual case like this can be brought to the High Court in Bahir Dar. I later contacted police officer Negus, now stationed in Durbete in South Achefer, but he declined to be interviewed.

Eventually, the family gave in. The grandfather still regrets that they accepted the compensation. He returned to the High Court the following week to ask whether he could still institute a lawsuit but was told this was impossible as the family had already received compensation. "It was because of the pressure from the Chinese side that we settled the matter," he noted. He felt terrible, especially for his daughter, Selam's mother. "She did not obtain justice."

After the mother and grandfather left, Police Chief Abebe concluded: "In cases like this, we consider the foreign nationality of the people involved and the significance of their project." Tana Beles, he explained, was "a national matter." By justifying this special treatment of foreign nationals working on large-scale infrastructure projects, the chief of police adopted the very same stance—at least in his conversation with me, a white foreign national—that Temesgen and other legal professionals resented and fought against in the courtroom.

China's contribution to Ethiopia's development and the Chinese managers' work responsibilities repeatedly surfaced as a bargaining chip in civil cases and mitigating circumstances in criminal suits. Some public prosecutors resisted claims for immunity or favorable treatment for Chinese nationals, yet they often hit a brick wall. One of the challenges in cases involving foreign nationals was obtaining untainted evidence.[94] Foreigners, including Chinese enterprise managers, were not averse to bribing eyewitnesses and expert witnesses or even the police officer drawing up the criminal investigation report. This happened with another traffic accident in North Achefer, in which a Chinese manager killed an elderly farmer.[95] The man was walking with his wife when a Chinese driver veered off the road and hit him. He died, leaving his wife unscathed. She witnessed the entire scene.

The case ended up on the desk of the state prosecutor, who sought to bring charges against the driver and asked the wife, the leading eyewitness, to give her testimony. She refused. The Chinese enterprise manager had approached her and offered compensation of eighty thousand birr (about 9,500 US dollars)—a generous amount in 2002 or 2003 (the prosecutor did not remember the exact year). "The money changed her mind," the prosecutor recalled.[96] "She reversed her statement to the police in court." Instead, she connected her husband's death to his character, saying that his restlessness was the cause of the accident. Recalling the events, the prosecutor smiled. He and his colleagues had laughed at the time, he admitted. As a blatant example of tainted evidence, the woman's testimony became a running joke in the prosecutor's office. Yet, the prosecutor regretted the events. The driver, a senior company manager, got away scot-free.

This case illustrates the fact that prosecutors also seek to prosecute foreign nationals even if the odds are against them. They are under pressure from different sides, not only the company or the Chinese embassy but also the regional government's executive branches or the Ministry of Foreign Affairs, which seeks to protect the interests of foreign contractors and investors. According to the prosecutor who prosecuted this case, the most crucial feature was that the victim or their family would be compensated. "Federal and state prosecutors have the discretion to discontinue criminal charges if the public interest is involved." This often happens when the case concerns a foreign party:

If there are legal proceedings against them, the Chinese complain to the government that it affects their work. They try to lobby government officials. The government, in turn, takes heed of these cases. If they are prosecuted for certain crimes, they may say that the project will incur delays. The Chinese are well aware of the interests of the government and take advantage of this. They may say, "How can we continue our project if this person is prosecuted? He is crucial to the project." . . . Even if the court gives a decision on a case, these judgments are rarely executed. We occasionally visit prison facilities. You will not find foreign nationals there, apart from individuals prosecuted for political crimes. You will not find foreign nationals who are held liable for ordinary crimes.[97]

The frank and forthright reflections of this public prosecutor, who has twenty-four years of work experience in Bahir Dar and other areas in West Gojjam, Amhara, convey the reality that immunity is often granted, whether it is asked for or not. If foreign nationals are prosecuted, the judgment may not be enforced. He also notes that the interests of the Chinese party and the government overlap: They seek to finish construction projects without delay. After such incidents, the Chinese national in question often remains in the country and may be sent to work on another project in a different region. The prosecutor added, "The government knows. They obtained permission from the government." This statement hints at the conspiracy between Chinese contractors and the government—a connivance against which many litigants and legal professionals, as I show in the following chapters, fight.

On whether he recalled specific cases subject to interference, the prosecutor replied: "Yes, but I prefer not to tell you the details. I don't know what happens after these cases have been judged. I can, however, say that there are many such cases." The prosecutor's reluctance to give concrete examples reflects the ambiguous nature of interventions in cases involving foreigners. The fact that the prosecutor did not want to go into detail betrays the fact that various interested parties—whether the victim's family, community, colleagues, or the public—disapprove of such actions. Critical observers like him hold that immunity is a right granted to specific individuals by law, not a token of gratitude.

CLAIMING AND GRANTING IMMUNITY:
SOME REFLECTIONS

There is a tug-of-war between opposing forces on cases involving foreign nationals like Binzheng Zhang, not least with expatriate managers who demand to be treated leniently or pardoned for work accidents in return for their contribution to development. To them, immunity is a privilege that is legitimately extended in return for their service to the country. Indeed, the Latin root of the term immunity, *immunas*, means exemption from service, with *im* meaning "non" and *munas* "service."

However, these managers were not the only ones who claimed immunity. As we have seen, government functionaries and police officers occasionally pardoned foreign nationals, as in the actions of police officer Negus, who urged the Ethiopian party to settle their case. Police Chief Abebe justified foreigners' privileged status by drawing on the same argument as the one advanced by Chinese enterprise managers, thereby pulling the case into the political realm. If one considers criminal cases like the homicide in Liben an issue of national importance that threatens to disturb diplomatic relations between Ethiopia and China, the fate of Binzheng Zhang is not surprising.

The boundary between interventions and invitations as incursions on sovereignty, discussed in the introduction, and between demanding immunity and extending it, is not always clear. Did the state prosecutor drop charges against Binzheng Zhang at the request of the Chinese embassy, or was it because he received a phone call from the Ministry of Foreign Affairs? Interventions by the embassy and the ministry are not unheard of in criminal cases, especially if the reputation of the Chinese community is at stake.[98] And if it was the legal decision of a single prosecutor based on his judgment, why did he draw on this argument? According to Temesgen, the prosecutor was probably bribed by the Chinese company and used the argument as an excuse, although he has not been able to verify this.

Similarly, did Emperor Menelik II drop the arrest of the Italian engineer who killed one of his assistants at the request of the Italian mission? Or did he make this decision out of caution to avoid upsetting the foreign diplomatic corps? Did Emperor Haile Selassie reach a compromise in the case of Thakur Singh of his own accord, or did the British consul pressure him? The reality often lies somewhere in between, as both sides seek to protect their interests, including maintaining workable relations with the other. More importantly, the convergence of the parties' interests encourages collaboration and complicity. Whatever the case, there are usually members of the public with competing interests to protect, whether they want foreigners to be treated on equal terms with locals and their sovereignty to be preserved or whether they are not averse to profiting from this ambiguity by seeking extralegal compensation. In other words, claims for and gifts of immunity rarely go uncontested.

The Ethiopian Plaintiffs

"Even the Law Saw It and Smiled"

On September 29, 2020, Berihun found a letter on the noticeboard stating that his contract had been terminated, together with those of eight coworkers. His employer, the China Communications Construction Company (CCCC), cited the reduction of work due to Covid-19 as the reason for the dismissals. Berihun knew better. He took the letter and rushed off to the Bureau for Labor and Social Affairs.[1]

Berihun worked as a crane operator for CCCC, the Chinese state-owned enterprise that constructed the new bridge over the Blue Nile in Bahir Dar. About a year earlier, he had returned to his hometown "to beg from the Chinese," as he put it.[2] As an ethnic Amhara, he no longer felt safe in Oromia, where he had worked previously. Like many young men, he came back to his home region to find a dearth of employment opportunities. Grudgingly, he agreed to work on a salary that was less than half what he had earned before.

Berihun candidly confided that he had challenged the CCCC managers on several occasions. He had witnessed the company cutting corners and could not remain silent. Born and raised in Bahir Dar, he felt a sense of ownership over the bridge, which would be inaugurated in May 2024. Recounting his occasional fallouts with managers, he acknowledged, "I put some pressure on them, simply because I was concerned about the bridge. It belongs to the residents of the city." The company had skimped on building specifications related, for instance, to the depth of the bridge's forty-eight pillar holes. The holes were required to be at least twenty-two meters deep. Chinese managers had, according to Berihun, bribed the Ethiopian consultant engineers into approving holes that were as shallow as eighteen meters. This way, the company, or the individual managers who had conspired against their enterprise, could save costs not only on excavation work but also on building materials, such as cement, steel reinforcement, and crushed stone.

The abrupt dismissals had followed a comparable confrontation. One of the Ethiopian concrete mixer drivers had noticed Chinese engineers reusing old concrete by adding chemicals and water to dilute the aggregate. He informed the materials engineer of the consultant firm supervising the project, who, in turn, asked the Chinese project manager for an explanation. Concrete has a limited lifespan between batching and curing. Ready-mix concrete should be placed within at most two hours of the mixing process. Chinese managers flatly denied that they had used old concrete. As the Ethiopian materials engineer failed to convince his Chinese counterpart, he disclosed his informant, the driver. Soon after this incident, the notice appeared on the board.

The Bureau for Labor and Social Affairs of Bahir Dar city called the Chinese managers to their office. After protracted negotiations, the company agreed to reinstate six of the nine mixer drivers and machine operators. Berihun, together with two others, was classified as a troublemaker, and the management refused to take him back. Seething, Berihun took his case to court.

DIGNITY CLAIMS

Upset about injustices inflicted on not just them as individual workers but more often as a collective, be it the city of Bahir Dar and its residents or Ethiopia as a country, Ethiopian plaintiffs like Berihun framed their grievances in terms of dignity.[3] By so doing, they situated their claims outside the workplace and the all-consuming realm of capitalist accumulation. The Amharic word for respect or dignity, *kibir*, captures both social recognition and a sense of inner worth.[4] In a context of global capitalism, *kibir* acquired a collective edge that was expressed in nationalist and, at times, racial terms, referring to Ethiopia's or (black) Africa's place in the world.

Dignity claims responded to the racial inequalities produced and perpetuated in the workplace and beyond. Rather than a byproduct or coincidental characteristic of capitalism, as Cedric Robinson posits, race is central to its workings.[5] The expansion of global capitalism, and the devaluation and dispossession of black people on which it has fed and continues to feed, is reproduced by Chinese subjects and corporations,[6] even if in distinct forms that build on existing hierarchies mediated by enduring modalities of whiteness and blackness.[7] Importantly, the discriminatory dynamics of racial capitalism, in its new as much as its old iterations, seep into all realms of life.[8] The devaluation of racialized subjects serves to justify not only the suppression of wages and the subjection of workers to managerial whim[9] but also the skimping on building specifications and putting at risk the safety of a dehumanized public.

In this chapter, I seek to expose the underlying structures of inequality that generate immunity in African–Chinese encounters and the new forms of racial capitalism that sustain it. I zoom in on Ethiopian employees, who make up the largest group of plaintiffs, and ask why they take Chinese corporations to court, even when doing so requires them to make substantial and risky investments. The dynamics of power and inequality unearthed in this chapter, if most pronounced in the employer–employee relationship, also apply to disputes between Ethiopian subcontractors and Chinese contractors, Ethiopian suppliers and Chinese customers, and Ethiopian lessors and Chinese lessees, some of which I will introduce later in the book.

Local employees of Chinese construction firms described devaluation as three interrelated processes: the denial of voice, the denial of face, and the denial of humanity.[10] The notion of value in devaluation, here applied to people rather than things or actions, articulates human worth realized through public recognition. Value, as David Graeber reminds us, only exists within webs of social relations.[11] As I will show, it resides in interactions *beyond* as much as within the realm of accumulation and the networks that structure it. Workers creatively resisted processes of devaluation as they opposed and withstood their own disposability through legal institutions.[12]

Not being able to preserve one's dignity on one's home turf stung the most and fueled a desire to right a greater wrong. Linked to place and a sense of ownership, dignity was thus closely intertwined with self-determination, or sovereignty.[13] "They [Chinese managers] act as if they are in their own country" and "We feel like immigrants in our own country" were oft-repeated statements, suggesting that corporate managers set the rules and oversaw their observation as quasi-sovereigns. Despite the minimal means available to them, workers managed, at least partially, to recoup value for themselves, others who suffered a similar fate, and, more indirectly, the greater entity that had been harmed. They did so by addressing in court the corporation and its accomplice, the state.

The silent second defendant, then, was a government that not only failed to protect its citizens from the excesses of racial capitalism but also refused to share its benefits and profits with them.[14] Instead, the state granted "foreign money" (*ye-ferenj genzeb*)—as global capital was talked about in popular parlance—immunity at the cost of its own people and their dignity. Over the past decades, the Ethiopian state's unprecedented investment in infrastructure, much of it built by Chinese contractors, has occurred against the backdrop of people's struggles to access basic needs. Public works, then, come to embody contestations between citizens and the state.[15]

As I follow these contestations from the construction site to the courtroom, I show how collective calls for dignity transform into individual claims for rights to fit a particular legal mold. Most disputes were not about unlawful dismissal per se—the issue usually formulated by the court in labor cases—but about the taking

of the worker's dignity over the course of employment through myriad devaluation processes. The reformulation of grievances into legal rights suggests that while
workers' dignity claims expressed a desire to think oneself outside the confines of
political economic structures, capitalism pulled them back in.[16] Even so, the court
victories obtained by Ethiopian plaintiffs partly achieved their disguised purpose
of restoring the dignity of the worker and that of a collective.

I start by unpacking the notion of dignity as it was perceived by the Ethiopian
employees of Chinese construction firms whom I met over the course of 2020—a
turbulent year that put the already precarious position of Ethiopian laborers further on the line. More than five years of ethnic strife had ground labor mobility to
a halt, leaving workers with few options but to accept worse employment conditions than they had accepted before.[17] Drawing on case files and courtroom observations, I furthermore capture moments in which dignity was rearticulated, as
Ethiopian workers confronted their Chinese employers in court. To be sure, given
the dependence of workers on their employer, there were obvious limits to recoup-
ing value. Yet, however minor the court victories were, they warrant attention. A
critical mass of court victories contributed to shaking the confidence of corporate
managers, instilling in them some caution, doubt, and occasionally fear.

DENIAL OF VOICE: "YOU HAVE A JOB"

Berihun was taken aback by the question asking whether he had tried to talk to
his Chinese managers. He hesitated. "They don't give you a chance to speak. If you
go to them, you might be fired. You don't have the right to ask questions."[18] Given
the precarious job market, even Berihun, who is normally outspoken, did not dare
approach Chinese managers, let alone speak up. If there was something that bothered him, he instead turned to the Bureau for Labor and Social Affairs, as he had
done when he found his termination letter on the noticeboard.

The reluctance of expatriate managers to listen to workers caused resentment.
Abel, a human resources officer who worked for the China Gezhouba Group on
the Gereb Giba Dam project near Mekelle, explained how the lack of communication caused confusion and disgruntlement among workers: "The Chinese dismiss
workers simply by saying 'Go! Go!' They don't communicate, leaving the worker
puzzled as to why he is dismissed. When a worker fails to adjust to the work culture of the Chinese, they are quick to fire him. Or when the worker fails to accept
an order right away, they simply fire him. These workers go to court as a result."[19]

The Chinese corporate culture forced employees, especially racial others, to bot-
tle up their feelings and swallow their concerns, as they quietly accepted decisions
and submitted to demands.[20] Talking back was risky. It could lead to dismissal.

Communication between Chinese managers and Ethiopian workers was mostly
one-directional. Chinese foremen used monosyllabic expressions, combined with
gestures, to pass on orders. Low-level managers who had been in Ethiopia for a

long time used a pidgin—a contact language largely composed of Amharic, Chinese, and English.[21] Even if the contact language smoothed conversations, its vocabulary remained restricted to serving its narrow function of labor management. It did not contain words to express nuance or feelings.

Apart from the language barrier and a corporate hierarchy that prevented words from traveling up, the pregnant silences and indirect speech that characterized communication between Chinese managers and Ethiopian laborers also resulted from the fact that words could reveal the exploitative nature of global capital in Chinese-managed enterprises.[22] Utterances could hurt the listener or risk the speaker's loss of face.[23] As a result, much was left unsaid.

Ethiopians who had worked with Chinese employers for a long time, however, discovered that they could communicate with managers through mediated and humorous words. Especially if they were expressed in the manager's native tongue, such mediated phrases were more likely to find a willing ear. Abel, who had taught himself Mandarin over the more than ten years that he worked for Chinese enterprises, acted as a linguistic broker. He mediated between Ethiopian employees and Chinese supervisors by expressing delicate matters for others. However, Abel, too, had to be careful:

> Sometimes workers ask me, "Why don't you persuade them [the Chinese]?" Honestly, I feel for them. Yet, we can't persuade the Chinese, simply because we are their employees too. They don't listen to us. They don't respect us. They don't really listen to what you say. If you say, "The law says this, please do this," or if you tell them that they should look after their Ethiopian employees in the same way as they look after their Chinese employees, they simply respond, "You have a job. You have a bed. You have food."[24]

When Chinese managers did answer, they typically threw the ball back into the workers' court. The complainants had no reason to be dissatisfied with the opportunities that management had so generously offered to them. "You have a job" was the usual reply to workers' protests and requests. Or "If you are dissatisfied, you can leave." This phrase brought an end to a conversation in which managers denied any responsibility. Note that Abel draws a link between the unwillingness to listen and the reluctance to give respect. Workers perceived management's denial of voice as an unwillingness to recognize a subordinate's dignity.

In some instances, Chinese managers did listen to Abel. Over the years, he had learned to create opportunities to be heard. One of his strategies was to add his voice to a stronger voice from, for instance, the Ethiopian client of the project, on whom the Chinese contractor depended for regular payments and political backing. During a conversation we had at the Dove Café, a grand cafeteria opposite the Tigray Supreme Court in Mekelle, Abel received a phone call from his Chinese line manager at the project management camp. He solicited Abel's assistance in the company's negotiations with their client, the State Water Resources

Bureau. The bureau had requested the contractor hire security personnel to be stationed at the reservoir to prevent its water from being "contaminated" by locals. Abel turned to Bereket and me, whispering, "I show you. They can really shout."[25] He switched on the loudspeaker and a cacophony of Chinese male voices blasted out of his phone. Apart from his manager, two other Chinese men participated in the heated discussion. Hiring extra security personnel meant additional expenses for the company, explaining the Chinese managers' hesitance. Yet, they could not decline their client's request. One of the Chinese managers suggested that the security guards could stay in the workers' quarters to save costs.

Listening thus far, Abel then chimed in, stating matter-of-factly that it was not an option to have the guards stay with the workers. He urged his managers to build a separate shelter without explaining why—perhaps to avoid potential questions from management about the validity of his statement. As I discuss in greater detail below, Chinese managers were often insensitive to the social distinctions among Ethiopian staff based on status of occupation and seniority. For this reason, the guards, who were often local community elders, needed their own accommodation. His Chinese managers gave in.

After he hung up, Abel grinned, "See. They want to eat you." Abel used the verb "eat" to describe the domineering attitude of his managers.[26] The metaphor of eating is widely deployed in reference to the grief that Chinese corporations inflict on members of the local community, whether in the form of denial, denigration, or the deaths caused by freshly laid asphalt, which encourages drivers to pick up speed, leading to fatal accidents. Abel nonetheless got what he wanted. He had not only preserved the dignity of the security personnel but also prevented disputes on this matter arising in the future. This incident shows that Abel did, in fact, persuade management to do something in a way that protected the interests of the workers. He knew that the Chinese managers were likely to compromise in this instance, just because the request came from a voice that could not be ignored: their client.

Another strategy of speaking up or talking back to Chinese supervisors was to do so with humor. Humorous words softened the content of what was being said, as Abel explained: "Once we were working on site. There was a quick-witted worker. He often quarreled with the Chinese. The Chinese told him to go. They said, 'Go!' He replied, 'You go! Me, this Ethiopia.' He meant that he is in his own country and that the Chinese were the ones who were supposed to leave, not him. The Chinese laughed. We laughed too."[27]

The laborer was allowed to stay on. Workers like him who accommodated the whims of Chinese foremen with a smile came to enjoy working with them and could stay on for years. Many, however, were uncomfortable with the Chinese management style. The managers' denial of voice stoked resentment. Owing to the denial of voice on top of the language barrier, it was, workers believed, impossible to sit down and reach a negotiated solution. Their answer to "Go!" was legal action.

DENIAL OF FACE: "THEY ASK YOU TO WASH THEIR FEET"

The denial of face, as a sense of social recognition or outer respect, manifested in the Chinese managers' lack of sensitivity about Ethiopian status hierarchies, despite the importance attached to protecting face in Chinese society.[28] When assigning tasks, expatriate managers frequently failed to make the social distinctions that mattered to the workers and from which they derived face. "If you are hired as a bar binder, they will ask you to carry poles," Berihun expounded with a whiff of indignation.[29] "Or they demand you to haul cement sacks. These workers are experts in one thing, but they have to do another thing. They even have to pump out toilets. If you refuse to do so, you will be fired."

Manual work has long been stigmatized in Ethiopian society, even though discrimination is officially banned.[30] The stigma of craftwork as dirty and craftworkers as not fully human lives on, as Daniel Mains shows in his work with unemployed young men in Jimma, Oromia, who decide to forgo an income to avoid losing respect.[31] Social pressure based on what is called *yilugnta*—self-conscious pride that is intricately linked to what significant others think—informs occupational choices as young men seek to maximize status rather than income.[32] Cleaning toilets was the worst, for it was considered not only a lowly job but also women's work, and therefore threatened to hurt a male worker's masculine pride.

Melashu, an interpreter for a Chinese private subcontractor at Gereb Giba, recalled with vicarious shame one incident that revealed Chinese disregard for professional distinctions.[33] His Chinese manager had hired his friend, a driver, on his recommendation. After having worked for a week, the driver saw a daily laborer struggling with excavation work, so he joined in to help. "It was kind of him," Melashu commented, adding resolutely, "but he should not have done it." The next day, the Chinese manager brought the driver a shovel and gloves and ushered him to the building site: "I'm embarrassed to tell you. My friend was made to dig for the entire week, by which time the manager had forgotten that he was a driver."[34] Melashu's friend could not bear the shame and resigned, to the incredulity of the Chinese manager.

Knowingly or unknowingly, Chinese managers routinely denied Ethiopian workers face, not only in, but also beyond, the workplace. Berihun and his former coworkers, Eyob, who was a welder, and Girma, who was a mechanic, also came from Bahir Dar and liked to dress well. They put on clean, fashionable clothes when they left the house each morning and changed into their work gear at the workplace. At the end of the day, they changed back into their fine clothes before returning home. Because the water tank was near the mechanic's workshop where Eyob and Girma spent most of the day, they asked a plumber to lead a water pipe from the tank to an open space next to the shed so they could take a shower.[35] One day, however, a Chinese manager walked by. Expostulating that the water was meant for drinking, he grabbed a saw and cut through the pipe. When recalling this incident, Eyob claimed, "They only want to see you in workwear."[36] By refusing the workers' desire to leave work clean and travel home with dignity, they denied them face.

The perceived denial of face was perhaps best captured by a remark by Girma, who had recently been dismissed for refusing to clean the toilets. "They want you to wash their feet," he grumbled.[37] As mentioned in the introduction, the Ethiopian practice of foot-washing symbolizes vertical power and embodies profound deference.[38] To wash the feet of a foreign employer epitomized the denial of face in Girma's eyes. His observations and objections correspond with those leveled by Zambian workers against their expatriate managers at the Chinese-run farms near Lusaka described by Di Wu.[39] According to Wu, tensions in Chinese management and Zambian labor relations arise from the conflicting directions in which attentiveness flows between superior and subordinate. Whereas attentiveness flows upward to those ranked higher in Chinese settings, meaning that workers are expected to display devotion towards the boss and keep them company in exchange for favors, attentiveness flows downward in the Zambian context, where the boss is expected to care for their workers in exchange for authority and loyalty. The contrast in these flows of attentiveness is a frequent source of misunderstandings. Ethiopian workers, too, complained that their expatriate superior did not display care.[40] They rarely greeted the workers, let alone asked how they were, appearing indifferent to their well-being.[41] Their Chinese managers, in contrast, expected the workers to display respect to them rather than the other way around. However, these cultural differences were lost in translation, causing conflicts and fueling grievances. Misunderstandings or not, these practices led to the perceived devaluation of workers.

DENIAL OF HUMANITY: "THEY THROW US AWAY, JUST LIKE SOCKS"

Closely related to the denial of face was the denial of humanity, or a sense of intrinsic human worth. "They respect you until you finish your job," Melashu said.[42] The bond between the Chinese managers and Ethiopian workers and the recognition the former gave to the latter, he explained, seldom extended beyond the workplace. "Once you have completed your job, you are nothing for them. They will not even talk with you for two minutes. . . . They use you and throw you away, just like socks."[43] Socks are the least valued item of clothing, and a wearer's relationship with them is fleeting. The same held true for the manager–laborer relationship. Melashu regretted that his Chinese managers were interested in him only as a worker, not as a person, and valued his labor power, not his worth as a human being. It is therefore not surprising that Ethiopians framed their demands in broader terms of dignity and situated these outside the capitalist realm.

Melashu had started working with Chinese companies more than ten years previously, when he joined the Tekeze Dam project near his hometown, Abiy Addi, in Tigray. He had since switched among Chinese companies, which took him from Bahir Dar to Welayta to Dire Dawa to Afar and back—places hundreds of miles apart. He had learned many trades from his expatriate superiors, from repairing vehicles to driving loaders and from operating excavators to maintaining the construction equipment for the dam. He owed them a lot, he confided. "They are hardworking people, but they lack humanity," Melashu concluded.[44] He had recently taken them to court as, in his eyes, management had crossed a red line by violating his dignity. Teaming up with two former colleagues, he had filed a case at one of the district courts in Mekelle and won.

Melashu, like other Ethiopian workers, couched his critique of Chinese managers in a language of humanity, or *sebawinet.* The Chinese supervisors, they explained, rarely displayed human emotions, at least not sympathetic ones such as compassion or gratitude. Worse still, they failed to treat workers as humans. Assaults to the workers' dignity were exacerbated by a perceived disregard for their health and safety. The staff were rarely equipped with hard hats, safety shoes, protective gloves, or reflective vests. "They may give you a fluorescent vest when a government official visits the site, or a higher manager of the Chinese company. The next morning you are supposed to hand it back," Berihun snorted. "It's just for the show. They do not care about safety." I should note here that the project management was equally lax when it came to the health and safety of its expatriate staff, who walked on the hot asphalt in canvas shoes and climbed concrete slabs without safety helmets.

Their perceived denial of humanity was further compounded by the meager wages paid by the Chinese companies, which, according to workers, were not enough to subsist on. Even though wages are not much lower than those paid by local companies, they are typically viewed as low in proportion to the presumed wealth of the Chinese multinational enterprises. "They [the Chinese] familiarized themselves with our economy," Melashu explained, describing the attitude of Chinese managers as shrewd.[45] "They came to realize that if they fire twenty workers today, they will find forty new workers tomorrow." Ethiopia's poverty, combined with its enormous labor surplus, led Chinese managers to regard workers as cheap, in the same way that the federal government promoted Ethiopian labor as "cheap" to attract foreign investors.[46]

The unstable political climate has further driven down wages, and the already precarious position of Ethiopian laborers in the construction sector has deteriorated as a result. Labor mobility decreased significantly in the wake of growing ethnic violence, well before the start of the civil war in November 2020. Many workers from Amhara and Tigray returned to their home regions in fear for their lives. Melashu, for instance, left Amhara in 2018 due to growing anti-Tigrayan sentiments that made him feel increasingly uncomfortable. Berihun no longer felt safe in Oromia, where he had worked on several projects, and he returned to Amhara. Owing to the decrease in mobility, labor has become plentiful and cheap, especially in Ethiopia's two northernmost regions. Chinese firms are aware of the precarious situation and the availability of labor, and, according to the critical Ethiopian workers, take advantage of it.

"I drive big trucks. I could drive to different corners of the country," Eyob explained.[47] "Instead, we prefer to stay here [in Bahir Dar]. But we have to cope on a discount salary, making us beggars to the Chinese."[48] Eyob uses the pronoun "we" to refer to himself and his coworkers on the Nile bridge project, all of whom are Amharas. The word "beggar" is a loaded term in Ethiopia. Begging is considered a shameful activity for an able-bodied man. As beggars to the Chinese, workers believed they were under the threat of losing respect as well as their dignity.[49]

Chinese managers acted as though they were in their own country, some held, disrespecting Ethiopia's sovereignty. They did as they pleased, skirting regulations and circumventing the law. A staff member of the Bahir Dar City Bureau for Labor and Social Affairs did not mince words when she reflected on the feedback she had received from workers on the Nile bridge project: "Frankly, they use workers like trash. They don't treat them with dignity. When we went for inspection and questioned employees [about their labor conditions], they had many complaints. They said, 'It feels like we are not living in our own country' and 'The Chinese act as if they are living in their country.' They boss laborers around. 'We feel like immigrant workers,' they said."[50]

Workers' self-portrayal as immigrant workers, alongside their depictions of managers as setting the rules as though they were in their own country, are telling of the way they perceive expatriate management. The female staff member of the bureau put her finger on the sore spot: "Ethiopian workers have pride in what they do. They don't want to be treated in ways that hurt their pride."[51] Only by granting workers their dignity, and autonomy as an intrinsic part of it, would Ethiopians work well. She had urged enterprise management to change their employment practices and was not surprised that many workers went to court.

In short, dignity harm, in the Ethiopian workers' experience, was an accumulation of the denial of voice, the denial of face, and the denial of humanity. This triple denial implied a refusal of managers to recognize the presence of the laborers as humans capable of giving an account of themselves and of the way in which they organized their lives.[52] The Ethiopian workers refused to accept dignity threats and sought to restore their dignity within the space available to them. The court offered them a relatively affordable opportunity to do so.

RECOURSE TO THE COURTS

The courts were the only institution to which Ethiopian workers could turn to hold their employer accountable for dignity threats. Due to the time and cost of litigation and the language spoken in courts—Afaan Oromo in Oromia, Tigrigna in Tigray, and Amharic in the other states and the federal system—workers native to the region in which they worked were more likely to enter litigation and see their lawsuits through to the end. The plaintiffs occupied various positions up and down the corporate hierarchy, including daily laborers, supervisors, mechanics, machine operators, drivers, administrative personnel, interpreters, and even lawyers. Litigation was, however, gendered. The plaintiffs were almost exclusively men. The mobilization of the law in the male-dominated construction industry contrasts with the more informal forms of protest and resistance initiated by the predominantly female workforce of Ethiopia's textile and apparel industries.[53] Female factory workers primarily vote with their feet and leave the job if they are dissatisfied or disgruntled.[54] Yet litigation seems to be also on the rise in the manufacturing sector.[55]

Sporadically, Chinese enterprise managers sued at the prompting of their Ethiopian legal advisors. They preferred to solve disputes out of court, mainly through negotiation or mediation by their in-house counsel. Painful court experiences had made them hesitant to return to courts that, in their eyes, "favored locals." The only reason they might pursue a lawsuit to its conclusion—even when the counterparty is willing to settle out of court—is to transfer responsibility to a neutral arbiter. This is particularly true for managers of state-owned enterprises, who may be reluctant to make decisions out of fear that they will have to justify their actions to superiors and face personal consequences if the dispute resolution leads to unfavorable outcomes. A court verdict conveniently absolves them of this responsibility.

Supported by the coercive power of the law and invested with the symbolic power of the state,[56] the courts created a platform on which judges compelled litigants, especially unwilling expatriate managers, to listen, thereby granting workers a voice, as I will show in chapter 5. This is not to say that Chinese enterprise managers willingly accepted the court's authority. They did not want to have anything to do with the courts and were, in the eyes of Chinese managers, not supposed to. After all, they had brought the development that Ethiopia so urgently needed.

The court, however, had little patience for arguments like these. It entertained in absentia if managers or other company representatives failed to come to court and often decided against them, forcing Chinese enterprise managers to take the court and, by extension, their own workforce, seriously. In short, national courts could hold Chinese corporations liable when other venues failed to do so. Court decisions were binding and were by and large enforced. Other organs may listen to complaints but are unable to act decisively. Although it is largely sympathetic to the laborers' cause, the Bureau for Labor and Social Affairs—a government body mandated to mitigate labor disputes between employers and employees—can only mediate disputes. Although they are recorded, the agreements they broker are not binding. Chinese management often eschewed the bureau, knowing it had little authority. They did not turn up at meetings or were slow to respond to the bureau's requests and suggestions.

Community elders, who traditionally carry much weight in Ethiopian society, were equally ineffective when it came to settling disputes with a foreign party. As outsiders, Chinese managers did not recognize, let alone respect, their authority, and they were not susceptible to the social punishments available to the elders to mete out, such as curses and ostracism. Furthermore, the Ethiopian media is not traditionally a medium through which grievances are addressed, especially when these grievances do not align with the government's point of view, which, workers believed, stood behind capital.[57]

Of course, the law, too, discriminates. It tends to favor the haves over the have-nots.[58] Like Chinese company managers, rank-and-file workers were unfamiliar with the system and had limited legal knowledge. They did not have the financial means to hire a lawyer and turned to scribes. Asking between fifty and two hundred birr to draft legal documents such as pleadings, scribes are Ethiopia's barefoot lawyers seated in shaded areas around the courthouse. Yet, scribes were not allowed to enter the courtroom, where plaintiffs were left to their own devices. Generally, however, pleadings drafted by scribes went a long way, offering judges important leads as to the source and nature of the dispute and the components of the claim.

Despite their unfamiliarity with judicial procedure and lack of legal knowledge, many laborers coped well enough in court as pro se litigants, not least because many lower-court judges took them by the hand, explained the process, and hinted at their substantive rights.[59] In fact, the first cassation decision involving a Chinese corporation that made its way, in 2009, into the corpus of precedents, published yearly by the Federal Supreme Court in Addis Ababa, concerns exactly this issue.[60]

In *Biniyam Geremew v. China Road and Bridge Corporation*, the plaintiff sued at the Fogera Wereda Court in South Gondar, Amhara, accusing the Chinese enterprise of wrongful dismissal.[61] Initially, Biniyam claimed a severance payment and two months' salary. The lower-court judge, however, allowed him to modify the claim to include awards to which he might also be entitled. In his modified pleading, he claimed a severance payment, a payment for the failure to give notice, compensation for unlawful termination, and compensation for vacation days he never received. Dissatisfied with the decision, China Road and Bridge Corporation appealed to the High Court, which decided that the amount of claim could not be increased and awarded the plaintiff the amount he had initially requested. After the state supreme court confirmed the decision of the high court, the Ethiopian worker filed for appeal at the Federal Supreme Court.

The cassation bench ruled that judges were allowed to give plaintiffs the opportunity to amend their pleading to cover all their rights with an eye to rendering a "just decision."[62] When laborers were unaware of their rights, judges could resort to this intervention. Occasionally, however, judges granted damages that the plaintiffs did not claim in their pleading, thereby going beyond the law (see chapter 3).

Court victories enhanced workers' morale. News about legal triumphs spread fast and inspired others to try their luck, so much so that workers, in the words of an irritated Chinese manager, "get hired to be fired to sue us in court." However, if a court case dragged on, litigation could become expensive, especially for those who did not have a support network on which to fall back.

WHY DID PLAINTIFFS GO TO COURT?

If we look beyond the legal argument in which dignity claims had to be cast to be accepted by the court, it was the restoration of dignity that mattered most to plaintiffs, more so than the assertion of legal rights set out in the country's labor law or the monetary rewards they may obtain. It certainly mattered to Melashu and his colleagues Abel and Tekeste, who filed a suit at the Hadenet Wereda Court in Mekelle. The three had been employed by Tiesiju Civil Engineering Group (CTCE), a Chinese state-owned company that was carrying out a project building a road from Quiha to Mekelle Industrial Park before the war. CTCE had failed to give the two interpreters and foreman an employment contract. "Tomorrow, tomorrow," his manager had responded when Melashu asked.[63] Because the company did offer him a decent salary of fifteen thousand birr, he decided to stay on. A few months into their employment, Melashu, Abel, and Tekeste's Chinese line manager made a mistake and was replaced with another Chinese engineer, who had worked for the company on another project.[64]

One day his new manager asked Melashu to collect all the workers before the end of the workday. "You, you, and you," his Chinese manager snarled, pointing his finger at him, Abel, and Tekeste. "We don't need you anymore. Get your outstanding salary and leave."[65] After this, everyone left. The manager, it turned out, then reinstated the workers who had worked with him previously. The dismissals, in other words, were related to a controversial changing of the guard and had nothing to do with the three men.

Melashu, Abel, and Tekeste tried to explain to the management that a dismissal without notice in this situation was unlawful. They met a grumpy manager, who sent them away. Subsequently, the three workers visited the Bureau for Labor and Social Affairs, which called the company management to their office. The Chinese foreman who came to the bureau stood firm, however, and claimed that the three had been employed as daily laborers and their termination was lawful. At that point, going to court was the only option left for Melashu, Abel, and Tekeste.

In court, CTCE went so far as to deny having employed the plaintiffs in the first place. The lower-court judge was swayed both by this argument and by the evidence provided to support it and ruled that the plaintiffs had not been employees of the company and were not entitled to compensation as a result. Melashu, Abel, and Tekeste then filed an appeal at the Mekelle High Court, which found that the workers had in fact been employed by CTCE and remanded the case. As Melashu recalled, "The company came up with this argument to escape liability. Even the law saw it and smiled."[66] The second time around, the plaintiffs won.

Melashu went to court because his employers had violated his and his colleagues' dignity. Even worse, they had done so in his home region, Tigray. His Chinese supervisors had acted as though they were in their own country. Worst of all, the company had not been willing to make a single concession. "If they would have paid us an additional month of salary, we would not have gone to court," Melashu said. The Chinese managers' unwillingness to compromise angered the men. It was the final straw. Looking back at his court experience, Melashu reminisced, "I never gave up on the law."[67]

The question of why workers brought their labor disputes to court can be fully answered only by also considering *whom* they sued. Chinese enterprises were taken to represent a rising global power that had become economically advanced and wealthy—a model for others to follow. Chinese multinational enterprises, workers believed, had the resources to create good working conditions and pay decent wages. Instead, they flagrantly failed to do so. "We are Africans. We live in a dark continent, and yet we have the capacity to evaluate them. They say the company is the fifth-largest contractor in the world," Eyob said about his former employer, implying that it ought to meet high standards.[68] Nor did "China" live up to its growing prominence in the world. Eyob added: "The Chinese are from the civilized world. China is in good shape, economically. The country competes with leading countries. But how can they treat workers this badly?"[69] Eyob, Melashu, and Abel answered this question in economic terms ("because Ethiopia is poor"); Berihun in racial terms ("because we are black").[70] The three workers spoke directly to the distributional inequalities racial capitalism produced.

In her research on working-class women in Antigua and Barbuda who take their children's fathers to court to pay child support, Mindie Lazarus-Black demonstrates that women are more likely to sue fathers who are considered "big men" and are thus expected to support their children because they are financially capable and because their social status dictates that they should.[71] They are less likely to bring suit against fathers who struggle to get by. A similar dynamic is at play in

Ethiopia. Chinese companies are expected to fulfil their minimal duties of paying proper wages and respecting workers. Dignity violations stung especially because Chinese multinational enterprises backed by global capital had the financial means to treat Ethiopian workers with dignity. Note that Eyob used the plural pronoun "we." He referred not only to himself and his colleagues but also to Ethiopians and Africans more generally, construing dignity as a collective good.

DIGNITY IN THE PLURAL

In the courts the plaintiffs often addressed broader concerns beyond their individual legal claims. They intended to right a greater wrong or at least draw attention to it. Even though the court narrowed labor disputes to the question of whether the plaintiff's contract had been terminated lawfully and to how much compensation they would be entitled if this were the case, the workers found an opportunity to raise more substantial issues and have them put on the public record.[72] In the case of *Abadir Abdulsemed and Tesfahun Abibual v. Konso Yabelo Asphalt Road Construction Company*, a labor case that went all the way to the Federal Supreme Court Cassation Division,[73] where it received a decision in May 2017, the plaintiffs shed light on their former employer's malpractices and, more indirectly, the dignity harm it had inflicted on them as well as a greater entity.

The case was first entertained at a lower court in Borena, southern Ethiopia. The plaintiffs, Abadir and Tesfahun, had worked as surveyors for CTCE, the Chinese state-owned enterprise that I introduced earlier, which was granted a contract to carry out the construction of the Konso–Yabelo road in 2014. Neither the plaintiffs nor the respondent seems to have been represented by counsel. The surveyors stated that they had been wrongfully dismissed after raising objections to a design change that, they claimed in their pleading, had harmed "the country's economy."[74] Their Chinese line manager had refused to listen. Annoyed by the surveyors' objections, he fired them.

The contractor presented a different reading of the events. In its response, it stated that the management had dismissed the plaintiffs because they failed to come to work for five days in a row, starting on October 6, 2015. On October 10, 2015, it posted a letter of termination on its noticeboard. Ethiopia's Labor Proclamation allows employers to terminate an employment agreement without notice when an employee is absent from work for five or more consecutive days without supplying a good reason. The termination, CTCE argued, had therefore been in accordance with the law.

During the trial, the plaintiffs' witnesses testified that when the surveyors came to work on the morning of October 6, 2015, a Chinese manager known as Mr. Tian prevented them from entering the workplace. Abadir and Tesfahun returned the next morning, when they were met by security personnel, who ordered them to leave. Despite these witnesses' testimonies, which showed that the plaintiffs had in fact come to work, the lower court ruled in favor of the company, stating that the termination was lawful.

Dissatisfied with the decision of the wereda court, the plaintiffs filed for appeal at the Borena Zone High Court, which decided that the plaintiffs had sufficiently proven that they were present at the workplace on October 6 and 7, 2015. It reversed the decision of the lower court, awarding Abadir 240,000 birr and Tesfahun 252,750 birr—about 170,000 birr short of the 665,500 they had originally claimed. CTCE subsequently took the case to the Oromia Supreme Court, which reversed the decision of the High Court and confirmed the decision of the wereda court, whereupon the plaintiffs appealed to the Federal Supreme Court Cassation Division in Addis Ababa. The Cassation Bench ruled that Article 27.1b of Labor Proclamation 377/2003, which states that the employer can terminate an employee's contract without notice on the grounds of "absence from work without good cause for a period of five consecutive working days," was not applicable, because the workers had appeared at work.[75] It did, however, change the damages awarded to each plaintiff to 45,000 birr for severance payments, in accordance with the contract they had signed.

Unfortunately, I have not been able to talk to the plaintiffs, so we are left to guess their motivations. Reading between the lines of this case, however, shows that Abadir and Tesfahun had attempted to speak up about the injustice done to a greater entity: "the country's economy." The company had not only rejected their voices when they raised objections and dismissed them for it, it had also violated respect for the country. Design changes could have a significant effect on the quality of the road and the safety of its users. Cutting corners in construction shortens the lifespan of the public utility in question, something of which Abadir and Tesfahun were aware, much like Berihun, who tried to raise awareness about design breaches at the project in Bahir Dar.

By classifying the surveyors as troublemakers, management had instead created an opportunity to dismiss them using a legally valid reason: their absence from work for five consecutive days. This shows that the company was aware of the conditions for the termination of a contract without notice and had attempted to use the law to its benefit. The plaintiffs won nonetheless, even though they may have been disappointed with the damages awarded to them by the Federal Supreme Court. The court ruled they were in the right, thereby giving them voice and holding the company liable.

This case is an illustration of a trend that became clearer in the courtroom, where plaintiffs, especially when they were not represented, veered away from the legal argument to address grievances that had little to do with the unlawful termination of contract or their request for overtime wages. What concerned them was their employer's treatment over the entire period of employment that had led to a confrontation that ultimately culminated in their dismissal. This treatment was often experienced as humiliating. Furthermore, humiliation was not limited to employment relations. Breaches of contracts or designs—which, as Melashu had it, Chinese firms could only do because Ethiopia was a poor country dependent on foreign loans and investment—hurt too. Dignity assaults were collectively felt, turning individual incidents into instances of national humiliation.

VOICE, FACE, AND HUMANITY RESTORED?

The experiences of the plaintiffs at court were, by and large, positive, even if few received the amount of compensation they requested. In the case of Abadir and Tesfahun, the plaintiffs had wanted to draw attention to the events that had led to their dismissal, even though the court had concentrated on the narrow legal question of whether their termination was lawful. The fact that we can nonetheless read the plaintiffs' story in the cassation court judgment shows that they succeeded, at least partially, in bringing to light the questionable practices of their former employer. It was there, on the public record.

Berihun's case was not yet decided at the time of writing, nor were those of Eyob and Girma. Berihun is hopeful, even though he has come to realize after attending pretrial meetings that the court is not necessarily interested in the complete story: "The Labor Proclamation does not focus on the rights of the workers. It doesn't give rights to the workers. . . . *The law does not raise the question of why the worker is fired.* It does not even give power to the different offices to put pressure on the companies. It seems that the Chinese have all the power. They even feel that this is their own country"[76] (emphasis added).

The law focused on the *how* question, not the *why* question. It thereby leaped over wider issues of injustice. What workers like Berihun cared most about were the events that led to their dismissal or resignation—events that they experienced collectively. Despite Berihun's disappointment about the legal framing of the dispute, the court did offer him a space where he could express what he had long wanted to say and an opportunity to regain respect.

Melashu, Abel, and Tekeste were triumphant about the outcome of their collective labor case, even though the court process took longer than expected due to the retrial. Melashu and Abel were each awarded 150,000 birr, and Tekeste, a foreman employed on a lower salary, was awarded eighty thousand birr, approaching their initial claim of 467,860. The court had not granted them pay for overtime and rest days, as they had failed to prove that they had been at work during those times.

The monetary award was first and foremost confirmation that they had been in the right and their opponent in the wrong. The plaintiffs had obtained vindication—and more. Over the course of the court process, they had recovered their voice, reclaimed face, and restored their humanity. Melashu was, moreover, jubilant at the fact that he had been able to force his foreign employer to respect the law, and with it, he had regained his dignity and that of the collective.

FIGHTING IMMUNITY AND IMPUNITY

In the eyes of Ethiopian workers like Berihun, Eyob, and Melashu, disobeying the law, demanding exemption from it, or making one's own laws amounted to disrespect for the sovereignty of the country and the dignity of its people. By comparing the degradation of a worker to the humiliation of a country and framing dignity as self-determination, they placed respect for the law on par with respect for something greater or more fundamental. Expatriates, they believed, acted as if they enjoyed immunity, or worse, impunity. Yet, why did Ethiopian disputants—whether they were workers, business partners, subcontractors, or suppliers—bother with the law?

Ethiopians referred to and mobilized the law to add weight to their judgments or demands for improvement. As Christian Lund shows, the law can be both a solvent and a solidifier.[77] By promising state backing for a claim, legalization solidifies claims as rights. If effectively asserted and enforced, rights compel competing claims to dissolve. Before the court, plaintiffs were forced to use the language of the law to transform dignity claims into rights claims. However, the outcome of this translation exercise was never entirely satisfying. By narrowing claims down to circumscribed individual rights, the law and the interpreters of the law, the judiciary, seemed to express little interest in the underlying collective dignity violations. Even so, as an instrument, the law could become potent and productive. Legal victories reinstilled a sense of confidence and dignity.

Construing dignity as a collective feeling, a social status, and a shared objective, the plaintiffs associated threats to dignity with past instances of national humiliation and a collective sense of being Ethiopian. Dignity, as I demonstrated in this chapter, is intrinsically social and affective. The worth of a person or group requires an audience that acknowledges it. Since the court was one of the few venues where workers could obtain recognition, they began to respect its language, reframing their claims into rights. Yet not all plaintiffs were successful. Some lost their cases when they failed to prove that they had been unlawfully discharged from work—that is, when they were unsuccessful in turning their dignity claim into a legal argument. Others, after hearing about court victories of fellow workers, went to court opportunistically and unprepared. Irrespective of their motivations and the outcomes of their lawsuits, the plaintiffs embraced the opportunity the court afforded to express their voice and recoup their value as a result, restoring dignity to themselves and others by speaking out.[78]

To be sure, disputants blamed not only Chinese corporations but also, and at times more forcefully, the executive branches of state for allowing expatriate managers to make their own laws. State and foreign corporate interests and visions converge, especially within the developmental state model that the EPRDF government espoused. When development is viewed as a collective good, citizens are expected to cooperate with the state to achieve it.[79] Even though the administration under Abiy Ahmed has adopted a different economic and governance model, citizens continue to pay the price for development—a price that workers like Berihun, Melashu, Eyob, and Girma felt they paid in dignity.

Lawsuits and their outcomes nonetheless resulted in tangible improvements. Chinese corporations adjusted wage levels and formalized employer–employee relations. Yet some of these changes have been negated by the deteriorating situation in the country, which has curtailed labor mobility and forced workers to accept lower wages and worse conditions, turning them into "beggars," as Berihun put it. This dire reality makes it easy for sceptics to argue that litigation does not change the dynamics of dependence, much less the global inequalities on which they are founded and the legal and political immunities they generate.

I disagree. We should not so easily dismiss the power of plaintiffs. Those who went to court were morally determined and driven by principled convictions. They had the guts to stand up against wealthy multinational corporations. Bear in mind that many firms feature in the top 250 of international engineering contractors, with four, including CCCC, ranked in the top ten.[80] They have the financial capacity to hire the best lawyers, and since the courtroom has become their "second office," as one in-house counsel joked, alluding to the time his employer spent on litigation, they have become repeat players in the legal system. Even if it took them taking a big company to court, Ethiopian plaintiffs refused to accept structures of inequality and injustice. Not accepting the world as it is, the plaintiffs mobilized a law that at times smiled at them, acknowledging support. They asserted agency in the tightest of corners, to borrow John Lonsdale's apt words,[81] as they wrote history under conditions that were not of their own making. The next chapter shows how their insistent and creative writing affected incremental changes as they smashed expectations of immunity and destabilized corporate authority.

3

The Chinese Defendants

"The Law Is on Their Side"

I have worked in the mining industry and traveled a lot in the past years, both over land and sea. I have been to many places. [I have seen] green jade seas and blue skies, bustling metropoles, wild steppes, and farmlands. I have experienced everything. In all, the Democratic Republic of the Congo (DRC), in fact many other African countries too, give you a feeling of a small horse pulling a big carriage. The big carriage stands for a perfect administration and a legal system left by the Western colonialists. The small horse stands for the country's backward economic condition, the quality of the masses, the level of education, and so forth. The small horse cannot pull this whole superstructure. To give an example, the labor protection policies of the DRC come from Europe. To be born, to grow old, to get sick and to die, the company cares about this process for all family members of a worker. Given the state of the economy of this country, there is no way this can be realized. In 2012, the DRC copied the value-added tax policy of the French. We didn't know how it worked and went to the tax bureau. The tax bureau said: "We don't know; please have a look at the manual." It's all right. Now is the time to cross the river by groping the stones, at last they will be able to implement it.[1]

Few reflections convey Chinese views of the legal system in African countries as well as this post on Zhihu, the Chinese equivalent of Reddit. Even though the author—an "old overseas" who has worked and traveled in various parts of Africa—writes about the DRC, his observations resonate with those of Chinese managers I met in Ethiopia. Implied in the metaphor of the small horse pulling a too-heavy cart is China's own experience and the widespread belief that the country only developed at the pace it did due to the initial absence of formal laws. Entrepreneurs who took the plunge and ventured into business during China's transition from a planned economy to a market economy in the 1980s and 1990s capitalized on legal voids concerning property rights, taxes, company regulations, and other areas to accrue financial benefits and create business opportunities. In the eyes of this man, the combination of the socialist model ("to be born, to grow old, to get sick") that China had long abandoned to make way for market reforms, and a set of complex laws copied from European countries, hold the DRC and other African countries back.

As China's economy developed, so did its regulatory environment. Yet African countries had not yet reached this stage. Their laws were too "rigid," "protective," or "complete"—adjectives that many Chinese engineers in Ethiopia also used—for the country's level of development. Their apprehension of litigation and their claims for exemption from legal process and prosecution, in other words, should be partly understood in light of these views. Law, many firmly believed, stood in the way of development—a belief that some Ethiopian political elites also stand by. Despite his criticism, the old overseas embodies the Afro-optimism that has countered long-standing Western Afro-pessimism. He had no doubt that the DRC will develop and the horse will grow big enough to pull the carriage. It is just a matter of time and, as he put it, repeating Deng Xiaoping's adage, "Now is the moment to cross the river by groping the stones." Deng, who led China's economic reforms in the 1980s, advocated a measured and gradual approach to development, which African countries should also take if they want to advance in the man's eyes.

In this chapter, I reflect on the perspectives of Chinese enterprise managers and consider, first, what led them to claim immunity in certain situations and, second, how they responded when their claims were dismissed and their justifications brushed aside. To understand why some managers requested exemption from legal process and prosecution—or, for that matter, sought to circumvent the legal system in other ways—we must consider their attitudes toward the law and their experiences of life and work in Ethiopia more generally. Frustrations with local courts were often part of broader narratives of suffering. Notably, previous court experience, legal consciousness, educational background, ideological leanings, language skills, and other factors influenced their stance toward the legal system, making Chinese experiences and perspectives diverse. Most of my Chinese interlocutors, however, viewed development as a gift and litigation as a form of ingratitude that disrupted the cycle of reciprocity.

Despite disappointment and despondence, some Chinese managers let go of their grudges. They began accumulating legal knowledge, inspiring others to do the same. Their learning curve, I show in the second part of the chapter, manifested in three interconnected shifts. The first was a move away from a stubborn self-help approach to embracing legal advice from Ethiopian lawyers. The second was a leap away from band-aid solutions to conflict prevention. The third was a shift from the skillful use to the occasional abuse of the Ethiopian legal system. Insistent instructions from Ethiopian in-house counsel or legal consultants, who, alongside judges, pressed expatriate managers to abandon claims for immunity and change their attitude, enabled and accelerated this learning process.

"ETHIOPIANS HAVE THE FIRST AND THE LAST WORD"

Much like Western travelers, missionaries, and scholars in eighteenth- and nineteenth-century Ethiopia, Chinese managers described Ethiopians as litigious.[2] "Ethiopians like to go to court" was a typical response when I asked about the surge in lawsuits. While some attributed this litigiousness to custom and character, others described it as a manifestation of the rights Ethiopian citizens enjoyed and their trust in the courts as an avenue to claim these rights. They often connected litigiousness to the democratic nature of governance in Ethiopia, measured against China's authoritarianism.[3] To Chinese interlocutors, litigiousness symbolized the assertiveness of Ethiopians. "This country is a democracy. The people are powerful," a deputy project manager explained. The readiness and boldness with which Ethiopians asserted their rights in court were for him the ultimate evidence of the power of the people. "Ordinary people have the first and the last word."[4] Indeed, lurking behind his sense of frustration was an appreciation of Ethiopian litigiousness and perhaps envy of the legal protections that Ethiopian citizens, in his eyes, enjoyed. (Whether Ethiopians would agree is, of course, another matter.)

Chinese managers commonly drew a comparison between Ethiopia and China and their respective legal systems, using the former as either a positive or a negative mirror image of the latter. Two narratives stood out. By depicting China as an authoritarian state that denied citizens' rights protection, the first glorified Ethiopian democracy and praised the country's courts as effective institutions for claiming citizen rights. By contrast, the second narrative either painted Ethiopia's justice system as too developed for the country's level of economic development, as the old overseas in the prelude did, or as lagging in the efficient and fair delivery of justice compared with China.

Known for his critical views of the Chinese government, a civil engineer representing the first narrative described the law in China as a piece of toilet paper. "In China, you can change the law as you like. We have seen it with the Great Firewall," he explained, referring to internet censorship. "The government made traversing the wall illegal. It simply adapted the law to its policies. Even the constitution can be changed in a wink, like Xi Jinping did to extend his term."[5] A law that political leaders can change to their liking cannot be called a law, he maintained. "They say China has a rule of law [fazhi]. But where is the law?" This engineer was equally critical of Chinese courts, which he depicted as corrupt and plagued by government interference. In other words, even if Chinese citizens had rights, they could not claim them.

"In China, the law will not help you get your rights. The local government will not help you either," another Chinese engineer once remarked. "The only way to get your right is to petition the central authorities in Beijing."[6] However, he continued, drawing on a word play, "After Xi Jinping came to power, *shangfang* [petitioning] turned into *jiefang*."[7] The latter concept refers to the interception and incarceration of those who seek an audience with higher authorities. "The central government realized that it could not solve all the problems of the people. . . . Instead of handling problems, the government turned to handling those who raise problems. Citizens [*gongmin*] have become criminals [*fanmin*] as a result." Indeed, the high tide of petitioning in 2000s Beijing was short-lived. Petitioners—now construed as criminals, in the words of the engineer—threatened to disturb the social stability the central government was set on preserving.[8] "Instead of seeking an audience in Beijing, they now seek an audience at the UN with the UN secretary," his colleague chipped in, laughing. This somewhat sarcastic statement suggests that Chinese citizens have come to depend on the international community to claim their voice and seek redress.

These critical narratives contrasted the lack of local channels to claim rights in China with the supposedly abundant options Ethiopian citizens had at their disposal, one being litigation. Some expatriate managers expressed genuine respect for the Ethiopian legal system, being convinced that China could learn from Ethiopia.

Other Chinese interlocutors, some of whom had a nationalist bent, evoked a different narrative. They applauded the efforts of the Chinese government to strengthen security through data governance and improve the delivery of justice, while construing the Ethiopian legal system as either too advanced for the country's level of development or underdeveloped. One young Chinese engineer reflected: "About ten to twenty years ago, the justice system in China was like that of Ethiopia. It was not perfect. Step by step, the system has improved, as has the quality [*suzhi*] of legal professionals. About ten to twenty years ago in China, we also feared the police. But we no longer do. Cameras have replaced the police. No police officer will pull you over on the street. Only, perhaps, to check whether you drive under influence."[9]

The digitization of China's justice system has, according to this engineer, eliminated its former ills, such as corruption captured by the image of police pulling drivers over. Many Chinese engineers complained about their inconvenient encounters with traffic police in Ethiopia and other African countries. This engineer construed petty corruption as a sign of underdevelopment.

When I caught up with him after his return from China for his annual holidays in 2019, he spoke excitedly about the development of online courts in his home country, which, he surmised, rendered justice more transparent and accessible. Since 2014, the Chinese government has implemented judicial informatization policies to render litigation more effective, transparent, and, allegedly, just.[10] It launched a campaign to build "smart courts"—an assembly of initiatives related to the automation and digitization of the legal process, including the introduction of algorithms in judicial decision-making and the establishment of online courts for the litigation of disputes arising from online transactions.[11] Even though the smart court program has faced some domestic pushback,[12] it has enjoyed widespread popular support and fueled pride in technological advancement and new digital infrastructure in mainland China and beyond. Chinese professionals carried this pride with them to Africa.

In short, while the first narrative criticizes the Chinese government and justice system by using Ethiopia as a positive example, the second narrative praises the Chinese legal system by depicting Ethiopia as lawless, akin to colonial depictions of Africa as a legal vacuum.[13] The latter hinges on a firm belief in development as a linear process in which poor countries gradually grow more prosperous, informal economies transform into formal economies, and weak state institutions become strong ones.[14] Prevalent among Chinese expatriates in Ethiopia, and, as Han Cheng cogently shows, development thinkers and policymakers in China,[15] this positivist assumption can also be applied to the development of the legal system, in which corrupt and malfunctioning African courts gradually mature into transparent and well-functioning ones, provided they are given sufficient resources and their actors are committed to change.[16] Of course, these two narratives represented two ends of the spectrum. What is more, they were likely accentuated in conversations with me, a white Western woman. I presented a suitable foil to express criticism of the Chinese government on the one hand and display pride in China and its political, economic, and technological achievements on the other.

CHINESE ENCOUNTERS WITH ETHIOPIAN COURTS

> We don't dig up their farmland or go to their villages and throw stones. We don't steal their cattle or their goats. We are here simply to make money. We even create employment and build infrastructure. Yet, local people think they can take everything from us. You would think that the officials from the local government or the judges of the local courts are educated enough to understand the value of our work. They don't.[17]

Enraged, this Chinese manager lamented that neither ordinary Ethiopians nor educated administrators and judges recognize the value of their contribution to the country's development. His tirade alludes to the contested nature of the social aims and benefits that are supposed to outweigh the value of imposing liability— the principle of immunity. He reverses the familiar narrative of giving and taking in international development interventions, arguing that locals take everything they can lay their hands on while refusing to give back, thus breaking the cycle of reciprocity. Chinese managers like him often connected their courtroom battles to the trials and tribulations they faced outside the court. Their complaints about the legal system were tied into more general narratives of suffering that construed Chinese managers ("we") as pitiful victims of Ethiopian greed.[18]

Irrespective of their views of the Ethiopian and Chinese legal systems, most Chinese professionals and workers I met felt that local courts were biased against them, which explains their aversion and attempts to circumvent the justice system by claiming immunity. "Ethiopians support Ethiopians," sighed one Chinese manager, telling me about the many cases her company, a private enterprise from Fujian, had lost in court.[19] She, like many of her expatriate colleagues, considered purportedly partisan judges and compromised judgments as two aspects of what she painted as an ordeal. Other Chinese interlocutors took partial judges and lost lawsuits as evidence that "the Chinese" are easily "bullied":[20] "Why Ethiopians are not afraid of the courts? They know that they will win in court. This has to do with the impression Ethiopians have of the Chinese. They believe the Chinese have a lot of money and happily spend it. It is easy to bully the Chinese. As soon as they are bullied, they will pay. Locals have come to assume that this will always be the case. In general, the Chinese are willing to bear wrongs. This can be an advantage, but it can also be a disadvantage."[21]

This engineer placed negative court experiences on par with everyday extortion at the hands of petty bureaucrats and police officers.[22] Chinese reflections on their position were, however, conflicted. While some ascribed instances of discrimination to Ethiopian opportunism, others blamed themselves or inferior members within the Chinese community for trying to solve problems with bribes, thereby creating perverted expectations.[23] In the eyes of the engineer quoted above, the willingness of Chinese "to bear wrongs" placed them in a vulnerable position.

An Addis Ababa–based Chinese project manager who had become a skilled litigant over the years described the diasporic community as a *ruoshi qunti* ("weak group")—an idiom used to typify the lower strata of Chinese society—when relaying his court experiences.[24] With limited access to financial resources and social connections, members of vulnerable groups are exposed to intimidation and exploitation by the powerful.[25] The Chinese in Ethiopia, the project manager felt, found themselves in a similarly precarious position. Their lack of assertiveness made Chinese nationals susceptible to everyday extortion, especially since Ethiopian state agents in his eyes tolerated everyday bullying, if they did not contribute to it themselves. Expatriate managers failed to stand up for themselves. Instead, they used cash. Indeed, as Derek Sheridan shows for Chinese traders and entrepreneurs in Tanzania, the vulnerability of Chinese nationals and the sovereign capacity of the state to detain were offset by the privilege of members of the Chinese community and their economic capacity to pay, rendering their status ambiguous.[26]

Chinese suspicions about allegedly partisan judges were not unjustified, one Ethiopian in-house lawyer concurred:

The courts do not treat the Chinese equally to the locals. They even treat the Chinese differently from Westerners. Western companies treat employees well. They pay good wages. For instance, at the Tekeze Dam project, there was a US consultancy company. China Gezhouba Group [CGGC] worked on that project as well. CGGC paid only seven thousand birr for a surveyor, whereas the US company paid 25,000 birr, at least four times more than the Chinese. Because of this, some judges had a negative view of the Chinese. It [was] reflected in the verdicts they gave. The federal courts are better than the regional ones. They are impartial. . . . It differs from region to region. There is a 50+1 rule [regarding evidence] in civil cases. Foreigners, especially when facing governmental organs, must provide more evidence, along a ratio of 60:40 or even 80:20, to win their case.

Identifying a causal link between Chinese enterprises' treatment of Ethiopian workers and the courts' treatment of Chinese enterprises, this former in-house lawyer believed that judges respond to injustices they observe outside the court. Often living in the community, judges identify with local workers and residents and sympathize with them as a result, even though they are rarely posted in their hometown and are regularly rotated. Either way, Chinese managers had to submit more or better evidence than their counterparty to win a lawsuit ("along a ratio of 60:40 or even 80:20"), instead of according to the common 50+1 principle. In some regions, this lawyer conceded, "being a foreigner is almost a crime."

However, local protectionism in the lower courts was often more complicated than the picture painted by this lawyer or Chinese managers. Racial prejudice intersected with class bias. Some judges tended to support indigent litigants. A lawsuit filed against China Geo-Engineering Corporation's overseas subsidiary CGCOC at Enbise Sar Midir, East Gojjam, in 2013, may serve as a pertinent yet painful example. The judge who entertained the case on appeal at the East Gojjam High Court relayed the case to Zewdu and me, growing sad as he spoke.[27] The dispute concerned a young man who had incurred a grave bodily injury at the CGCOC-managed road-building site. According to the hospital statement, the worker had lost 75 percent of his physical capacity. He was represented in court by his father, a farmer. The judge had vivid memories of the older man, who entered the courtroom for each hearing carrying his son on his back. The worker claimed a paltry 23,000 birr (four hundred US dollars) in damages.

"Everyone asked themselves how the plaintiff could have requested so little," the judge recalled.[28] Compensation in cases like these is calculated by considering the amount of capacity lost, the plaintiff's daily wage, and the number of years left until retirement. "The amount [claimed] would not even suffice to cover living costs for one year." The judge reckoned that a scribe had written the pleading based on the suggestions of the father. If there had been a discrepancy between the amount written in numbers and in letters, the judge explained, the court could have exerted some discretion, but the pleading was crystal clear. It stated "23,000" and "twenty-three thousand" (in Amharic).

The Enbise Sar Midir Wereda Court awarded the plaintiff three or four hundred thousand birr (5,200–7,000 US dollars); the judge could not recall the exact amount. CGCOC appealed to the East Gojjam High Court, arguing that the decision of the lower court contained an error of law. By law, the court cannot grant plaintiffs more damages than they claim. The company's motion was substantiated, the judge admitted. "We waited to give a final verdict for a long time. We were reluctant to issue a verdict. He asked for 23,000 birr. By law, we could only award him 23,000 birr."[29] It was one of the most painful rulings this judge had ever issued. "Even if three or four hundred thousand birr is significant, it is still not enough considering the gravity of the injury." The plaintiff did not file for appeal.

This could be an extreme case, yet it is representative of verdicts reached by lower courts that go, as the judge put it, "beyond the law."[30] Lower courts often award higher amounts of damages than higher courts, at times for legally questionable yet morally understandable reasons. In this case, the lack of access to legal advice on the part of the plaintiff and his father led to injustice. Acutely aware of this, the lower court granted an amount of compensation it deemed fair, disregarding the amount the plaintiff had claimed and thus stepping "beyond the law." The judge who recalled this episode mentioned the "deep pocket principle," which the court occasionally observed in extracontractual cases in which compensation was calculated based on equity. This principle implies that the risk and its costs should be borne by the party that is best able to shoulder them. In all lawsuits, the Chinese enterprise had a deeper pocket. Judges in lower courts stood close to the community and were aware of the living conditions and hardships of Ethiopian plaintiffs. Appeal was the only way to overcome local protectionism.

Apart from viewing the surge of litigation as a form of discrimination, many expatriate managers also saw it as a sign of ingratitude. The candid comment of a Chinese grader operator illustrates this stance: "These black people don't realize we are here to help them. Local workers don't appreciate the fact that they have a job. . . . If we Chinese were not here to build a road, people could never have left this area."[31] The act of leaving a region stands for development. Many Chinese interlocutors described the areas surrounding their infrastructure projects as lacking opportunities. They believed that what they did—bringing development—was an act of goodwill and generosity that should be reciprocated with gratitude. If development is a gift,[32] any form of opposition, including litigation, naturally becomes a form of ingratitude.

Yet what kind of gratitude were locals expected to express? In everyday encounters, gratitude meant cooperation and understanding. In the courtroom, gratitude amounted to exemption from liability. If belligerent Ethiopian litigants and partial judges had recognized the value of Chinese-led development, they would have spared them the trouble of going to court. I should note here again that as with perceptions of the legal system, attitudes toward litigation differed. Some Chinese actors declared war on a system they described as hostile and continued filing claims for immunity, while others began to learn to litigate and came to appreciate it.

FROM SELF-HELP TO LEGAL ADVICE

Chinese enterprise managers who let go of their grudges gave up on attempting to gain immunity. They began to accept and adapt to the regulatory environment, shifting from an "against the law" attitude, in which they saw the law negatively as an unreliable, overbearing system, to a "with the law" attitude, in which they envisaged the law as a game in which they could manipulate the rules to advance their interests, to borrow Patricia Ewick and Susan Silbey's classic concepts to encapsulate evolving legal consciousness.[33] This altered approach meant, on one hand, that judges' efforts to enact their jurisdiction and have litigants respect it had borne fruit. On the other hand, this meant that expatriate managers started playing with the law and taking advantage of the legal system, drawing on individual resourcefulness and corporate resources. However, learning the ropes of litigation was a gradual process. In their early dealings with the courts, companies chiefly resorted to self-help.[34] Their expatriate managers drafted statements of defense with the help of Ethiopian administrative assistants and attended court hearings with local interpreters. Over time, Chinese liaison and human resource managers started learning by heart relevant articles in Ethiopian labor law, such as those relating to the dismissal of workers.[35]

Some expatriate managers stayed on top of their lawsuits, even if they lost most of them. Others, especially managers of privately owned Chinese subcontractors, were much less committed to following up on cases, not least because liability would likely fall on the contractor. They put court summonses aside and subsequently forgot about them or threw them in the bin. Management typically hired lawyers only after the fact, when they faced an overwhelming number of cases or a particularly challenging lawsuit. One manager of Zhongmei Engineering Group, a provincial-level state firm from Jiangxi, experienced at first hand the limits of this self-help approach. His company had faced a series of extracontractual disputes in the aftermath of a car accident that injured and killed more than thirty workers who had been standing in the back of the truck that shuttled them between the town and the construction site.[36]

One of the reasons managers initially clung to a self-help approach was their lack of trust in Ethiopian lawyers. They feared that local legal experts would conspire with local community members. Such suspicions were not unfounded. A few in-house counsel did plot against their employer by entering deals with potential litigants. Experiences of broken trust made it even harder for management to engage local lawyers. The transfer of trust is, however, central to legal representation.[37] Lawyers frequently requested to see documents that could help them win a case, many of which were classified as confidential by management and were only intended to be seen by selected Chinese eyes. Lawyers compelled Chinese managers to lay out the cards they would otherwise keep close to their chests. However, some Chinese managers came to appreciate the work of Ethiopian lawyers, especially when they began winning lawsuits. For one, court victories dispelled distrust. Consequently, trusted lawyers became central to revamping Chinese managerial practices and improving relations with various Ethiopian parties, from laborers and subcontractors to suppliers and government bodies.

Meanwhile, lawyers made expatriate managers aware of the possibilities of the legal system, especially the right to appeal. Chinese companies often fared better in higher courts. Appeals also extended the life of cases, exhausting the resources and testing the willpower of Ethiopian plaintiffs. On discovering the magic of appeal, expatriate managers became determined to take all cases to the Federal Supreme Court. Sometimes they did so against their counsel's legal advice. "In some cases, I told them, an appeal does not make sense," one lawyer recalled, laughing.[38] "Our witnesses had testified against us, and there was no error of law. Even then, they pressed upon me, 'Please do it.'"

Two lawsuits, a labor case filed against China Communications Construction Company (CCCC) in the Afar region and an extracontractual case instituted against China Civil Engineering Construction Corporation (CCECC) in Dire Dawa, illustrate why Chinese enterprise management insisted on filing for an appeal, even though the chances of obtaining a better result or having the application for appeal accepted in the first place were slim.

Ashenafi Hailemariam, a former driver for CCCC,[39] sued his Chinese employer in October 2016, requesting compensation for unlawful dismissal. He worked for the Chinese enterprise between November 2015 and October 2016, earning 4,500 birr a month. During his employment, he suffered from abdominal pain and sought treatment. When the pain did not subside, he requested sick leave. His Chinese employer, however, did not accept the doctor's note and instead fired Ashenafi, who claimed two months of outstanding salary, medical expenses, and compensation for unlawful dismissal—65,750 birr in total.

In its statement of defense, CCCC, represented by counsel, countered that the driver had left the job on his own initiative. His line manager had rejected the health certificate because it did not show that the illness was incurred during the period of employment.

The Abala Wereda Court in Afar awarded the plaintiff three months' salary and sixteen thousand birr for medical expenses—29,500 birr in total. Dissatisfied with this decision, CCCC took the case to the Zone 2 High Court in Abala, which dismissed the appeal, as did the Supreme Court of Afar in Semera.[40] The company subsequently applied for appeal at the Federal Supreme Court in Addis Ababa, which requested an additional statement of claim and response before entertaining the case. It ruled that Ashenafi had left the job on his own accord after completing medical treatment, despite his Chinese manager's request to stay on. Since

Ashenafi had worked for his employer for just over a year, he was not entitled to a severance payment. Furthermore, the court did not classify the driver's illness as incurred at the workplace and did not extend compensation for medical expenses. Finally, the court granted Ashenafi a mere 4,500 birr of unpaid salary.

For a multinational enterprise like CCCC, the financial stakes of this case were low. It nevertheless decided to bring the case to the Federal Supreme Court. By so doing, the company gained its right and, perhaps more importantly, showed its willingness to fight until the end. One of CCCC's managers recalled one case, entertained in 2017, that stemmed the tide of labor suits that had begun in 2014, when a plaintiff won three hundred thousand birr in damages with which he bought a house in Mekelle. After this court victory, workers began to see the court, in the manager's words, as a source of instant wealth creation and an opportunity to transform one's life, motivating others to try their luck as well. The 2017 case concerned a driver requesting 130,000 birr in damages for wrongful dismissal. The Ethiopian plaintiff won in the lower courts but lost in the Tigray Supreme Court and, subsequently, the Federal Supreme Court. The process took more than a year and ended in July 2018, but it was worth it, the manager acknowledged: "Our persistence started discouraging workers from taking their case to court."[41]

Another example of the success of an appeal was *CCECC v. Tewodros Demse Weldeyesus*,[42] an extracontractual case initially filed by Tewodros Demse Weldeyesus against one of the two Chinese state firms contracted to build the Ethio-Djibouti Railway, along with a truck driver and a truck owner as second and third respondents, respectively, at the Federal First Instance Court in Dire Dawa. Before its completion, the railway was put into emergency operation to transport grain and other food supplies to drought-affected areas in the Somali Region. The plaintiff incurred an injury while carrying sacks of wheat from the train to a vehicle parked beside the train door. The vehicle's tailgate connected the truck to the train. When Tewodros stepped on it, it broke and pulled him to the ground, causing a significant injury. He claimed 176,000 birr in medical expenses.[43]

The First Instance Court of Dire Dawa ruled that CCECC and the truck owner were jointly and severally liable. Dissatisfied with this decision, CCECC, represented by counsel, took the case to the higher court, which confirmed the lower court's decision. Next, the Chinese company filed for appeal at the Federal Supreme Court cassation division, which detected a procedural error in how the lower courts had entertained the case. Whoever claims compensation for an injury must substantiate that they suffered the injury as a result of the act or property of each respondent separately. Tewodros had sufficiently proven that the truck owner was at fault due to the defect on the vehicle's tailgate,[44] but he failed to demonstrate that CCECC was liable too. The cassation division did not change the decision regarding the truck owner, Mezgebu Temermiro, yet stated that if Tewodros or Mezgebu sought to hold CCECC accountable, they must file a new case, presenting adequate evidence.

In this case, CCECC escaped liability altogether. Chinese managers often com-plained that they were easily sued and held liable because they had deep pockets. This might have been true in this case, even though it is unlikely that the lower court judge came to the decision deliberately, let alone maliciously.

While they often lost in the lower courts, Chinese firms started winning more and more cases in the higher courts with the assistance of Ethiopian legal experts. Over time, Chinese managers grew familiar with the forums of dispute resolution in the regions where they were based and started weighing their advantages and disadvantages. In the Somali Region, for instance, management favored custom-ary dispute resolution as they sought to remain on good terms with the pastoral communities living near construction sites. Calculating costs and benefits, they rejected customary settlement if the damages awarded to the counterparty in court were lower than those agreed to with community elders.

Growing legal literacy among Chinese managers was apparent, too, in their increased familiarity with judicial processes and procedure.[45] Managers started keeping files, documenting activities, requesting letters of approval from local government agencies, and collecting evidence even before they were sued. Quick learners with strong social skills were assigned to deal with disputes. As a result, certified civil engineers, quantity surveyors, and contract managers became liai-son officers, occupying themselves with court litigation for most of their work-ing day. They handed over their engineering, surveying, and management work to more introverted colleagues. While some staff loathed their daily dealings with the court, others took an interest in litigation. A few came to see litigation as a game.

Trained as a civil engineer, Peng was one of the Chinese managers I met in Ethiopia who began taking a keen interest in law. During one of his annual trips home, he attended legal training in Beijing relating to overseas enterprises and familiarized himself with Chinese and Ethiopian labor laws. Instead of grum-bling about the law and the courts, as many of his colleagues did, he respected the law and urged his colleagues to do so too. Peng picked up more than the basics by handling a growing number of court cases as a company represen-tative and interacting closely with a team of Ethiopian in-house lawyers. He learned, for instance, as he explained to me, that trials in lower courts were crucial because appellate courts drew on the evidence presented there and did not consider additional evidence unless they explicitly requested it. He selected witnesses strategically, favoring Ethiopians, especially local administrators with a degree of authority; he knew that the judges would give their voices more weight. Perhaps most importantly, he recognized the benefits of local legal expertise and urged project management, initially apprehensive about hiring local professionals, to recruit Ethiopian lawyers. By advancing employment and contracting practices and compelling Chinese management to adhere to the law and embrace its possibilities, the lawyers provoked another shift, from trying to squash disputes when they erupted or after they had escalated to preventing them from happening in the first place.

FROM BAND-AID TO CONFLICT PREVENTION

Seeking to reduce the time they spent in court, Ethiopian in-house counsel initiated the move to conflict prevention. They concurred being fed up with court litigation and "roaming around the court," in the words of a female lawyer based in Addis Ababa.[46] They found sympathy with Chinese managers who looked to improve managerial practices and corporate public relations to try to reduce the number of lawsuits brought against their corporation. Bringing company practices in line with the law was a significant step toward conflict avoidance. From the start, in-house lawyers exhorted Chinese managers to contact them before making consequential decisions. When their legal advice bore fruit, corporate management gradually left to their legal experts final decisions on everything from the recruitment and dismissal of staff to the drafting of contracts with subcontractors and suppliers.

While Ethiopian in-house lawyers sought to enhance legal awareness and improve compliance, Chinese managers opted for a different approach. "In China we have three concepts: *qing* (emotion or sentiment), *li* (reason or logic), and *fa* (law)," a design engineer from Guizhou who spent two years in the Central African Republic before his company transferred him to Ethiopia explained. "We solve problems with the first two, but we are unfamiliar with the last one."[47] Chinese unfamiliarity with the law and their preference for using *qing* or *li*, in his eyes, explained their initial frustrations with the legal system, and even though they began recognizing the law's importance and the advantages of adhering to it, most managers bet on honing interpersonal bonds with Ethiopian laborers, subcontractors, and other contractual parties to prevent disputes and smooth interactions.

I asked several Chinese managers what their company had learned from litigation in Ethiopia. Some mentioned that negative court experiences encouraged them to settle disputes amicably through what they referred to as *xietiao* before they ended up in court. Comprising the characters *xie* ("be united" or "cooperate") and *tiao* ("change" or "tune"), this verb is usually translated into "harmonize" in English. Based on compromise through mutual or, in practice, often not-so-mutual concessions, harmonization was achieved with the help of Ethiopian interpreters and facilitators. Essentially a conflict-prevention mechanism, *xietiao* was used to iron out friction with an eye to achieving common objectives and shared understanding.

Engineer Zhang explained that harmonizing employment relations required *renqing* ("personal favors") and cultivating *ganqing* ("affection") between Chinese managers and Ethiopian employees.[48] These principles also held true for other types of relationships—for instance, between the corporation and the community and the corporation and its subcontractors and suppliers. In her treatise on interpersonal relationships in reform-era China, Mayfair Yang describes *ganqing* as standing "for the emotional commitment in such long-standing and intimate social bonds as those found between a parent and child, husband and wife, close friends, teacher and student, and certain favorite relatives."[49] *Ganqing* captures a deep emotional feeling that contains a shallow level of instrumental calculation— lower, for instance, than *renqing*, which is a form of intimacy built on mutual personal favors. In manager–employee relationships, an emphasis on affection conceals expectations of duty and the power differentials embedded in these often-unvoiced expectations. By symbolically breaking the boundaries between the private and the public realms and "befriending" Ethiopian staff, Chinese managers, as Jenny Chang shows for Chinese-managed workplaces in Zambia, attempt to harmonize relations and overcome, or simply obfuscate, relations of inequality.[50]

One Chinese project manager in Ethiopia was widely praised for his *xietiao* skills. Most of his projects, such as the Debre Berhan Industrial Park, were a striking success due to his engineering expertise, management style, and, above all, people's skills. During the relatively short construction period, the company faced only a handful of lawsuits. One of the Chinese engineers pointed out that, apart from the low number of lawsuits filed against the company, the absence of theft was evidence of this manager's peaceful and cordial relationships with the local community. Pilfering on Chinese-run construction sites abounds. For this reason, Chinese companies typically purchase more building materials than they require for a project. The fact that this company had piles of building materials left after finishing the Debre Berhan project, which it donated to the local government, was held to be telling of the project manager's mastery of *xietiao*. The number of court cases and the level of theft were taken as barometers of a local community's positive or negative perceptions of the Chinese community.[51]

"Disputes that the law cannot solve can be settled through amicable relations," an engineer turned liaison manager pointed out.[52] "The law should be the last resort." He held that cultivating sympathy and affection could strengthen management–labor relations and reduce the number of court cases.

An expression of *renqing*, gift exchanges were believed to generate affection and loyalty. A young Chinese project manager who oversaw the construction of a road in CMC, a newer middle-class neighborhood in eastern Addis Ababa, went so far as to give part of his monthly allowance to his Ethiopian staff to maintain good relations with them. He did so, he explained, based on performance or *biaoxian*, which was intimately connected to loyalty and being at the ready service of one's superiors.[53] He gave local employees something extra at the end of a workday or before dispatching them to run errands. "For me, five hundred birr means little. For them, it means a lot."[54]

Relations with their Ethiopian clients—for instance, the Ethiopian Roads Authority or Ethiopian Electric Power—were maintained in a similar fashion. The same project manager explained that contractors sought to avoid court litigation and arbitration: "If there is something [wrong], we will go straight to the boss." Informal negotiation was the norm. Only if they could not solve the matter with the client would they reach out to third parties, such as higher-level officials. He mentioned the story of a European contractor who surprised the Ethiopian Roads Authority with a big claim at the end of a project. The authority promptly made the company ineligible for future tenders. The incident served as a cautionary tale for Chinese companies, encouraging their representatives to solve matters peacefully through negotiation. In the project manager's understanding, arbitration could be as risky as litigation in an open court, even though it occurred behind closed doors. Problems should be solved subtly by "pulling [in] the boss for a chat." He concluded our conversation with the adage that while "Chinese people like taking detours, Europeans like to go straight."[55] Taking a detour or winding road refers to seeking alternative ways to solve a dispute, preferably through private channels and in a nonconfrontational way. Going straight, in his rendering, meant using arbitration or litigation to reach a win-or-lose outcome.

Chinese managers' attempts to improve relations with Ethiopian clients, business partners, and employees through the cultivation of sympathy and understanding went hand in hand with the efforts of Ethiopian counsel to align company practices with the law. Chinese enterprises began to use written employment agreements in line with legal templates and to grant severance payments. They started paying overtime according to the rate stipulated in the labor proclamation and even went as far as lending money to workers in need—a local practice that fell under the employer's responsibility. This changed attitude was a far cry from Chinese managers' earlier attempts to claim immunity in the presiding judge's office or the courtroom. However, as soon as they accepted litigation and learned to litigate, expatriate managers also discovered ways to use the court system to their advantage.

LEARNING TO USE AND ABUSE THE COURT

Chinese managers who had been in Ethiopia for a significant time learned not just to use but also to abuse the court system. I take "abuse" to mean the use of legal methods toward questionable ends and of illegal methods that fit a legal mold with the aim of feigning compliance. Ethiopian lawyers played a vital, if ambiguous, role in the adoption of these practices. While some stood squarely with expatriate management and even engaged in dishonest activities for them, others took it on themselves to improve company practices and render them lawful, resisting managers' attempts to play the system.

I will reflect on five practices that my Chinese interlocutors divulged or to which Ethiopian interlocutors alerted me. First, expatriate managers began deploying the right format and tone to get what they wanted from the court and benefit from their standing. Second, they started taking advantage of the rights Ethiopian law granted them as foreign investors. Third, they learned to exhaust the counterparty, using technically lawful yet morally dubious methods to force them to give up and drop their claims. Fourth, in collaboration with or at the initiative of their Ethiopian lawyers, some Chinese managers developed ways to get ahead of the law and exploit legal loopholes. Finally, management used illicit means to strengthen their case for trial.

Slowly but surely, Chinese firms, especially large state-owned enterprises, started coming out ahead, if not in all cases.[56] Increased legal literacy aided this process. Expatriate managers, moreover, learned to push the right buttons when they sought to speed up court proceedings. The following letter, sent by the state-owned China Railway No. 3 Engineering Group to the Amhara Supreme Court, is illustrative of Chinese firms' increased communication skills, coupled with legal savviness:

> Case number: 51285
> Ginbot 28, 2011 [June 5, 2019, Gregorian calendar]
>
> To the Amhara Supreme Court
> Re: Construction Works of Pawi Junction—Renaissance Dam Road Upgrading Project; Lot 1: Pawi Junction—Km 69.
> . . .
> Issue: Change of the adjourned date
> In the case between Desalegn Zeleke Ferede Construction PLC and China Railway No. 3 the court adjourned the hearing. Our company would like to request to adjourn the case to a closer date.
>
> Our company has worked in different parts of the country for the last 12 years, fulfilling contractual agreements with ERA [Ethiopian Roads Authority]. It has completed a lot of road construction work.
>
> This project is crucial for the Grand Ethiopian Renaissance Dam (GERD) and of high priority to the federal government. We were awarded the contract to construct a road from Pawi Junction to GERD. Beyond serving the project site's residents, this project has immense value to the construction of GERD. It provides a road for the transport of building equipment to the site of GERD. As it has this advantage, it is among the projects to which ERA gives due attention.
>
> As most of the soil is black soil (seen from that it easily cracks) and it is rainy season now, it [further delays] will affect the quality of the asphalt. This will have an impact on big lorries that transport materials to GERD and other areas.
>
> On top of this, it may be a cause for traffic accidents. It may have an impact on the work. The applicant failed to complete their contractual agreement to carry out their activities according to ERA's standards and constructed a detour [road] of poor quality. It moreover failed to complete work on the main road. The parts it did complete were of poor quality.
>
> Taken together, this [the subcontractor's poor performance] has resulted in problems related to transports to GERD. We are willing to wait for the adjourned date and correct our mistakes and pay the compensation stipulated by the court. However, we are encountering car accidents and traffic jams. Because of this, we

need to send [in] our machines, incurring unnecessary expenses. In addition to this, we have been given repeated notice from ERA [to continue construction activities].

Therefore, in order to finish our cases and as we are already finished the issues from our side, and in order to avoid creating any problems for road traffic, we request the court to adjourn our litigation for Sene 12, 2011 [June 19, 2019, Gregorian calendar]. We are willing to settle this issue in good faith. We are sending ten pictures that show the problematic state of the road.

The respondent
China Railway No. 3 Engineering Group Company Limited

The lawsuit between the Chinese contractor and its Ethiopian subcontractor to which this letter refers concerned a common contractual dispute. The Chinese state-owned firm withheld payments due to underperformance. The local construction firm went to court to claim this sum. This case was eventually settled out of court after the Chinese company offered to pay 1.5 million birr.

The letter writer uses various rhetorical techniques to convey the good reputation of the company, the importance of the project, the urgency of the construction activities, the reasonability of the request, and corporate morality and goodwill. Establishing the contractor's status by mentioning its twelve-year record of accomplishment, the letter foregrounds the company's contribution to the development of the country's infrastructure network. It continues by underlining the significance of the national project the company serves by constructing the road: the GERD. The firm's managers must have known this dam was the country's most celebrated project at the time. Built to alleviate Ethiopia's energy shortage, the dam on the Blue Nile has from its inception ruffled feathers across the international community. Egypt strongly objected to its construction and continues to oppose its operation. For this reason and because of the project's grandeur, the dam has become a symbol of Ethiopian national pride, rendering its building and operation synonymous with establishing and maintaining the country's sovereignty.[57]

To give more weight to their request for a change of date and the company's authority, the letter furthermore mentions federal government organs. It subsequently paints the corporation as benevolent, indicating that it cares for the safety of road users and the community at large.[58] It depicts the corporation as a moral actor in contrast with the counterparty, decrying the latter for delivering substandard work and forgoing the guidelines provided by the Ethiopian Roads Authority. By vilifying the subcontractor, it takes the moral high ground. In the final paragraph, the letter writer conveys the company's patience, expressing its willingness to wait for the appointment date and settle the dispute. By adding that circumstances make it hard to do so, the narrator offloads responsibility onto external circumstances or force majeure. The letter includes photographs as visual evidence.

In sum, the letter shows that expatriate managers have learned to use the right format, tone, and vocabulary in their correspondence with the courts. They have grasped that formal written documents are more likely to find a willing ear than informal visits to the office of the presiding judge and that mentioning federal authorities gives weight to their request, as does the provision of evidence.

As a second strategy, Chinese companies have started to avail themselves of the opportunities that local laws afford them as foreign investors or contractors. A senior lawyer who had worked with many Chinese firms in the construction and manufacturing sectors relayed how some enterprises abused the lawful concessions extended by Ethiopia's investment proclamation, such as tax holidays:

> For example, a company has worked as "ABC Company" for three years. For these three years, the company will not pay income tax. Then, in the fourth year, they make ABC Company inefficient. They will start another company, "XYZ Company," doing the same work, and get another tax holiday. They are not entitled to a tax holiday when they do the same job with the same shareholders, only with another name; the law says they should not get a tax holiday. There is even a chance for the company to get a tax holiday for the third time. Some companies exploit these kinds of benefits.[59]

These and other practices regularly presented this lawyer with a conundrum: Should he continue working with clients who engage in such practices? Should he forsake his commitment to the cause of his client? Should he participate in unlawful practices? This Addis Ababa–based lawyer had a significant client base and could afford to drop firms engaged in suspect practices. He occasionally did so. Ethiopian lawyers in need of cash could not afford to be this selective.

Yet another strategy with which Chinese executives became increasingly skilled was taking advantage of the sluggishness of the legal system. One method was to drag out cases and wear the plaintiff down emotionally and financially. Ethiopian migrant workers often lacked a support network in the region in which they worked and could not afford protracted court proceedings, especially when they remained unemployed throughout this period. In addition, employment opportunities in some areas were limited. This was the case with projects in the Omo Basin in southern Ethiopia. Internal migrant workers from Welayta and Sidama—two of Ethiopia's primary migrant-sending regions—and northern regions like Amhara and Tigray often drop their claims when they move away.

To stem a rush of lawsuits, the public relations manager of a Chinese private firm in the Omo Valley, in consultation with the company's lawyer, developed techniques that either helped them win in court or forced the plaintiff to capitulate. He did so lawfully, through appeals, as described above, and, less sympathetically, by not showing up at trial, dodging the execution of judgments or coaxing witnesses into withdrawing their testimonies.

An Ethiopian facilitator working for this company and involved in these practices himself attempted to justify them: "The law assumes that employers exploit their employees."[60] Having just witnessed a spike in lawsuits, he sympathized with his Chinese employer and pointed to the opportunism of local workers: "The law is on the side of the laborers. Many laborers know this to the extent that they have started to play with the law. They use the law to their advantage." While Ethiopian workers have grown bolder in mobilizing the law against Chinese corporations, expatriate managers have also stepped up their game.

As a fourth strategy, company managers strengthened their position contractually in anticipation of court cases that might be instituted against them. Within the remit of the law, for instance, they fiddled with wages to minimize the compensation they would have to pay should a worker win a court case for unlawful dismissal. If a company hired an employee for six months on a salary of 1,500 birr per month, one lawyer illustrated, they would give him only three hundred birr in actual salary; the remaining 1,200 birr would be offered as benefits.[61] Should the employee take legal action for unlawful dismissal, the court would calculate compensation according to a salary of three hundred birr a month. A worker's maximum compensation is six months' salary, which makes the compensation 1,800 birr only. The lawyer remarked that this strategy discouraged workers from going to court in the first place.

The former in-house counsel who detailed these practices disclosed a decisive role in devising them. He, like the facilitator mentioned above, was quick to offer a justification for what he realized could be viewed as a suspect practice: "Local laborers have a poor work attitude. They cheat and steal. The law protects these lazy workers and thieves."[62] The lawyer laid blame on locals' work ethic, while praising the discipline of Chinese supervisors. A better attitude on the side of Ethiopian laborers, he believed, would prevent discord and disputes. Even if practices like these were technically lawful, they could be perceived as morally dubious for exploiting the workers' lack of legal knowledge. Moreover, they fed on a crowded labor market in which workers had little option but to accept unfavorable terms.

The fifth strategy, using illicit methods to navigate the legal system, was unambiguously unlawful. Chinese managers, for instance, cultivated loyalty through cash gifts and prodded witnesses into giving false testimony in court. A Chinese project manager confided that while his company never bribed judges ("we would not dare"), it routinely bribed expert witnesses to testify in a way that strengthened their version of the truth.[63] Expert witnesses are usually called to court to estimate, for example, the damage caused to a house by the vibration of heavy road-rollers or to farmland through the illegal dumping of sand or waste materials.

While some of the methods described above were lawful but morally suspicious, others were flatly unlawful, such as coaxing witnesses to give false testimony. I want to conclude with one lawsuit that, in my eyes, epitomizes the legal skills Chinese managers accumulated over the years. When one of Zhongmei Engineering Group's local subcontractors defaulted on paying for the building materials Zhongmei had provided, the Chinese firm went to court, despite the arbitration clause in its contract. Surprisingly, the High Court in Afar rejected the preliminary objection raised by the subcontractor that the court did not have jurisdiction over the case. The bench decided in favor of the Chinese company, awarding it the requested sum of three hundred thousand birr.

The local subcontractor subsequently took the case to the Afar Supreme Court in Semera, which confirmed the decision of the High Court. Undeterred, it then filed an application for appeal at the cassation division of the Federal Supreme Court in Addis Ababa, arguing, again, that the Afar courts did not have jurisdiction to hear the claim. The cassation bench overruled the decisions of the lower courts in Afar, reasoning that they indeed should not have proceeded with the lawsuit due to the arbitration clause in the contract, leaving the dispute unresolved. Eventually, the two parties came to a resolution through negotiation.

Why did the Chinese company take this case to court? Zhongmei's former in-house counsel explained that his employer had sued the subcontractor to buy time and force the subcontractor to negotiate.[64] In addition, the court had placed a restraining order on the building materials, further increasing the pressure on the subcontractor to pay for them. The Chinese company feared that the subcontractor would disappear without paying the money. Zhongmei's lawyer concurred in an interview that it had not been his idea to take this case to court. In fact, he had discouraged his Chinese line manager from doing so[65] and sat down with his managers to discuss the matter. Shortly before the meeting, he received a phone call from the general manager of the subcontracting company, who pledged to resolve the dispute through negotiation. The Chinese management nonetheless pushed on. "I never thought that the court would reject the preliminary objection. The court must have been eager to entertain the case. It might be related to the benefits they could accrue. . . . They claimed jurisdiction and started entertaining the case."[66] The benefits to which the lawyer alluded are bribes. Indeed, Zhongmei's liaison officer admitted that they regularly paid bribes because, as he excused himself, the judges in Afar were hungry for them. Alternatively, the judges might have been keen to assert their jurisdiction. Either way, the court ruled in favor of the Chinese company.

This case reveals the confidence Zhongmei's managers had gained over years of dealing with the courts in Afar. Their assertiveness was equally demonstrated by the fact that they ignored the advice of their Ethiopian in-house counsel and went their own way. Eventually, they got what they wanted, not from the court but from using the court to their benefit.

STRATEGIZING WITH AND AGAINST THE LEGAL SYSTEM

The spectrum of newly adopted strategies detailed above exemplifies expatriate managers' growing legal consciousness. "I learned a lot about the law, especially about judicial procedure," a Chinese manager based in Addis Ababa readily admitted.[67] "I now know how to find witnesses and what kind of witnesses. I know more or less how to win a case. If I lose, I appeal."[68] His confidence reflected the extensive experience he had accumulated. For years, he had dealt with court matters alongside his duties as a civil engineer. Young and energetic, he sucked up tough legal lessons and began to obtain court victories with the help of legal professionals.

Faced with a litany of lawsuits, this project manager and his counterparts across Ethiopia gradually conceded control to Ethiopian lawyers, who aligned company policies and practices with the law, prompting a shift from reverting to self-help to soliciting legal advice and from using band-aid solutions to furthering conflict prevention. Instead of claiming immunity or circumventing the court, Chinese managers began confronting the legal system head-on. Noncooperation made way for cooperation, reluctance for assertiveness, despondency for hopefulness, and dismay for openness.

This significant change in attitude, whether merely performed or not, signaled the success of Ethiopian plaintiffs and the judiciary in enacting their jurisdiction, thus forcing multinational corporations to answer to the court and accept liability in line with their verdicts. As I will detail in chapter 5, Chinese litigants initially posed a true threat to judicial authority, confronting it with objections, protests, walkouts, appeals to higher authorities, and unpleasant and (at times) offensive behavior in the courtroom. Yet, judges' attempts at disciplining recalcitrant litigants garnered results, as evidenced in this chapter. Chinese respondents began heeding court orders and observing judicial procedure. They learned the ropes of litigation and grew increasingly savvy. Indeed, legal subversion was the flipside of managers' increased familiarity with the law. Yet as newly minted repeat players in the Ethiopian legal system, expatriate enterprise managers did respect most of the laws and procedures. Having explored the perspectives of the Ethiopian plaintiffs and Chinese defendants, the next chapter turns to the relationship between them and the inequalities that generated opportunities for claiming immunity.

4

Immunity Through Inequality

In July 2013, Ethio Telecom signed a 1.6 billion US dollar contract with Chinese telecommunications corporations Huawei and ZTE to expand the country's mobile phone infrastructure and to introduce a 4G broadband network in Addis Ababa and 3G services throughout the country. This deal brought Huawei to Mekelle, Tigray, in May 2014. The telecommunications giant concluded a tenancy agreement with Milano Hotel to accommodate its staff. Soon after Huawei moved into the hotel in the summer of 2014, during Ethiopia's rainy season, its relationship with the Ethiopian landlord began to deteriorate. Tensions built over the first year until they erupted, culminating in an attempt by the Chinese staff to leave without notice and two court cases that, combined into one, received a decision in the Tigray Supreme Court in 2017.

To understand the structural inequalities that generate the conditions for claims for immunity, I trace the evolution of the dispute between the Ethiopian tourist hotel and China's telecommunications giant from the signing of the lease contract to the court verdict and its aftermath. Structural inequalities create moments in which the party with the upper hand can define the terms of the relationship and the exceptions to these terms. These transpired not just in everyday interactions between the Ethiopian lessor and the Chinese lessee but also in their written agreement. However, as soon as one of the parties to a private contract goes to court—in this case, Milano Hotel—the bench comes not just to adjudicate the dispute but also to mediate the power disparities between the disputants. As well as unpacking these disparities, I explore the power of the court in balancing them out. The communicative function of the court,[1] I demonstrate, lends judges expansive discretion to reshape relationships between unequal parties, especially those who do not share a language, cultural codes, or normative repertoires. By exercising discretion, the judiciary simultaneously asserts its jurisdiction.

I should note that my reconstruction of the events described in this chapter is necessarily incomplete. I was not present when the dispute arose and evolved into a lawsuit, nor did I witness the trial. My interpretations are based on interviews with the presiding judge, the lawyers for Milano and Huawei, and the hotel manager, in addition to analysis of the tenancy agreement, the judgment, and case file documents, including written evidence put forward by the parties. This chapter describes a legal dispute that differs from the cases involving Ethiopian employees and Chinese employers discussed in chapter 2. Huawei purchased a service, and the tourist hotel and telecommunications giant were simply business partners. In contrast, the relationships between Chinese employers and Ethiopian employees were characterized by a higher degree of interdependence and a more pronounced power imbalance. Even so, *Milano Hotel v. Huawei Technologies* shares similarities with other disputes in Ethiopian–Chinese interactions—similarities that offer insight into the inequalities underlying claims of immunity and the role of the court in mediating them.

THE DISPUTE

Milano's general manager had learned through acquaintances that Huawei was coming to Mekelle and recommended that the Chinese firm stay at his hotel. One of the oldest hotels in Mekelle, Milano has a majestic yet forlorn feel to it. Guests are welcomed at the entrance with a statue of a golden prancing horse with a rider armed with spear and shield and a reception area with dark wood fittings and stately traditional Ethiopian furniture. Despite the grand entrance, most of the bedrooms are sparsely furnished. The fanciest hotel in the city when it opened in the 1990s, Milano has since been surpassed by more luxurious establishments. Competition was fierce in the hotel sector before Mekelle was hit first by Covid-19 and then by a devastating civil war. "We needed them at the time," Milano's manager said of Huawei when Bereket and I spoke with him in August 2020.[2] "We had little experience with hosting companies. We hoped their arrival would give us the chance to attract more companies in the future." Huawei was new to the region. The existing mobile phone network had been installed by its competitor, ZTE, in the first decade of the 2000s.[3]

Looking back, Milano's manager concluded that the main source of the dispute had been the contract, signed on March 21, 2014. Keen to seal the deal, they entered it in a rush, he admitted. The manager had initially looked at the contract as a mere formality, believing the terms could be discussed as they went along. To Huawei's staff, who were dissatisfied with the services the hotel offered, the contract became the pivotal proof that their expectations were justified and their rights unmet. As communication worsened and ground almost to a standstill, the contested contract became the cornerstone of the relationship and the ensuing dispute. In sum, the lack of a common language meant the parties put more emphasis on the contract than they would have in a situation in which both parties were Chinese or both Ethiopian.

The leased space included twenty bedrooms, a kitchen, a dining hall, and two office areas.[4] The lease stretched from June 1, 2014, to May 31, 2016. The parties agreed on the daily rate of 292.50 birr per bedroom, including taxes and service charges, and a monthly rate of 37,215 birr for the conference room, 20,250 birr for the kitchen, and 13,500 birr for the dining hall. Milano provided a small office facing the road free of charge. Payments were to be made following a six-month cycle.

Drafted by Huawei, the contract reflected the power inequalities among the parties who signed it. The agreement extended the freedom to unilaterally alter the terms of the contract only to the Chinese lessee.[5] It locked in the price of the rent over the lease period and beyond, if the lessee sought to extend it.[6] It furthermore granted the lessee the liberty of withholding 10 percent of the rent should services fail to meet a loosely defined standard and held the lessor responsible for theft, expecting it to cover any losses.[7] While the hotel was required to give sixty days' notice for termination of the contract,[8] the occupant was allowed to extend, renew, or terminate the lease agreement with thirty days' notice.[9] It is clear that at each turn the Chinese lessee set the terms of the lessor–lessee relationship and could alter most terms as it wished.

Furthermore, the terms of the lease poorly fit the conditions on the ground. They required the tourist hotel to make substantial changes to its sparsely furnished rooms to meet the configuration set out in the contract. As well as a bed, Milano was to provide a table and a chair, a closet with at least five coat hangers, white and clean bed linen, mosquito nets, access to Wi-Fi, hot showers, and an electricity supply. Round-the-clock hot water and electricity were a lot to ask for in a place where water shortages and power outages were a regular occurrence.[10] Like most hotels, Milano has a generator to provide backup power, but water shortages are impossible to absorb, especially when they last for one or two weeks, as they occasionally did during my eight-month stay in Mekelle. The contract did excuse the lessor in case of a force majeure but left undefined what this entailed.

As well as the unequal and not entirely realistic terms of tenancy, another problem was that the contract was drawn up in English—the third language of Milano's staff and the second language of their Chinese counterparts. Although the hotel manager's conversational skills in English, accumulated over more than ten years working in the hotel business, were solid, he admitted in our interview that his reading skills were not sufficient to fully grasp the content of the contract. On the Chinese side, only the legal department at Huawei's office in Addis Ababa, not the engineers on-site, had a full understanding of the contract's content. As a result, communication about the contract and more generally between the parties went from Mekelle to Addis Ababa and back by email. Communication was thus mediated through, first, a foreign language; second, mediators with legal knowledge; and third, the medium of electronic messaging.

Jay Ke-Schutte shows how Afro-Chinese encounters are mediated through what they call the "Angloscene" and describe as a historically imbricated manifestation of Western hegemony.[11] Interactions between Ethiopians and Chinese, too, are compromised by the use of English—the only language the two parties had in common, if they can be said to have a common language at all. English in Ethiopian–Chinese encounters at once enables and disables communication. It permits the parties to communicate with one another, while creating misunderstandings that potentially jeopardize their relationship. Debunking the idea that English is just a language and whiteness just a race—to which liberal discourses tend to appeal—Ke-Schutte shows that English is a far from neutral language, as it stratifies its speakers according to fluency. English, moreover, intersects with other vectors such as whiteness or ideals of cosmopolitanism. In the relationship between Milano and Huawei, from the start the latter had greater access to English and, in this case, legal English. Race further reinforced the inequalities in the relationship.

"Each time they raised a defect, they referred to the contract," Milano's manager reflected.[12] "We did not expect that the contract would disadvantage us. We trusted them. . . . We did not notice that the contract was drafted to benefit the Chinese company." Milano signed the contract without the assistance of a legal expert. One of Huawei's managers had listed a few requirements in his conversations with the hotel manager, and the hotel owner, who spent a significant part of the year in Italy, had simply gone with what his trusted manager said. Note that Milano's manager accords agency to the rental agreement ("the contract") and depicts it as having turned against the hotel in favor of its Chinese drafters. While to him the contract had been a mere formality that established the initial relationship, Huawei took the contract as the basis of their relationship and the "go-to" document, especially when they found themselves disappointed with the services the hotel offered.

What was not mentioned in the contract was that Huawei would bring its own chef. It was the kitchen, shared with the hotel, that became the first source of confrontation. Although not mentioned in court, this issue caused tensions to heighten from the start. When he learned that the Chinese company had its own chef, Milano's manager hesitated to let the chef use the hotel kitchen and did not offer him another space. The cause for the manager's concern were rumors about the Chinese diet. In Ethiopia, neither Ethiopian Orthodox Christians nor Ethiopian Muslims eat pork. The consumption of donkeys—widely used as pack animals—is also frowned on, as is that of dog meat and insects, which the Chinese were rumored to eat.

Of course, these stories did not necessarily represent reality. When I lived in Chinese camps, the only delicacies I was served that went against Ethiopian customs were pork and camel meat.[13] The Chinese camp residents largely refrained from eating things that were considered unacceptable. Given the rapid circulation of rumors and the disgust they conveyed, the manager was worried that his Ethiopian guests would leave or stay away when they learned that Milano's meals were contaminated. "They even wanted to bring in a pig, slaughter it in the courtyard, and bring it into the kitchen. We said 'no.'"[14] This was the only issue on which Milano stood firm, at least in the manager's interview with Bereket and me. It was an objection motivated by visceral disgust and community pressure. Yet pork is so central to Chinese cuisine that chefs cannot exclude it if they are to avoid reprimands from their managers. It is highly likely that the Chinese chef smuggled in some pork.

INDIRECT COMMUNICATION

Communication was heavily mediated throughout. Rather than relaying their complaints directly to Milano's manager, the Chinese staff informed Huawei's head office in Addis Ababa, whereupon the head office wrote to Milano's manager via email. This indirect form of communication may have saved the face of those who communicated with one other by avoiding direct disagreements, but it created misunderstandings that remained unresolved and fed into frustration. Sporadically they did have a formal meeting when the hotel owner or a manager from the head office was in town. Then the parties sat together and could see eye to eye.

The indirect communication between the Ethiopian hotel staff and the Chinese engineers and support staff resonates with observations of Afro-Chinese interactions by other scholars, such as Cheryl Mei-Ting Schmitz in Angola and Di Wu in Zambia.[15] In her discussion of a dispute between a laid-off Angolan worker and his former Chinese managers, Schmitz reveals the workings and purpose of indirect speech in relations that are permeated by racialized inequalities.[16] She does so while reflecting on her own role as a translator. Schmitz found that the Chinese managers and the Angolan worker alike shied away from voicing things that they deemed unethical. Instead, they preferred to communicate indirectly and shift the burden of interpretation to the addressee. Chinese managers attempted to evince a sense of respect for their employee's dignity. Indirect speech helped the Angolan worker—seeking compensation for what he defined as a workplace accident—to appeal to his former employer's goodwill. Indirect speech does not necessarily lead to miscommunication, Schmitz notes: "When speech is understood by both speaker and addressee to be indirect, and contextual cues are agreed upon, indirectness does not necessarily pose a problem for the transmission of meaning."[17] Ultimately both her translation—in which she, too, negotiated between "attempted kindness and unavoidable cruelty"—and her interlocutors' indirect speech failed, as the Chinese managers were structurally incapable of avoiding harm to the laid-off worker. In other words, indirect communication and noncommunication did not reduce inequalities, let alone mitigate opportunities for immunity resulting from them.

Indirect speech, however, preserved peace and prevented discord.[18] As such, it served an important function. Some speakers carried a heavier burden of communication and interpretation than others, such as Milano's manager and Huawei's Ethiopian liaison officer. This burden became progressively heavier as rising tensions led to impatience and the breakdown of polite, indirect speech. The manager told us:

> We thought that the arrival of a big company could benefit us in many ways. Sadly, the reverse happened. We entered into the agreement in a rush. They delayed payments. We sent receipts to Addis Ababa, but the headquarters delayed their payments. . . . We wrote letters of request. They told us that this and this happened. They came up with excuses. You wonder how such a big company can do this. I have worked in the hotel business for many years. Customers who come from Europe or the US or other African countries . . . of course they should not have to have any complaints, but if they do, the way in which they express their complaint and how they approach you is with respect. These customers buy a service from you. They do not buy *you*. This was not the case with the Chinese. The Chinese are like, "You have to do this!"[19]

After several months, the tone of speech changed and accentuated the power disparities, as Huawei began using rental payments as a form of control. Respectful requests made way for curt commands reminiscent of the one-directional speech between Chinese managers and Ethiopian workers on a construction site. The statement "they do not buy *you*," which the hotel manager used to suggest his Chinese guests acted as though they had bought him rather than the service he provided, revealed the dignity threat lurking beneath increasingly tense interactions. Huawei's staff, he believed, failed to treat them with the respect that service providers deserve from their customers, regardless of racial or national background.

The hotel manager's remark also suggests the loss of ownership, which can be construed as a form of devaluation, as described in chapter 2. Like the Ethiopian workers who take their employer to court, the manager described his client as a "big company" whose behavior ought to be more responsible, if only because it had the resources to be so. To stress the severity of the Chinese managers' disrespect, he compared Huawei's staff with customers from Europe, the United States, and other African countries, who he alleges are courteous when raising complaints.

Milano's manager felt he had satisfied all the requests his Chinese guests raised. To us, he underscored that the hotel had even made generous gestures. He had, for instance, offered a deluxe room free of charge for a higher-level manager who came to visit the project. Here again, the dynamic between giving and taking comes to the fore. While rebuking claims that he had been inhospitable by taking, the hotel manager stressed how unstinting he was by giving. Huawei had likely deployed similar terms. Its managers may have argued that they had accepted terms less favorable than in the contract and that offering the deluxe room was the least the hotel could do in return.

BREAKDOWN OF COMMUNICATION

Worsened communication eventually devolved into its complete breakdown, leading to Huawei's departure in the dark of night—or "escape," as the judge and the hotel manager called it.[20] On standby that night, the manager was awakened by noise. Alarmed, he found Huawei's staff packing their technical equipment and personal luggage and loading it into their vehicles. Enclosed by trees, the hotel's parking area is barely visible from the street. During the day, blue tuktuks, known as *bajaj*, line up outside on the street waiting for customers. The hotel overlooks a roundabout that connects Ageazi Street to Mekelle's main artery leading around the hills. If you walk down the street to Romanat Square, you hit the Tigray Supreme Court midway. Afraid that Huawei would leave without paying the outstanding rent, the hotel manager asked the Ethiopian drivers of the company's vehicles to stay put and his security personnel to prevent any cars from leaving the premises.

Huawei's departure caught the hotel manager by surprise. The expatriate managers had not indicated to him that they intended to leave, nor had they sent notice of termination of their lease contract. The Chinese staff insisted on leaving and grew frustrated when they were barred from so doing. Emotions ran high, even leading to a physical altercation with one of the Chinese managers, who "tried to kick me with a karate kick," the manager recollected.[21] He called the police immediately. The Tigray Police Commission was conveniently located across the road from the hotel, and the police arrived swiftly. The officers demanded that the Chinese staff members take their suitcases back upstairs. They did so reluctantly.

"There was nobody to mediate," Milano's manager regretted.[22] Communication proved impossible without mediation. On their arrival, however, the police took on the role of mediators and managed to stem animosity. When everyone calmed down, the hotel manager and his Chinese counterpart went to all the rooms with a checklist, following the standard checkout procedure, to see whether any damage had been incurred or anything was missing. After this, the Chinese staff were allowed to exit the premises. Their departure left a bitter taste among the hotel staff.

I have not been able to talk to any of the Huawei staff who were based in Mekelle at the time and am left to guess why they chose to leave the hotel in the middle of the night. Judging from numerous interactions between Ethiopian workers and Chinese managers, as well as the Ethiopian subcontractors and Chinese contractors I observed firsthand, I reckon that the Huawei personnel sought to avoid confrontation and save face by leaving unseen. I often witnessed situations in which Chinese managers opted for noncommunication over a potential confrontation to prevent disputes from escalating.

Exploring the interactions between expatriate and local workers at Chinese farms near Lusaka, Zambia, Di Wu shows how and why Chinese managers adopt indirect speech in communication among themselves and with their Zambian counterparts. They do so to protect social relations, as careless wordings threaten to break the harmonious relations that Chinese managers seek to maintain at all costs.[23] Resorting to indirect speech is a way to preserve one's face and the face of the addressee. Furthermore, opening a communication gap allowed the speaker to escape responsibility. By creating such a gap, Chinese managers put the burden of communicative cooperation and interpretation on the African addressee. This led, at times, to major misunderstandings. Speakers did not always understand the cultural cues implied in speech. In many instances, including this one, communication gaps had the opposite of the intended effect. Indeed, the silent departure led to an explosive confrontation.

Milano's owner, a seasoned businessman, decided to take the dispute to court and claim outstanding rent and compensation for the additional purchases the hotel had made for Huawei, the loss it had incurred by closing the hotel bar at the company's request, and the damage to the dining hall. The hotel was unable to call Huawei back to the negotiating table. Only the court could reestablish communication between the two wrathful parties.

As many socio-legal scholars have long shown, disputants take their case to court when compromise-based forms of dispute resolution, such as negotiation and mediation, no longer work.[24] Sally Merry and Susan Silbey, for instance, describe a disputant's turn to court as the point at which "the grievant wants vindication, protection of his or her rights (as he or she perceives them), an advocate to help in the battle, or a third party who will uncover the 'truth' and declare the other party wrong."[25] In these instances, one of the parties, often the weaker one, seeks a neutral party that can facilitate and direct communication, someone who can, moreover, give an authoritative interpretation of the dispute—one that gives them the "truth."

Until today, the hotel manager and owner remain in the dark about why Huawei left and did so abruptly. Even Huawei's lawyer did not have an answer. He doubted whether his client had given him the full story: "The Chinese raised the poor quality of the hotel. To me, this is not persuasive enough. I don't think that the hotel has bed bugs. But this is what the Chinese said. You bring to court what your client tells you. You will not rent a room and experience it yourself and then argue [in court]. I am not convinced by their argument, but this is what they said. They said that they will prove it with evidence."

Huawei demonstrated the infestation of bed bugs through witness testimonies. The bed bugs became a powerful symbol of the poor services its staff had received. Yet Huawei's attorney disputed this, even hinting that it was a lie. By so doing, he protected the reputation of the hotel and the dignity of its staff and owner. Huawei's Ethiopian lawyer decided to take the middle ground in our interview. He insisted, however, that he had represented his Chinese client in court as best he could.

THE SUMMONS

Huawei's staff rejected the court summons by showing the door to the person who delivered it. After Milano had proved that the summons had been duly delivered, the court began proceedings in absentia.[26] Huawei's head office in Addis Ababa found out about the court case when it received a letter from the Commercial Bank of Ethiopia stating that it had frozen 3.5 million birr of the company's assets. This was after Milano had filed the first lawsuit together with an injunction request on April 26, 2015, when the Chinese staff were still living at the hotel premises. Ethiopian representatives of the company traveled to Mekelle for negotiations and engaged a local lawyer (their in-house counsel in Addis Ababa presumably did not speak Tigrigna).

The lawyer Huawei had enlisted, a solo practitioner with a small office in Kebele 16, went to the registrar's office to request a copy of the pleading but his request was declined. He wrote a letter to the court, arguing that the summons had in fact not been duly delivered. It should have been sent to Huawei headquarters in Addis Ababa instead of its office at the Milano. He also mentioned the likelihood of miscommunication between the parties, pleading for understanding on the part of the court. "The defendant is a foreign company," he wrote in his letter.[27] "It is difficult to say whether the person who rejected the summons was aware that it concerned a court summons. It is hard to establish whether this was made clear to him in his own language," he pointed out, thereby suggesting that the language barrier had caused an innocent misunderstanding, even if the rash reaction of the Chinese manager who refused to accept the summons might suggest otherwise.[28] "The plaintiff may have given the summons to any Chinese, but 'any Chinese' does not necessarily mean the defendant," he further contended. "A Chinese worker and an Ethiopian worker are the same. Both are employees of the company. The court summons shall be delivered to the appropriate organ or person." The lawyer may have propounded that the summons ought to be delivered to an Ethiopian member of staff who could have understood the document. It is, however, unclear whether Huawei had Tigrigna-speaking management staff in Addis Ababa. To prove Huawei's innocence, he stated that the Chinese company had reached out to him immediately on finding out about the lawsuit; it was not necessarily "disobedient to court summonses." He concluded by requesting the court allow Huawei the right to respond. "The philosophy of the general interpretation of law states that procedures, unless there is gross negligence, shall not violate substantive rights."[29]

The court accepted the letter of apology and began proceedings anew. Either way, the threat of litigation prompted a change in the Chinese firm's attitude.

Huawei immediately deposited 1.3 million birr into the plaintiff's bank account. This move testifies to the court's power to boost the leverage of the weaker party and reshape the relationship between the parties in the process. Likely fearing reputational damage as much as a lengthy legal battle, Huawei's head office solved the issue within a day. If Milano had not taken the step to court, the Chinese company might have dragged its feet or perhaps transferred only part of the sum. The court forced the firm to fulfill its obligations as a lessee. By so doing, it recalibrated power inequalities and denied the telecommunications giant the opportunity of immunity it had generated by mobilizing these inequalities and inscribing them in the contract.

I had earlier witnessed the strategic use of the threat of litigation by Ethiopian disputants. They used the threat to compel their Chinese business partner, client, or employer to give in to demands or reach a compromise. The threat of litigation also helped start talks in the first place. Courts encouraged the parties to communicate not only in the form of scripted courtroom conversations but also outside court with an eye to avoiding drawn-out proceedings. In the dispute between Milano and Huawei, the communicative function of the court indeed extended beyond the courtroom. The institution of a court case and the potential of a legal dispute brought the parties back to the negotiating table. During the proceedings, the hotel owner and his Chinese counterparts met in Addis Ababa to settle the dispute. Yet, these well-intentioned and hopeful efforts were in vain. Milano's owner had little sway, and Huawei held on to the terms of the contract.

Both parties accused the other of being overly litigious, each claiming they had intended to solve the dispute amicably. Huawei, its legal representative stressed, had tried to settle the dispute through negotiation. "The Chinese do not like to go to court," he explained.[30] "They do not believe in the legal profession or the judicial system. They don't think that they will be treated properly by the court." To Huawei, solving the matter through negotiation was a strategic choice. "To tell you frankly, it is not easy to work with them as a lawyer. Luckily the people from Huawei were good people."[31] Huawei had been a relatively easy client to work with, given its extensive international exposure. Huawei's international experience can also be read from its contract with Milano, which is much more sophisticated than other contracts I have seen signed by Chinese companies and Ethiopian counterparts.

For Milano, it was the first time it had brought a lawsuit. "I had never attended court," the hotel manager said. "I worked with many counterparts, from waiters to CEOs. I prefer to negotiate and take things easy. I don't like courts. It was my first time."[32] The hotel owner had wanted to solve the dispute through negotiation, according to Milano's lawyer, who described him as a "patient man":[33] "He even said during the court proceeding, 'I don't really like litigation. I can quit at any time.' He used to tell this to the Chinese: 'You spoiled my hotel, and you tried to leave in the middle of the night, as if you are thieves. It is not good for your reputation.' This is what he said to them. To us, he said that, if we can and the Chinese pay us, we can quit the case. 'We don't want to fight a big company.'"[34]

The owner of Milano, here described by his lawyer, must have been aware of Huawei's sensitivity about its reputation. Huawei might have been equally reluctant to air its dirty laundry by having the dispute adjudicated in open court. For this reason, it deposited the outstanding fee as soon as it learned about the case. According to Huawei's lawyer, however, it was the hotel owner who was intent on "knocking on the door of the court."[35] Communication turned bitter yet again. The parties accused one another of sowing animosity.

To Huawei, the source of the dispute was Milano's failure to meet the requirements stipulated in the contract and the poor services provided as a result. To Milano, it was Huawei's failure to pay the rent in a timely fashion. "The case went to court because they did not make the payments according to the contract," the hotel manager explained.[36] "We repeatedly requested them to make the payments. . . . We tried to solve the dispute through mediation. We were willing to compromise and went to Addis Ababa for negotiations." The Chinese managers on the ground did not have the corporate mandate to negotiate the terms in the contract and, apart from the project manager, had likely not even read the document, as I observed on other projects. Negotiations, however, came to naught. Milano filed a second lawsuit on September 8, 2016.

MILANO HOTEL V. HUAWEI TECHNOLOGIES

The judgment reads that Milano requested compensation for damage incurred to the dining hall that Huawei had remodeled as an office space with desk islands separated by gypsum walls, additional services the hotel had provided, losses suffered from the closure of the hotel bar at Chinese management's request, and outstanding rent, amounting to 1.8 million birr.[37] In its response, Huawei argued that it had not damaged the hall and that its staff had cleared and cleaned the hall before departure. The additional services—including the provision of boilers for hot water and extra tables, chairs, and white bed linen—had been listed under the "bedroom standard configuration" provision in the contract. Furthermore, the hotel had closed the bar by mutual agreement due to "unreasonable noise." Huawei furthermore contended that it had made all payments, apart from 3,192 birr for additional services, which it was willing to make should the court request it to do so, the telecommunications company stated in its response.[38]

The witnesses for the plaintiff—the hotel manager, another Ethiopian staff member, and the wife of the hotel owner—underscored the magnanimity of the hotel in making the Chinese guests comfortable. The defendant's witnesses—the Chinese project manager, another Chinese team member, and a Chinese computer scientist—underlined the poor services the hotel had provided. I quote the testimony of the Chinese project manager at length, as I did not have the chance to interview him. His testimony exudes the frustration he and his colleagues must have felt:

> They [Milano Hotel] failed to provide 24-hour hot water and clean sheets, blankets, internet, office chairs, and bedroom chairs and tables. The hotel was required to provide all this according to the contract. The doors of the rooms could be opened with one key. There was not always water. We had trouble with the toilets too. We repeatedly asked to make improvements according to our contract. They promised to fix these issues within a day. We did not get a solution. The internet was not working. There were cables but no internet. There was no hot water. At night, we were attacked by bed bugs. We requested several times to solve these problems. They did change the bed sheets. There were no tables and chairs in our bedrooms, only at the office. We agreed to use the hall . . . as an office, by installing gypsum partitions. We attached them to the walls, but we did not change the layout of the space. We did not request the hotel to buy anything beyond the contract.
>
> The plaintiff requested of us the payment of the first term. [We had agreed that] if there is a problem with the service, 10 percent will be deducted, and so we deducted this amount of money. The service we received was poor. As for the internet, our company installed its own internet, by communicating with the relevant organ [Ethio Telecom]. There is nothing that the plaintiff provided to us. Because we wanted to terminate the contract, we sent a letter to the plaintiff by DHL on May 22, 2015, European Calendar. On May 25, 2015, European Calendar, we sent an email and on May 30, 2015 we gave an in-person notice to the owner of the hotel that we want to terminate the contract. However, the owner of the hotel . . . refused to sign. After two months, when we were about to leave the hotel with our properties, we were prevented from doing so by the plaintiff's staff. We left the gypsum walls of the partitions. The plaintiff agreed to that. As for the list of other properties, we completed the hand-over in writing together with the manager of the company, the first witness of the plaintiff. After that, we left the hotel.[39]

The defendant's witnesses testified that the services provided by Milano did not meet the requirements stipulated in the contract (note that the word "contract" is mentioned five times in this extract). The dissatisfaction of Huawei staff with the hotel's services seemed to be the main source of grievance, but was it the reason for their unanticipated departure? It was rumored that Huawei's project had been completed before the expected end date.[40] In the final weeks, staff occupied only a few of the bedrooms on the top floor. Renting an entire floor, including office and kitchen space, no longer made sense financially.

To the court, the main issue of contestation was whether Huawei had terminated the rental agreement with or without the mandatory prior notice. Milano argued that it had not received notice by email or in person. The letter delivered by DHL was a request to extend rather than terminate the contract. Huawei, in contrast, alleged that it had given notice, mentioning the DHL letter and an email sent on the same day. The defendant brought a computer scientist as a witness to testify that the email had been received by the hotel—a move that aroused suspicion.

The presiding judge divulged in our interview with him that he suspected that the email—a print copy of which Huawei submitted as evidence—had been forged. He pointed to a discrepancy between what was written in the email and the testimony of one of Huawei's witnesses. The court decided that Milano had not received prior notice and demanded the defendant pay 492,930 birr in restitution for unpaid rent. All Milano's other claims were dismissed.

Describing both parties as "stubborn," the presiding judge sensed bad blood between them.[41] Even in court, where the parties were compelled to look the other in the eyes, communication was far from smooth. This was partially the court's fault. It had been unable to find a neutral Mandarin interpreter and allowed one of Huawei's managers to translate from Chinese to English, whereupon the court interpreter translated from English to Tigrigna. "God alone knows whether what the witness said was the same as what the interpreter interpreted," the judge told us.[42] He could have understood the gist of an English testimony, but this was much harder with one in Mandarin. Language had been one of the main challenges for the judge in this case. He suspected that the Huawei manager who interpreted the testimonies of his colleagues had twisted them to the company's advantage. Double translation was common in cases involving Chinese parties. Sometimes the court was able to find a neutral interpreter. More often, it requested that an Ethiopian or Chinese member of staff of the company interpret. Double translation notwithstanding, the judges reestablished communication between the parties.

REFLECTIONS

There was no clear winner in *Milano Hotel v. Huawei Technologies*. Huawei won on some issues, while Milano came out as the winner on others. Both Huawei's lawyer and Milano's manager claimed they had obtained a court victory. Huawei was spared paying 2.3 million birr, while Milano still received a fair share of what was an exaggerated claim. The threat of litigation had, moreover, helped the hotel owner obtain the rent for the last cycle of the lease. Given the power differentials between the parties inscribed in the contract, it is unlikely he would have been better off without the court's intervention.

Huawei had an advantage not only in determining the nature of the relationship between lessor and lessee but also in negotiating the terms that defined this relationship. The Chinese corporation effectively set its own rules and granted itself the power to divert from them. Relentless competition in the hospitality sector in Mekelle further reduced the hotel's bargaining power. If the rooms would not have been occupied by Huawei, they might have sat empty. Milano found itself in a position in which it had to resort to litigation or threaten to put pressure on the Chinese party when it refused to meet the hotel midway. When communication broke down, Milano was left with no option but to turn to court. The conflict had become serious enough to warrant the intervention of someone who could give a binding and enforceable decision. Only the court, with the coercive backing of the state, could force the parties to continue their conversation, if in a formal setting and scripted manner.

To Milano, the court provided the only avenue to take on a foreign multinational corporation. The biggest challenge, Milano's manager reflected with the benefit of hindsight, was the contract: "It was binding and not drafted in a way that we understood or in a way that we wanted it."[43] However, the hotel manager was not all negative about his experience hosting the telecommunications firm. His eyes lit up when we asked him what he had learned from his Chinese guests:

> I was envious. They are very hardworking. One Chinese had four or five laptops in their room. They are multiskilled. One Chinese can be a technician, a network distribution engineer, and a carpenter. I was amazed seeing them do all these tasks. I know our hall well, but I never pictured the hall in that way. I was surprised to see how they turned the hall into a fancy office in a few days' time. They were the ones to do this. As a citizen, although they are contracted by the government to work on these things . . . I understand that at the end of the day the network is for us. I do have respect for them. I tried to help them. I tried to make their stay comfortable.[44]

Note that the hotel manager switched gears when adopting the identity of a "citizen" instead of that of lessor. He expressed appreciation for the installation work the Chinese team carried out. When providing compliments and reflecting on the contributions made by the Chinese firm, he distanced himself from the lessor–lessee relationship and his personal relationship with Huawei's staff. Ultimately, he admitted, the work the telecommunications firm carried out in the region was for Ethiopians. As a citizen, he reiterated the argument that Chinese activities ought to be seen as a national benefit or a gift to the nation (hence his reference to citizenship). However, his everyday interactions with Huawei's staff were different. He experienced the power differentials and the structural impasses they engendered firsthand. He tried to develop a relationship with his Chinese guests beyond the contract and was successful to some extent. The hotel had invited them to coffee ceremonies—an Ethiopian sign of hospitality—"yet they did not have time. They simply eat, drink, and work."[45] When the dispute turned sour, the contract was all there was to hold onto in the relationship, and it was set out in unequal terms, allowing one party to set the rules and determine the exceptions to them.

EMPTY CONTRACTS

To the bench, *Milano Hotel v. Huawei Technologies* was a straightforward contractual dispute. The judges could refer to a detailed contract that set out the relationship and its terms, if in English. The case was certainly easier than some other contractual disputes between Chinese and Ethiopian parties that ended up in court for which the only evidence of a relationship was what judges and lawyers variously called an "empty contract," a "one-page contract," a "contract without a beginning or an end," a "contract with nothing to hold onto," or a "toilet paper contract." Empty contracts lacked basic elements, from the time and place of the contract's signing, which are critical to determining the period of limitation and jurisdiction, to provisions explaining the nature of the relationship, the rights and obligations of the parties, the deliverables, and a termination-of-contract clause. A "toilet paper contract" was a scrap of paper with a few words jotted on it, easily forgotten until an unforeseen dispute arose between the parties, who were left with no option but to go to court. Empty contracts, however, lent the court extraordinary discretion, giving the judges the freedom to fill the silences in these documents in a way they deemed fair or otherwise saw fit, thereby shaping the relationship between the parties.

An Ethiopian lawyer based in Addis Ababa relayed her amusement at having entertained a case in which two Chinese parties met in court. They had concluded an agreement with what she called a "one-page contract":[46] "What they said was basically 'X and Y agree to carry out this and this construction work. The amount of payment is this.' That's it." She and the court were left to (re)construct the relationship between the parties and had significant discretion in so doing. This was true, too, for disputes between Ethiopian and Chinese parties. The lawyer indicated that her Chinese client had hired Ethiopian laborers using similar one-page contracts before they brought her on board. She began preparing templates for various types of employment agreements as well as for contracts with suppliers and subcontractors. "I told them, when you are about to sign a contract, send it to me first." She reckoned they heeded her advice in 75 percent of cases, but "sometimes they are in a rush and sign an empty contract."[47] By engaging in important transactional work, Ethiopian lawyers like this one improved Chinese business operations, especially regarding human resources and external relations. As mediators and translators, lawyers also smoothed communication.

Many Chinese corporations learned the consequences of an empty contract the hard way in open court, as had China Wu Yi. The overseas arm of the Fujian Construction Engineering Group had signed an agreement with an Ethiopian subcontractor for the construction of ditches along its project road in Afar in northeastern Ethiopia.[48] The drafter of the contract had forgotten to include a time and place. When a conflict arose over the subcontractor's work and the payment due, the Ethiopian construction firm filed suit against the Chinese contractor in the Supreme Court of Tigray, the region bordering Afar. China Wu Yi's lawyer, enlisted by the company after the fact, regretted the course of events, but could only shake his head over it.[49] With considerable international exposure, China Wu Yi should have known better, he believed. The company was completing the Zemen Bank headquarters in Addis Ababa and had successfully finished several projects in neighboring Kenya, such as the makeover of the Jomo Kenyatta International Airport.

Smart and savvy, China Wu Yi's lawyer attempted to take advantage of the omission in the contract by filing a request for a change of venue as a preliminary objection. If the case could be heard in Afar, he suspected, the company would stand a better chance of winning. "In Afar, the company has established relations with local authorities," the lawyer explained.[50] "Here in Mekelle they are on their own." The lawyer did not disclose to us where the contract had been signed. Given that the subcontractor was based in Mekelle, the closest city to the project site, it is highly likely that the contract was signed there and fell under the jurisdiction of the Tigray Supreme Court.

The conflict between China Wu Yi and its Ethiopian subcontractor arose from a unilateral decision by the contractor to reduce the payment promised to the subcontractor. It cited poor performance but did not communicate this to the sub-contractor, likely to avoid a confrontation. Unsurprisingly, the subcontractor was not pleased to discover it had received a lower payment than initially agreed on. China Wu Yi's lawyer admitted the company had failed to make the advance payment, with the result that the subcontractor did not have enough funds to rent the machinery required for the work. The local subcontractor eventually suspended construction due to a lack of funds.

Unaware or unaccepting of the predicament of the local construction firm, Chinese management wrote a letter to the Mekelle-based company, ordering it to finish the work. When the subcontractor did not respond to the letter, China Wu Yi carried out the work itself and decided to pay only 25 percent of the agreed contract price to the subcontractor. How much work the subcontractor had completed was contested and had to be established by the court. Another issue was that because the contract lacked a date, it was unclear when the ninety days the subcontractor had been given to complete the work would end. China Wu Yi could not provide hard proof (as in written evidence) that the subcontractor did not finish the work in three months. It was questionable whether witness testimonies would suffice.

Of course, an empty contract could easily play in the favor of the Chinese con-tractor *outside* the court. It allowed the party with the upper hand to set the terms, as Huawei and China Wu Yi had done, and determine exceptions to these terms. As Carl Schmitt and Giorgio Agamben pointed out,[51] the sovereign not only makes the rules but also has the power to decide on exemptions from these rules. Private contracts signed between unequal parties generated a quasi-sovereign, one that could claim de facto and, at times, de jure immunity. Indeed, some private contracts, such as those between the Export–Import Bank of China and the Kenyan government mentioned in chapter 1, stipulate that the state, as a party to the contract, concede its sovereignty. The parties to the contractual agreements discussed in this chapter do not enjoy de jure immunity; however, by diverting from the rules they set themselves, they claimed de facto immunity. The material disparities and power inequalities that mark the rela-tionship as inscribed in the contract and that negotiated beyond the contract enable stronger parties to do so.

Aware of such practices, the courts largely prevented them from happening provided plaintiffs requested their intervention by filing lawsuits. The lawyer for the Ethiopian subcontractor was confident it would win the case, even though "the contract is full of gaps."[52] Yet, their Chinese opponent was wearing them out. They raised the question of jurisdiction as a preliminary objection, and he first had to prove through witness testimonies where the contract was signed. Should the case be entertained in Afar, it would become difficult for the subcontractor and drain its limited budget.

Worse still, China Wu Yi had concealed its local financial assets, making it hard, if not impossible, for the subcontractor to find the right bank account on time and have a freezing injunction placed on it. Indeed, the fast transfer of money between bank accounts was a common tactic to evade injunctions and default on the payment of damages. In Ethiopia's decentralized banking system, it was not always easy to find the bank accounts that the counterparty had open in other regions. Many Chinese companies have infrastructure projects in several parts of the country and multiple local accounts, if all with the Commercial Bank of Ethiopia, as regulations stipulate. In sum, if the subcontractor won the case, it was unclear whether the court's judgment could be enforced. This shows the limits of the court's authority. At the end of my fieldwork in December 2020, the case was still pending. It was delayed, first by Covid-19, which resulted in the partial closure of the courts, and later by the civil war.

Whether China Wu Yi stood to benefit from the gaps in the contract with its Ethiopian subcontractor *inside* the court is questionable, if we leave aside the possibility of China Wu Yi evading the payment of damages. As this case indicates, communication gaps were not only common in everyday interactions on building sites or in engineers' offices but also in writing. The silences left in daily communication echo and extend those in the contract. When a serious disagreement arose and one of the parties brought the case to court, the judges were left to fill the gaps. The emptier the contract, the more discretion judges had to shape the nature of the relationship between the disputing parties and determine their rights and obligations.

CLOSING THE COMMUNICATION GAP

The court effectively closed the communication gap between the Ethiopian and Chinese disputants. As such, it possessed a communicative function that drew the parties to court and enhanced the discretionary power of judges. In chapter 2, we saw the everyday communicative impasses on a building site up close. The indirect nature or lack of communication not only gave rise to disputes but also caused them to spiral out of control, leaving Ethiopian workers with no option but to take their concerns, accusations, and grievances to court. Similar dynamics are at play in relations that appear more equal at first glance, such as those between an Ethiopian lessor and a Chinese lessee, an Ethiopian subcontractor and a Chinese contractor, and between Ethiopian and Chinese business partners.

The communicative function of the court manifested in several ways in *Milano Hotel v. Huawei Technologies* and other cases I have discussed. First, the court established a platform or venue for communication. Even the threat of litigation could suffice to bring the parties to the negotiating table and restore communication. The formal setting of the court and the scripted nature of courtroom conversations had an equalizing effect on power relations, as I will further illustrate in chapter 5, even though they never entirely erased the power differentials. Judges' ideological leanings and backgrounds influenced how they conducted proceedings and ruled on cases, as I will demonstrate in chapter 6. Interventions from third parties could, moreover, sway them to decide cases in certain ways. Yet, regardless of subtle and perhaps less subtle biases, the court (re)established communication.

Second, where communication had largely been indirect, the court eliminated some, if not all, mediation by bringing the parties together in one room. Of course, courtroom conversations are mediated by the judge, and translation is part and parcel of courtroom speech. Yet what was shunned in interactions between the parties was voiced in court. At trial and in pretrial and posttrial hearings, the court compelled parties to communicate with one another in a direct fashion, forcing them to say "on the record" what commonly remained "off the record."[53] In other words, where communication on the building site, in the manager's office, or in the mechanics' workshop was often indirect, communication in the courtroom was, quite literally, "on the record." What was said was recorded on tape and in writing, stored in the court archive, and made accessible to the public. Disputants could voice their grievances and interpretations of events to the counterparty and the interested audience in public hearings. The court became a confrontational space as a result.

Furthermore, the bench gave a binding interpretation of disputes and, by extension, the responsibilities and duties of the disputing parties. It cleared miscommunication, if not necessarily the underlying structures and sentiments that caused it, by giving a decisive interpretation of events. The combined linguistic, cultural, and social barriers to communication made the court's communicative function even more crucial. In fact, parties in Ethiopian–Chinese encounters often did not even try to come to an understanding and went straight to court, thus skipping the negotiation phase. In extracontractual cases, plaintiffs and defendants might even meet for the first time in court. In such instances, the court established rather than reestablished communication and was able to shape the relationship between the parties significantly.

FROM CONSTRUCTING CONTRACTS
TO CLAIMING IMMUNITY

The discretionary power thrown in the lap of the Ethiopian judiciary enhanced their authority and emboldened them to assert jurisdiction and reclaim sovereignty. Private contracts, whether signed between employer and employee, buyer and supplier, or lessor and lessee, become public when at least one party goes to court. Of course, determining the content of private contracts such as the tenancy agreement between Milano Hotel and Huawei Technologies and demanding exemption from state law are two different things. However, the determination to hold onto (unequal) terms in private contracts, unspoken norms, or everyday practices—some of which are in noncompliance with state law—can easily evolve into claims for immunity, as they did in Ethiopian–Chinese interactions. Corporate managers assumed they had not just the upper hand in relations with their Ethiopian counterparts but also the advantage to negotiate with state actors, including the courts. They leveraged power disparities in their relationships with state institutions, legal or executive, as much as with their employee, business partner, or lessor.

Private contracts revealed the increased astuteness of Chinese corporations like Huawei. Chinese enterprises with less international exposure were still learning, as can be seen from the empty or one-page contracts they entered into, reminiscent of the period of reform and opening in China, when oral promises and mutual trust often sufficed to seal a business deal.[54] With the increase of legal experience and in-house legal capacity, this has changed dramatically—yet, not for all Chinese companies operating in Ethiopia. Given the diverse range of enterprises, from central state-owned firms to small businesses, company practices and responses to Ethiopia's local regulatory environment differ. However, I found out through interviews and observations that state-owned firms and individual businesspeople could be equally adamant about deserving to be exempted from local legal processes.

The bench resisted litigants' demands for immunity, as I will show in the following chapters. By so doing, it reset the terms of the relationship not just between the disputing parties but also between its jurisdiction and the foreign litigants it ensnared. The court's communicative function was critical to this endeavor.[55] It not only drew actors in cross-cultural disputes to court but also gave judges additional discretionary power. The communication gaps between the parties, including the silences left in their written agreements, expanded judicial discretion and ultimately extended jurisdictional power.

Enacting Jurisdiction, Reenacting Sovereignty

Most judges held vivid memories of the first Chinese cases they entertained, as did Judge Gidey.[1] Gezhouba Group (CGGC), a Chinese state firm, began road-building activities in Sheraro, a town near the border with Eritrea, around the time he assumed his post at the Sheraro Wereda Court in 2009.[2] CGGC had been awarded the first lot of the Shire–Sheraro–Humera Road Project, funded by the Ethiopian government. As construction work began, the court was flooded with labor cases filed against the Chinese company. The first were the most memorable.

The earliest lawsuit was a collective labor case brought by a group of Ethiopian laborers who had been abruptly dismissed by Chinese management. The plaintiffs requested compensation for unlawful dismissal. On receiving the court summons, the Chinese company failed to submit a written response. The deputy project manager nonetheless turned up to the pretrial hearing. When Judge Gidey asked what had happened, the Chinese manager snorted, "It is our right. We do not want them, and so we sent them home."[3] The judge asked: "Did you fire these workers?" "Yes. We have come here to work, but they [the laborers] don't work. We are dissatisfied with them. That is why we fired them." The manager confirmed all the facts presented by the workers and effectively conceded that their dismissal had been unlawful. He showed no remorse. The court granted the plaintiffs compensation for the illegal termination.

On receiving the verdict, the workers filed for execution, and the judge set a date for the parties to come to court. The deputy manager, however, failed to show up on the scheduled day. Instead, he made a phone call to the federal authorities (most likely the Ethiopian Roads Authority), who contacted a state official, who subsequently called the court, demanding the file be closed. The Chinese project manager threatened to abort the construction work.

The court president stood firm, stating that this was a court case, not an administrative matter. "If you pity the Chinese, you must pay on their behalf. These laborers shall not be left uncompensated," he told the official. "This was our stand," Judge Gidey recounted. "We also raised the issue of human rights violations. The dismissals were not just dismissals. They were heavy-handed dismissals. They had beaten the laborers before sending them home." The court refused to close the case and gave the Chinese manager a second chance to attend court to pay the damages awarded to the plaintiffs.

When the deputy manager appeared on the appointed morning, he declared he would not pay. "We don't get money from the Ethiopian government for such payments," Judge Gidey recalled him saying. "Do you have money?" he inquired. "Yes. We have money." The judge took this statement as a refusal to pay and ordered the manager's arrest. In line with Ethiopia's Civil Procedure Code, Gidey explained, litigants who refuse to pay may be taken into custody for up to six months or until they pay. The manager was ushered out of the courtroom by police. Within twenty minutes, another Chinese man appeared in court. He dutifully made the payment. The file was closed.

The involvement of the police must have shaken the deputy manager. In the second case against CGGC, an individual labor case, the Chinese project manager appeared in court. He, however, was equally uncooperative. At the first hearing, he announced in English, "I don't speak English. I speak Chinese. I need an interpreter." The judge agreed, promised to find an interpreter, and adjourned the hearing.

Judge Gidey had hoped to find a neutral interpreter, such as a government worker who spoke Chinese, but failed to find one. He had no option but to allow an Ethiopian employee of the company who spoke Chinese to act as an interpreter. At the next hearing, the Chinese project manager objected to the interpretation: "I did not say this! You are misinterpreting it." He announced this in English and effectively confirmed, yet again, that he did speak English. Exasperated by the untoward behavior of the Chinese project manager, Judge Gidey demanded an apology and started entertaining the case in English and Tigrigna.

The episodes above illustrate Ethiopian judges' first encounters with Chinese company managers. While courtroom scenes like these still arise when trials involve new arrivals, they have become less frequent since the 2010s. Most Chinese enterprises, especially state firms, have since improved their in-house legal capacity and are now typically represented by Ethiopian lawyers in local courts.[4] Foregrounding perspectives from the bench, this chapter explores how judges have gradually confirmed and reinforced their jurisdiction. They have done so by resisting informal and ad hoc claims to immunity and by asserting the importance of legal process and procedural respect. The authority of the bench was frequently tested by subversive practices like those described above—practices which, when enacted by foreign nationals, posed a significant threat to judicial sovereignty. Yet through their refusal to entertain unsolicited requests and their firm response to defiance, judges managed to consolidate their authority and uphold national sovereignty.

In this chapter, I draw on extensive interviews with judges and former judges who witnessed claims to immunity first hand. Their eyewitness accounts, however, have been affected by the passage of time and the fading of memory. Judge Gidey had penned down his experiences in Sheraro in a journal he has since lost. Nevertheless, many of the courtroom scenes remain vividly etched in his memory and in those of other judges. I, too, witnessed informal requests for exemption from legal process, both inside and outside the courtroom, though few were as striking, and at times staggering, as those described by Gidey and other judges in this chapter.

DISCIPLINING CHINESE ENTERPRISE MANAGERS IN THE COURTROOM

Several elements of the labor cases recounted by Judge Gidey repeatedly surfaced in other judges' recollections of their first experiences with Chinese litigants, such as their disrespect for the court and the judges, their ignorance of and disregard for judicial procedure, the appeals to government authorities, and the use of language to escape liability. Over time, however, judges managed to instill discipline in Chinese litigants through subtle rhetorical acts or cruder measures, such as arrests and occasional charges for contempt of court. By claiming their authority to hear a case and give a verdict, judges resisted Chinese claims to immunity and asserted their jurisdiction.

The communicative function of the court mentioned in the previous chapter is critical to this process. The court's power to facilitate communication as much as adjudicate conflicts makes it a pivotal mediator in Ethiopian–Chinese encounters. However, before the courts could exert authority and enable communication across radical linguistic, racial, social, and cultural differences, they had to familiarize litigants, especially recalcitrant expatriate managers, with court protocol and compel them to observe it. At the most basic level, judges taught Chinese litigants to not ask questions and speak only when requested. Most importantly, they made Chinese litigants listen to them *and* their Ethiopian opponents.

As the recollections of Judge Gidey show, Chinese managers were initially hesitant to acknowledge, let alone accede to, the court's authority. The process of disciplining was protracted. Chinese managers' disrespect for Ethiopian legal institutions started with disregard for the summonses brought to them. They ignored the subpoenas, refused to accept them, or tore them up in fits of fury.[5] If they did accept the court summons, they failed to attend court, confused the dates, or forgot about the appointment altogether. No-shows were common. They were an annoyance for the judge, who had to adjourn the hearing, and the counterparty, who dutifully attended the hearing and incurred additional costs.

From the 1990s to the first decade of the 2000s, few Chinese companies were represented by an Ethiopian lawyer. Instead, like the deputy manager and the project manager in Sheraro, they represented their enterprise themselves. They communicated directly with the judges—sometimes quite literally walking up to their elevated bench to voice their opinion.[6] On other occasions, Chinese managers attempted to circumvent the court by appealing to federal authorities, using the threat of withdrawal to solicit their support. Whether they could use these methods successfully depended on individual judges, especially the presiding judge or the court president. Sometimes their efforts panned out in the ways the Chinese defendant wanted. More often, they did not. In the Sheraro case, the manager's appeal for sympathy ("We have come here to work") and accusation of unfair treatment ("We don't get money from the Ethiopian government for such payments") was disregarded, not least because the Chinese managers had been harsh in their treatment of the workers, touching the judge's nerve. If circumvention was no longer an option, they opted for subversion, such as playing the language card or feigning ignorance.

In the eyes of Judge Gidey, few Chinese managers were interested in solving disputes amicably. The plaintiffs of the collective labor case had initially taken their complaint to the Bureau for Labor and Social Affairs. Mandated to mediate conflicts between employers and employees, the bureau had tried to talk with company management. It received a curt reply: "We are building your country. This is not our concern."[7] Realizing they could not help, the bureau's staff suggested the workers sue.

"I don't think that the Chinese have ears for conciliation," Judge Gidey reminisced.[8] This explained not only expatriate managers' hostile stance but also why so many disputes came to court. The image of "having no ears" captures the attitude of Chinese managers, many of whom were reluctant to listen, not only to the workers' demands and the mediators of the labor bureau, but also to the judge.

At his bench, Gidey forced the expatriate managers of CGGC to tone down their approach. His request for an apology from the project manager and his order for the deputy manager's arrest are examples of how the court, including the judges and their authoritative way of communicating, reinforced by the elevated platform from which they speak and the formal setting of the courthouse, exerts authority and compels disputants to conform with written regulations and unwritten norms. By so doing, they leveled the playing field. They created a platform that granted voice and visibility to both parties, enabling direct communication.

However, the enforcement of discipline was gradual and, at times, painstaking. It was a continuous process that did not stop with one Chinese manager. The high turnover rate of Chinese company managers and the constant arrival of new Chinese firms in Ethiopia meant that disciplining was never finished.

I describe Ethiopian judges' efforts to compel litigants to respect judicial procedure and courtroom etiquette, combined with the behavioral changes they affect, as *disciplining*. A continuous and unfinished process, the disciplining of litigants in Ethiopian courts, however, stopped short of having an all-encompassing impact on the behavior of Chinese litigants—captured by Foucault's "*surveiller*."[9] As outsiders who enjoy a degree of immunity granted to them by invitation from the federal government and by virtue of their physical mobility, Chinese litigants were never total subjects. They could escape the disciplinary regime through successful appeals to state authorities or simply by leaving the country. However, they did not easily walk out of the courtroom. Judges were considerably efficacious in transforming litigants' *outward* attitudes. Even if this attitude was merely performed and did not necessarily reflect litigants' inner thoughts, many Chinese managers came to observe the judges' commands.

MUTING DISOBEDIENT VOICES

Judicial procedure and courtroom etiquette enhance professionalism and preserve the court's authority. "Courts are respected if they are respectable" is how Therese Clarke captures it.[10] She argues that holding parties to the same standard of conduct increases fairness and formalism, which are integral to impartiality. The courts are held in considerable regard in Ethiopia, and many ordinary citizens enter a courtroom with a degree of deference. However, many Chinese litigants lacked this attitude, at least initially. Some were—as the altercations in the Sheraro court demonstrate—dismissive of the courts and disdainful of the judges. How, then, did judges go about disciplining litigants who were mostly unwilling and mistrusted the court? For a start, they compelled litigants to adhere to the codes of conduct regarding courtroom communication. They taught Chinese parties how and when to speak. Most importantly, they instructed them to dim their voice and listen. Judges and other court personnel, such as registrars and court reporters, also reined in what they classified as inappropriate behavior, from picking quarrels with court staff to smoking on the court premises.

Courts deploy basic rules of conversational exchange, such as turn-taking, as John Conley and William O'Barr show in their classic study of language and power in American courtrooms.[11] Yet courts alter conversations in significant ways. The judge acts as a referee who oversees the turn-taking process and monitors the substance of what is being said. Litigants and lawyers cannot address one another directly. All spoken words go through the judge.[12] Whereas in the US justice system, substantial power is vested in lawyers, in the Ethiopian legal system, which is based on the civil law legal tradition, most authority resides in the bench. Ethiopian judges ask questions and manage the topic under discussion; they can rebuke anyone who strays from it. Lawyers are also granted opportunities to pose questions in pretrial hearings, when the issues of the case are determined, or during cross-examination, but usually after the judges have finished asking theirs. In sum, courtroom talk is not only highly formalistic and controlled but also marked by a power imbalance between the judge and the litigants. It was exactly this power imbalance that mitigated the power disparities between Chinese and Ethiopian disputants.

Chinese parties, like their Ethiopian counterparts, learned to observe the conversational rules of the court. The judges corrected their speech in four ways. First, they compelled them to adhere to the question-and-answer pattern and only ask and answer questions when they allowed them. Second, the judges squashed Chinese litigants' attempts to bargain in pretrial hearings and trials. Third, they forced litigants to refrain from commenting, whether through verbal statements or emotional gestures. Last, they demanded litigants adhere to etiquette concerning nonverbal communication and their behavior in court more generally.

Judges noted that Chinese litigants had the habit of asking questions. "When they come to the court, they don't tell the court what the court wants to hear from them. Instead, they request the court to listen to *them*," a judge based in Bahir Dar, Amhara, remarked.[13] "They ask all sorts of questions, such as 'Why do we need to state the date when we make a payment?'" Judges deemed some of these questions inappropriate or even disruptive. For a start, they upset the question-and-answer format and thereby challenged the authority of the court. "They demand the court to listen to them rather than that they listen to the court!" the judge laughed.[14]

A lower court judge explained that some Chinese defendants were unaware of the court's mandate. "This is a district court. How can we be called? The court does not have the mandate to call us," a lower court judge recalled an expatriate manager of China CAMC Engineering saying.[15] Before the civil war, this company had carried out construction activities in the contested region of Welkait. Its expatriate managers were new to litigation. Because the Ethiopian Sugar Corporation had invited CAMC to build a sugar factory, the manager contended, federal authorities ought to settle the matter. "No law obliges us to come to this court," the judge recalled him stating unflinchingly.[16] The judge subsequently detailed the mandate of his court to the Chinese manager, explaining that the Ethiopian labor law granted lower state courts the jurisdiction to entertain any labor case, whether it concerned a foreign party or not.

Judges based in other regions recounted similar courtroom episodes. For example, a judge based in East Gojjam once ordered the police to bring a Chinese manager to court under arrest to pay damages awarded to the Ethiopian plaintiff in a labor case.[17] Upset, the manager raved: "This is an unlawful court. How can the court order the police to arrest me?!" After the manager had calmed down, the judge explained the mandate of the court and detailed the provisions in the country's civil code that permitted the arrest of litigants when they repeatedly failed to appear. The judge silenced the agitated manager and made it clear that there was a set of rules and procedures to which he should adhere.

Either unaware of the unwritten rules about courtroom talk or unwilling to accept them, Chinese parties continued to pose questions, whether about court procedure ("Why do we have to give a written response?"), the court proceedings ("Why do we have to turn up again?"), or the fairness of the verdict ("Why do you consider him unlawfully dismissed?"), until they had learned to refrain from asking questions. By asking questions, they risked antagonizing the judge, which, in turn, could influence the court's decision.

Bargaining was yet another tendency of Chinese enterprise managers that judges sought to suppress. Chinese parties sometimes tried to reach an agreement, not with the counterparty in civil cases or the prosecutor in criminal cases, but with the judge, proposing a transaction in which each would give and take to reach a settlement. Bargaining is, however, uncommon in Ethiopian courts. Litigation is not about giving and taking, much less about striking a compromise. Court decisions are nonnegotiable. These attempts suggested that the litigants who engaged in them were reluctant to accept the judge's command. Often bearing a moral or accusatory undertone ("We are building your country"), attempts at bargaining not only concerned court judgments and decisions but also judicial procedure.

Attempts at bargaining should, however, be understood with an eye to the negotiated nature of justice in mainland China.[18] Chinese judges consider not just the parties and their arguments but also a host of other factors related to the lawsuit and its outcome, including social stability, political hierarchies, and economic development—to which Chinese managers fervently argued they contributed in Ethiopia. The negotiated nature of justice also manifests in the continued importance of mediation inside and outside the Chinese courtroom.[19] In Ethiopia, however, trials are adversarial in nature and bargaining at trial is prohibited. Bargaining in court, then, can be seen as a cultural practice carried over to Ethiopia, aside of a manifestation of ignorance or rebellion.

Third, judges compelled litigants, Chinese parties included, to remain silent during court hearings and refrain from giving commentary—before, during, and after hearings. Adhering to courtroom etiquette included refraining from giving unsolicited comments and requests. The court punished failure to do so. For example, one judge recalled that, after hearing the witness testimonies, a Chinese manager snorted "*wishetam, wishetam*" ("liar, liar" in Amharic).[20] By using Amharic, the expatriate manager clearly sought to convey a message to the bench and the audience. The judge, however, reprimanded the manager, calling for discipline.

Initially, Chinese managers had greeted him amicably at the start of a hearing ("Hello, Judge! How are you?"), the lower court judge remembered, or they had stood up during a hearing to voice their opinion or walked out of the courtroom.[21] Acts like these were born of resistance as much as ignorance. Once, a Chinese manager came to ask for the judge's phone number, to call him for legal advice the next time he encountered a dispute. The judge clarified that providing legal counseling was not part of his job. He chuckled about the incident, blaming it on the Chinese manager's lack of legal awareness. Other judges were less tolerant of such incidents.

Sometimes the relationship between Ethiopian judges and Chinese litigants resembled play. Playfulness, however, had a serious undertone and could quickly transform into hostility.[22] Throughout, the judge had the upper hand. An arrest or a contempt of court accusation could follow an initially forgiving gesture. Litigants had to play according to the court's rules. By calling for silence or telling off litigants, judges forced them to listen to the judge and the counterparty.

To be sure, the transformation in behavior that judges sought to achieve in Chinese enterprise managers through disciplinary measures was performative.[23] In the courtroom, conduct and outward representation enjoy precedence over inner conviction or feelings. Whether judges were resigned to the fact that they were unable to exert much influence over litigants' thoughts, it was the outward presentation and conformation to the rules that ultimately mattered, not only in speech but also in demeanor.

COURTROOM ETIQUETTE

Rules of etiquette also encompass nonverbal communication and conduct inside the court premises. Posters listing prohibited acts—such as carrying weapons or *dula* (sticks used for walking and self-protection), chewing gum or khat, smoking cigarettes, or answering phone calls during court hearings—are attached to the walls of courthouses across Ethiopia.[24] Drawn up in the court language of the region, the lists are not necessarily accessible to foreign nationals. Foreigners are nonetheless expected to respect court etiquette, although judges are generally more lenient toward them.

A lower court judge recalled finding a Chinese manager smoking at the courthouse entrance and admonished him.[25] "But there isn't a no-smoking sign," he remembered the manager sputtering as he threw away his cigarette. Other judges were more accepting of this type of violation. "They used to smoke at court, but we were patient with them," another lower court judge recounted.[26] "We told them to smoke away from the courtroom. Smoking at the court is punishable with one year of prison." Whereas the former judge construed smoking as a violation of courtroom etiquette, the latter saw it as a cultural practice. He and his colleagues had resigned themselves to the habits of Chinese managers. "We let it be. It's their culture. We were patient with them." However, this judge detested Chinese disputants entering the courtroom during the trial and reprimanded them for it.

Generally, legal representatives are held responsible for their client's behavior in the courtroom. If litigants are not represented by lawyers, however, they themselves will be under greater scrutiny. Yet a breach of etiquette does not necessarily amount to an accusation of contempt of court, punishable by law. The judge may reprimand the litigant or request an apology. There is a fine line between acceptable and offensive and thus unacceptable conduct. Slouching in one's chair, as some Chinese managers did as a sign of uninterest, will not be punished; making a scene in court might be. Loudness may be construed as a breach of etiquette and result in a reprimand. Quarreling with the judge is more likely to be punished. Ultimately, it is at the judge's discretion where to draw the line.

When I once accompanied a Chinese manager to court to interpret at the hearing, I had to cringe when he made a loud throat-clearing sound and spat on the ground in the courtyard.[27] In Ethiopia, spitting is not done publicly, let alone in formal settings. Even in China, one does not normally spit in a courthouse. The conduct of the Chinese manager was perhaps intended to subvert the court and its formalities. The manager had been in a foul mood the entire day, grumbling several times that "Ethiopia does not have a rule of law" and "Ethiopia does not have a proper legal system." His bad temper was evident throughout the hearing as he reclined in his chair. The judge was visibly annoyed, as the manager and I had failed to turn up to the previous hearing. He let the behavior pass nonetheless.

Demeanor assumes a vital role in judicial decision-making beyond what counts as admissible evidence, such as witness testimonies, written documents, photographs, recordings, and physical evidence.[28] Demeanor is arguably even more central in cases involving Chinese, where judges often base their decisions on interpreted testimonies. Double translation from Chinese to English and English to one of the Ethiopian court languages (Amharic, Afaan Oromo, and Tigrigna) is prevalent. None of the judges I met understood Mandarin. Readable without linguistic competence, the facial expressions of Chinese defendants and witnesses were essential as indicators of sincerity, intent, or other inner states. Demeanor is, however, a poor indicator, not only because body language is ambiguous but also because it is culturally marked and can thus be easily misinterpreted.[29]

I have not encountered instances where a Chinese party was held in contempt of court. I did hear a story from the Ethiopian interpreter for CAMC Engineering, whose predecessor had been charged with contempt when he accompanied the Chinese human resource manager to the Supreme Court of Tigray. His phone rang during the trial, for which he was sentenced to one month in prison. In Ethiopia, as elsewhere, there are two forms of contempt: criminal and civil.[30] Anyone who in the course of a judicial inquiry, proceeding, or hearing "insults, holds up to ridicule, threatens or disturbs the Court or a judge in the discharge of his duty"[31] or "in any other manner disturbs the activities of the Court"[32] can, at the judge's discretion, be held in contempt of court. The court can immediately try the person for contempt and punish them with a prison sentence of up to one year or a fine of up to three thousand birr (fifty-two US dollars).

Civil contempt is a refusal to aid justice—for instance, by failing to comply with a court order. According to Article 448 of the Criminal Code, these acts are punishable with simple imprisonment for up to two months and a fine of one thousand birr or less. Ethiopia's Civil Procedure Code grants judges even more discretion, stating that "any president of a court or presiding judge may take such action as may be necessary to ensure order in court and the administration of justice under the provisions of this Code and may summarily punish with a fine any part, pleaders or another person who is guilty of improper conduct in the course of any proceedings."[33]

Some Chinese managers' behavior could easily amount to contempt of court, and we are left to speculate whether judges would be as lenient with Ethiopian company managers. For instance, the two managers in Sheraro violated, rather forcibly, judicial procedure and courtroom etiquette. They refused to heed a court order, displayed disrespect throughout the court proceedings, and picked quarrels with the judge. All these acts can be classified as contempt of court. However, judges were generally more forgiving when it came to foreign litigants, who were assumed to be unaware of the rules. In fact, some judges, including Gidey, admitted they had gone the extra mile for the Chinese litigants. At other times, however, they lost their patience.

RESPONDING TO CLAIMS OF IMMUNITY

Occasionally, judges reverted from the carefully scripted courtroom conversation to enter an argument. Judge Gidey recalled one such incident, in which a Chinese manager had walked up to him and threatened: "You are raising liberal rights and human rights, but you live in poverty. We are here to develop your country."[34] Gidey countered: "You are constructing this road for *your* benefit as much as ours. Therefore, you ought to respect our laws in the same way that you don't want the laws of your country to be violated." The project manager's assertion that liberal rights and human rights are incommensurable with the country's level of wealth reflects a conviction shared by many Chinese investors in Ethiopia and beyond,[35] one that rests on the idea that economic development in China was able to take off and flourish precisely because the country lacked clear laws and systematic enforcement.[36] Taking China as a model for Ethiopia, the manager implied that only when Ethiopia relaxed the enforcement of its laws would the country be able to spur development and escape poverty.

For his part, Judge Gidey linked the Chinese manager's attitude to Ethiopia's poverty.[37] He, along with other colleagues, condemned the federal government's feeble stance toward foreign investors. The government's desire and, at times, desperation to attract foreign direct investment and thereby fuel the domestic economy gave rise to preferential policies and concessions for which ordinary Ethiopians, he believed, ultimately paid the price. Had he given in to pressure from higher up and suspended the labor case, the workers would have borne the brunt and been left uncompensated.

Some judges ascribed the attitude of Chinese company managers to ignorance, others to arrogance. "They simply lack legal awareness," a lower court judge explained.[38] "That's why they do things that are not allowed as soon as they enter the court." This judge compared Chinese managers with Ethiopian farmers. "They confuse the courts with the police. They are not well-educated," he observed.[39] "There are only a few Chinese who have a degree. The rest of them are educated up to grade 10, 12, 7, 8." The judge referred to the managers of Chinese subcontractors who frequented his court, many of whom had started their career as builders and had, at most, completed vocational training.

This young judge was forgiving, even though the behavior of some Chinese litigants could easily be construed as contempt of court. Chinese respondents in his court had ignored his orders, voiced objections, and walked out in the middle of a trial. Yet he and his colleagues had been as strict with Chinese litigants as they were with their Ethiopian counterparts. They issued warnings and instructed them in legal procedures and courtroom etiquette. Most importantly, they taught them when to speak and when to listen, gradually cultivating the appearance, at least, of respect.

Other judges were less forgiving and ascribed expatriate managers' attitude to sheer arrogance. A former senior judge explained that some managers who had spent significant time in Ethiopia were shrewd.[40] They knew the legal system through and through and had found ways to circumvent it. He connected the boldness of managers from China directly with the country's ascendance to the world stage and Ethiopia's dependence on Chinese investment. This judge attributed unsolicited claims for immunity to global inequalities:

> There is a tendency. It's related to the country's poverty. They seek to take advantage of it. They tend to have decisions be made in favor of them by making political noise. They don't need a legal system that is independent, impartial, and competent. They try to make profit by making political noise. This is what we see in practice.[41]

What this judge describes as "political noise" puts tremendous pressure on the legal system, as it blows straightforward contractual and labor disputes out of proportion, drawing attention from government officials and embassies. If claims for immunity were delivered from an attitude of superiority and expressed in an overbearing manner, they rapidly degenerated into gestures of disrespect toward Ethiopian courts and their jurisdiction.

"I'm a judge," was the curt reply of a judge to my question of how he dealt with baseless claims to immunity.[42] His supposedly self-explanatory response was representative of those judges who sought to uphold the core principle of judicial independence. Yet many acknowledged that doing so could be challenging in practice, complaining that foreign litigants attempted to turn ordinary disputes into what they called "political cases." Lawsuits became political as soon as routine legal proceedings were disrupted by interventions from the litigants or third parties, who were often government officials. In these instances, the stakes in the case and its outcome were no longer limited to the disputing parties or the defendant in criminal suits.

"These politicians are scared that the foreigners' feelings will be hurt," a former judge in Mekelle, Tigray, explained.[43] During the course of his tenure as a judge, he had seen many foreign nationals in court: Eritreans, Sudanese, Somalis, Indians, Pakistanis, Italians, and Chinese. Due to the many infrastructure projects they carried out in the region, the most frequent foreign attendees to court were Chinese. Chinese company managers, he remembered, routinely paid him visits.[44] "They want to speak with you in person. They want to talk to you about their case in your office," he recounted, adding firmly: "You don't listen to them. Partiality starts from there." Their complaints could be related to the speed of the court proceedings, the scheduling of court hearings, or the judges on the bench. Most often, however, they entailed a request to close the case because "we cannot afford to halt the work" or "we are developing your country."[45] On most occasions, he managed to resist pressure coming not just from the parties to a case but also from government officials. As a presiding judge, he shielded his two colleagues on the bench by remaining silent about the visits and calls he had received. Only once pressure was so fierce that he requested to be taken off the bench. No longer in a position to give a neutral decision, he preferred to give no decision at all.

"My stance is that it is good to attract foreign investment, but just as they have laws in their country, we have laws here too." Foreign firms must abide by local laws. Pressure from government officials, the former judge said ruefully, often led to cases being taken out of court and settled through negotiation. He reported a typical phone conversation with meddling officials:

> "We settled the matter, and so you must close the case," they demand. I always ask why. "They are foreign investors. We should not scare them off with such cases," they say. I reply, "FDI [foreign direct investment] does not mean modern colonization. Investors ought to follow the procedure. Everyone must follow the same procedure. If there is a dispute, it must be entertained by an independent and impartial court. Whether the case will be decided in favor of the investor or the other party will be determined by the case itself and the evidence brought to the court. A judge must be independent and impartial." This is my position. My response is simply, "No."[46]

Referring to the overbearing attitude of foreign investors and their disrespect for the local legal system as "colonization"—using the English word and thus highlighting it as foreign to a country that has never been colonized—he criticized above all interfering government officials. Unlike colonizers, investors must refrain from writing their own laws. It is the responsibility of the state to not encourage them to do so. Disputes that come to court ought to be settled by the court, he said, as he established the scope of his jurisdiction. Cases like this come to court for a reason. Often disputants have failed to settle the issue through negotiation, or the plaintiff—in this case, the weaker party—does not dare to address the matter without the help of a neutral party. Taking the case out of court may thus deprive the plaintiff of justice.

The judge singled out for criticism not just the failure of the government's executive branches but also the hypocrisy of foreign parties: "Is an impartial and independent judiciary not one of the conditions for investment mentioned by foreign companies?" Foreign investors demand that there is an independent judiciary in the countries in which they invest, and foreign loans list judicial independence as one of their conditionalities, yet the foreign parties are the ones who flaunt these very principles when they are subjected to them. This hypocrisy alone drove him to fight for judicial independence and protect his jurisdiction.

RESISTING CLAIMS OF IMMUNITY

Often judges stood firm. An Amhara Supreme Court judge recounted a case he had entertained at the Dessie Bench.[47] The lawsuit concerned an Ethiopian subcontractor who had sued a Chinese contractor for overdue payments, claiming compensation of 6.6 million birr. The Chinese state-owned firm objected to the freezing order issued by the court after the case was instituted. The judge remembered that at first, a Chinese manager had come to his office requesting the lifting of the freezing injunction, which is a standard legal practice that prevents the respondent from disposing of their assets until judgment is obtained. "The court is becoming an obstacle to Chinese activities," the judge recalled the company representative saying when he visited his office. "It was a simple contractual disagreement," the judge explained, still put out about the incident.

Realizing that the presiding judge would not bend, the representative tried his luck with the court president. He, too, refused to retract the freezing order. The Chinese firm subsequently reached out to the regional president, repeating the argument that the court had become an obstacle to their activities and, ultimately, was compromising the friendly relations between Ethiopia and China. In a letter to the court, the regional president stated that many construction projects in Amhara were behind schedule. While the country was developing, Amhara was lagging. The reason, the letter suggested, was that the courts failed to properly adjudicate cases like this one. It recommended, the judge recalled, that "the court shall come up with speedy and amicable solutions that will not disadvantage the company."

To the judge's dismay, the federal government also backed the Chinese firm with a letter of support. Yet rather than swaying him, these letters and requests made the judge more determined to see this case through:

> We warned them and requested them to stop writing such letters. We can consider it contempt of court. We can impose a penalty for disturbing our court activities. In fact, they have become an obstacle for us. I was the one who issued the freezing order. You see, when we [Ethiopians] sue a company like that, government officials join them [the Chinese]. We warned them. They requested the court to lift the injunction. It was in Dessie. By the way, I can give you more examples of such cases.[48]

The judge disregarded both the Chinese representative and the government officials who tried to interfere with the court proceedings, referring to his power to impose a fine or jail term for contempt of court.[49] Note that the judge here turns the tables, accusing the company and the government of constituting obstacles to the judicial process, rather than the other way around. In this case, the court went ahead with the proceedings and gave a verdict.

Sometimes, however, this judge did sway to pressure. Even today, he regrets a ruling he gave as a presiding judge in a criminal case involving the expatriate employee of a Turkish corporation contracted to build the railway from Awash to Weldiya. The man was driving a concrete mixer truck when he ran over an Ethiopian pedestrian in the Weldiya area. The driver fled the scene, when, he claimed, bystanders threatened to set his vehicle on fire. The victim's family and police followed him as he sped back to Dessie, even firing at the truck. Upon arrival at his camp, the driver was handed over to the police and put in custody. Following police investigations, the public prosecutor instituted proceedings, charging the suspect with negligent homicide.

During the twenty days that the driver was held in custody, the police and the public prosecutor received a number of letters from the company, the Turkish embassy, and government offices, pleading with him to grant the accused bail. He was father and husband to a family who lived far away in Turkey, they wrote in defense of the accused. Meanwhile, the local administration established a reconciliation committee to reach an agreement over compensation for the victim's family. Revenge killings, albeit in decline, still exist in the area. Without such an intervention the Turk could have been executed by the family.

As soon as the lawsuit was instituted, the court received letters pleading with him to discontinue the case. The letters stated that it negatively affected the country's foreign investments and relations with Turkey. The court nonetheless proceeded and found the suspect guilty, sentencing him to four years and two months in prison. Yet they granted the man parole, citing mitigating circumstances related to his health and family circumstances. "Because of all this blah blah blah brought to the court, we decided to grant him parole," the judge explained. "They were very happy. The manager announced in front of the court, 'I would like to invite you all for lunch.' I warned him, 'This is a court.'" The decision to release the convict on parole left the judge conflicted:

> It puts our legal system into question; the ways in which we treat foreigners differently. Is it right to give in to so many excuses? I have many questions in this regard. By the way, the pressure is not easy [to deal with]. The pressure comes from different sources: from the company, the family, the government, the embassy. The most touching thing was that the man talked about Skyping with his family and that they were crying together. I felt compassion towards him. By the way, the accident was gruesome. The [victim's] body was severely damaged.[50]

Had the accused been Ethiopian, they would not have been let out on parole. The pressure, combined with his compassion toward the accused, had swayed the judge and his colleagues. Even though the court had insisted on entertaining the case and giving a verdict, the external demands made on them did have an impact on the final decision. Interventions were hard to ignore altogether.

The above reflections reveal the power of judges and their limitations. If they usually succeed in enacting their jurisdiction, they occasionally fail to give a verdict due to pressure. Even though the Amhara judge proceeded to entertain cases, he was not entirely satisfied with the ruling he and his colleagues issued. Even though the former Tigray judge insisted on entertaining claims against foreign firms like any other case, he was forced to withdraw when a routine case became a major political case. The limits to resisting claims for immunity and brokering sovereignty in the process can be explained by the fact that judges are embedded in the administrative structures of the court, the state bureaucracy at large, and the broader social and political environment. They must answer to their superiors and respond to outside requests to keep their job or position on a bench. Furthermore, retaliation may affect them and their family members—a threat that was the last straw for the Mekelle-based judge. He resigned to start work as a lawyer. Most of the pressure came from the long arm of regional and federal government offices rather than foreign litigants, or, in many cases, their interventions and impositions were the hardest to resist. Having to navigate a plethora of insistent and intense pressures, however, further motivated judges to enact their jurisdiction.

Furthermore, judges' attempts to prevent cases from being taken out of court and their efforts to discipline non-complacent disputants have been aided by the sheer number of cases brought to court. Intervening parties simply cannot keep up with, for instance, more than one hundred pending lawsuits involving Chinese parties in a single court. (Courts near infrastructural projects commonly must deal with a volume of cases of this order.) Most civil cases, such as labor, contractual, and extracontractual disputes, have become routine. The only cases that continue to attract interventions are typically those with the potential to tarnish the reputation of the Chinese community, such as criminal cases (e.g., rape, homicide, and sodomy), as well as family cases like disputes over child support, which suggest transgressive sexual behavior that spoils the image of not only individual hardworking Chinese engineers but also the Chinese community at large.[51] In most civil cases, however, "you can just treat them [Chinese] like Ethiopians," as a judge put it.[52]

TAKING THE COURT SERIOUSLY

Gradually, Chinese company managers started observing judicial procedures and courtroom etiquette. In Sheraro, CGGC management began submitting statements of defense, drawn up initially by Ethiopian administrative staff and later by lawyers in Shire. They began to "take the court seriously" or "respect the court," as judges described it,[53] even though they still lost most cases. Continued losses in court, however, reflected their employment practices on the construction sites as much as, if not more than, their lack of court experience or, as they claimed, the partiality of Ethiopian courts. Following an initial period of disciplining, Chinese parties appeared in court, heeded court orders, presented evidence, brought witnesses, and listened quietly to the judge and the other party. Even so, respect for the court and the judge remained largely performative. It did not necessarily translate into genuine appreciation, let alone admiration. Chinese managers continued to grumble about the courts. Instead, respect manifested itself in proper conduct in the courtroom and beyond, which, for most judges, sufficed.

"Nowadays they show respect. They respect the court orders," the Amhara Supreme Court judge reflected.[54] "If you order them to appear in court, they will appear. If you request the managing director to come to court, he will come. If he is not in the country, he will write a letter." If a party cannot attend court on the appointed day, they must write a letter of apology stating the reasons for their absence. The change in behavior signaled that Chinese litigants had familiarized themselves with legal procedure and observed it. When asked whether Chinese managers trusted the court, the justice replied firmly, "No. They do not trust the court. They *respect* the court. They are generally dissatisfied."[55] Continued complaints leveled by Chinese litigants were not lost on him. In his eyes, trust and respect were two different things; the latter could be shallow and performed, the former could not. Trust required belief.

Chinese litigants learned to keep a low profile in court. In the Sheraro cases, the fact that the Chinese manager had shown no remorse and, worse, openly claimed that his corporation was entitled to breach the law agonized the judge. Remorse can be interpreted as acknowledging fault and can influence a court decision. It is intertwined with judgments of blame.[56] Chinese litigants learned to adopt a respectful attitude. In other words, they familiarized themselves with the courtroom conduct that would help them obtain a favorable outcome. "These days they sit quietly at the back of the courtroom," the Amhara State Supreme Court judge noted, smiling.[57] Saying this, the judge exuded satisfaction. He and his colleagues had managed to subdue the arrogance and temper the confidence of Chinese enterprise managers. As such, they had been successful in enforcing their jurisdiction, even if this had not been a smooth process.

Growing respect for the court went hand in hand with increasing respect for the law. An overwhelming number of court cases has forced managers of Chinese companies across Ethiopia to reconsider their employment conditions, improve documentation and bookkeeping practices, and make site managers aware of the consequences of trespassing and dumping soil or waste on land not designated for such purposes.

Chinese managers also began collecting evidence, even before a lawsuit was filed against them. Taking photographs of the construction work and the surrounding farmland became routine. If one of the workers stole building materials, the company could demonstrate when and from where the steel bars or cement were stolen and assist the police and the prosecutor. If a farmer sued the company, claiming that a change in the lie of the land had damaged their crops during the rainy season, Chinese managers were able to provide visual evidence to show that the crops had barely been damaged. Some managers even made videos of workers lazing about. If these workers took their company to court, claiming that they were unlawfully dismissed, management could present evidence of their failure to carry out the tasks they were supposed to according to the employment contract.

One labor case entertained by a lower court judge in Welkait illustrates the growing legal awareness of Chinese enterprise managers.[58] The defendant, a Chinese company involved in constructing the Karema irrigation dam, part of a sugarcane development project, was sued by one of its former Ethiopian laborers for unlawful dismissal. The company had been in Ethiopia for some time and was represented by a lawyer; the plaintiff was not. A scribe drew up his pleading. In its written response, the Chinese defendant stated that management had dismissed the employee for inefficiency at work. The plaintiff countered that he had fulfilled his obligations.

Had the plaintiff been inefficient? And, if he had been, would this be a legitimate reason for lawful termination of his employment agreement? These were the two issues posed and investigated by the court. The judge acknowledged that it was a challenging case for the defendant, who carried the burden of proof and had to convince the court that their member of staff had been inefficient. In other words, the company had to prove inefficiency. Expatriate managers had, however, learned from previous losses in court. They knew that photographs counted as admissible evidence and had started capturing napping workers on camera. In their statement of defense, they listed a video of the plaintiff resting in the shade and a picture of him taking a nap on the construction site, in addition to Ethiopian witnesses, all of whom were employees of the company. The plaintiff brought witnesses too.

During the trial, the Chinese defendant claimed that the plaintiff had slept during work time—proof of his inefficiency. Its witnesses confirmed that the worker had received several warnings from management. (When an employee displays unacceptable behavior, their employer can only dismiss them lawfully after issuing three warnings.) Apart from confirming that the employment relationship between employer and employee lacked a written contract, the plaintiff's witnesses stated that the plaintiff had carried out his duties. They argued that the video and the photograph had been taken *after* work when the plaintiff was napping, tired from heavy labor in high temperatures. Ultimately, the court ruled that the dismissal had been lawful and the plaintiff was not entitled to the compensation he claimed. It classified the worker's naps during work time as inefficiency and an indication that he had not performed his tasks according to the contract. This case is the ultimate example of the learning curve of Chinese companies, which I discussed earlier.

A high court judge in Mekelle explained that after the Chinese manager of a construction firm in Abiy Addi, where he was once based as a judge, was brought to court under arrest, the company began to make timely payments for damages awarded to the other party.[59] Companies sometimes paid right after he issued his verdict, with the result being that the plaintiff did not even have to open an execution file. More recently, however, the Chinese attitude had changed. The judge lowered his voice: "They have become familiar with the system and started to resemble some of our Ethiopian litigants."[60] His eyes smiled above his turquoise face mask as he added, "I don't know if it is true. This is what I heard." A closer look at a series of compensation cases at the high court in Abiy Addi confirmed his suspicion. After the completion of a nearby project, when the engineers of the Chinese state-owned enterprise had left the area, their lawyer, at his initiative or the prompting of his Chinese managers, started delaying payments of compensation, even going so far as to hide the company's financial assets. This change in attitude was, for the judge, a sign of their increased familiarity with the Ethiopian legal system. With the help of their lawyers, Chinese company managers learned not only to use but also to abuse the system.

Overall, however, the judges' efforts to discipline Chinese corporations and their managers bore fruit. The latter started engaging with institutions they initially had not wanted anything to do with and circumvented if they could. They began to take the court seriously. However, Ethiopian judges adopted different approaches to entertaining cases with a Chinese party. They were not neutral adjudicators. Their ideological leanings and experiences with Chinese litigants informed their judgments—as I will show in the next chapter—as they became participants in national debates about the Chinese presence and the role of Chinese investors in Ethiopian society.

6

Dimming Some Voices, Amplifying Others

When Bereket and I arrived at the Hintalo Wajirat Wereda Court in Adi Gudem in August 2020, people filled the court premises. Ensconced in the shade of trees, they waited expectantly, chatted cheerfully, or debated animatedly. During the annual period of downtime, the judges were busy with what were known as "Covid cases," in which defendants, primarily young men, stood trial for violating the emergency decree regulations aimed at preventing the spread of the virus. Of all the states in Ethiopia, Tigray had implemented the strictest policies. Most of these rules enforced social distancing and applied to the public transport and service sectors. Three-wheeled motorcycles known as *bajaj*, for instance, were permitted to carry just one customer, and minibuses half the number of passengers they usually carried. Besides Covid cases, the lower courts entertained only lawsuits that were classified as urgent, such as divorce cases and a range of criminal suits. Even though labor disputes counted as urgent, the Hintalo Wajirat Wereda Court entertained few these days. This had once been different. In 2016 and 2017, the court had been flooded with labor cases filed against a Chinese company involved in the construction of the unfinished railway from Weldiya to Mekelle—the second tranche of a railroad intended to connect the capital of Tigray to Awash, Afar, where it joins the Addis Ababa–Djibouti line.

"The court no longer looked like a court," a former judge recalled, describing the crowded premises he encountered in 2016 when he was transferred to Adi Gudem. "It looked like a marketplace." On some days, he received more than ten new labor cases. During this period, Bereket and I gathered from handwritten court dockets, 179 Ethiopian employees of the Chinese enterprise or one of its subcontractors had sought legal redress, the majority within a window of six months.

All plaintiffs were men except for a woman cleaner and a kitchen assistant. The majority came from various districts in Tigray, a dozen from regions farther afield, including Addis Ababa, Oromia, Amhara, and what used to be the Southern Nations, Nationalities, and Peoples' Region.[1] They had filed 134 labor cases, twelve of which were collective lawsuits by up to nine plaintiffs. Five cases had been taken out of court and were resolved through conciliation. The remaining 122 received a court judgment.[2]

In this chapter, I home in on the wave of litigation that beset the lower court in Adi Gudem and the judges who presided over it. I do so to shed light on how judges weighed, and came to participate in debates about, immunity. Their views on Chinese corporations and the governance of global capital were influenced by legal, political, and personal considerations that transpired in their decisions. If all the judges were disappointed with the uncooperative and, at times, obstructive attitudes of Chinese enterprise managers and resisted claims of immunity, they did not necessarily see eye to eye on how much leeway the government should give to foreign corporations and what kind of policies were suitable to regulate them.

Of course, we cannot read judges' minds. It is hard, if not impossible, to evaluate the extent to which numerous factors—legal, political, economic, cultural, psychological, or otherwise—influence a judge's decisions.[3] Instead of measuring these influences, I evaluate how, when, and why judges exercise discretion to amplify some voices and dim others.[4] Judicial orientations, or biases, manifested especially in three realms. First, the Ethiopian legal system and the contested nature of precedent more specifically allowed judges to define the relationship between employee and employer in contrasting ways, with significant implications for the outcome of labor cases. Second, judges' ideological views on the role of the state in protecting vulnerable groups in society against powerful others, whether domestic or foreign entities, played a significant role amid heated debates about global capital. Third, judges' everyday experiences with disputants could further influence their rulings.

Set in Adi Gudem, a bustling town on the road to Mekelle in northern Ethiopia, the chapter dissects the decisions made by four judges based at Hintalo Wajirat Wereda Court when the wave of Chinese labor cases hit. I will refer to them as Judge Mengesha, Judge Yohannes, Judge Kahsay, and Judge Mehari. Judges Mengesha, Yohannes, and Kahsay served at Hintalo Wajirat Wereda Court for overlapping periods, while Judge Mehari occasionally acted as a stand-in. I draw on 134 case files and interviews with three of the four judges, in addition to a scribe who had penned pleadings for Ethiopian plaintiffs, and a Chinese engineer who had witnessed firsthand how Ethiopian laborers came to outsmart company management, as he described it, by mobilizing the law against them.

Before I turn to the events and the disputes to which they gave rise, I briefly introduce the project from which the court cases originated. Launched in 2015, the Weldiya–Mekelle Railway project was one of the infrastructure projects that fell victim to changing political winds in the lead-up to Prime Minister Hailemariam

Desalegn's resignation in 2018. Funds dried up as early as 2017. The Chinese contractor, CCCC, aborted most of the building work shortly after. The political weight pulling the project, the EPRDF-led government, fell into disrepute.

No one to whom I spoke on the Ethiopian or the Chinese side knew exactly what had happened to the funds, but many speculated about it animatedly. The Export–Import Bank of China (China EXIM Bank) had initially committed to extend a loan for the project. Chinese engineers concurred that the project would not be viable, let alone profitable. It was a political project that connected the home base of the TPLF, the leading party in the EPRDF, to the capital. In one Chinese manager's sarcastic words, the railway was no more than "a toy of the government."[5] However, the Chinese contractor continued pumping money into the project to keep some of the building works going in the hope that funds would be forthcoming in the foreseeable future.

When I met a Chinese project representative in Addis Ababa in January 2020, company management was debating whether to pull the plug altogether. In March 2020, however, a ray of hope boosted their morale. The controversy surrounding the Grand Ethiopian Renaissance Dam—under construction on the Blue Nile River since 2011—turned US President Donald Trump against Ethiopia, with him accusing the country of building a dam "that stops water flowing into the Nile" and warning that Egypt "will end up blowing up the dam."[6] President Trump publicly expressed support for Egypt. Amid Ethiopian anger about Trump's stance, Tan Jian, then Chinese ambassador to Ethiopia, snatched his chance. Let down by the United States, the Abiy administration was likely to become more empathetic toward its adversary: China. It did. Ambassador Tan persuaded the prime minister to continue supporting the project with about three hundred million birr per month—just enough to keep it going.[7] However, Covid-19 and the civil war in Tigray would soon throw spanners in the works.

MOBILIZING THE LAW

When laborers flooded the courts along the length of the railway, one of which was the Hintalo Wajirat Wereda Court, construction work was still going at full pace. The first labor case, *Weldehib Gebre-Hiwet v. CCCC*,[8] was instituted on February 16, 2016, by a metalworker employed by the Chinese contractor. The plaintiff claimed he had been wrongfully dismissed. He visited the Bureau for Labor and Social Affairs before taking the step to court. The bureau wrote a letter to CCCC, urging management to pay the worker's outstanding salary. The company failed to respond, after which Weldehib sued. Since no representative of the Chinese enterprise turned up to the hearings, the court entertained the case in absentia and decided in favor of the metalworker from Tanqua Abergele, a small town near Tigray's border with

Amhara, who had moved to Hintalo Wajirat for work. Judge Mengesha granted him 32,800 birr plus 1,800 birr for litigation expenses. Soon enough, other workers followed in his footsteps, bypassing the bureau altogether. In the subsequent Ethiopian calendar months of Megabit, Miyazia, and Ginbot (between March 10 and June 6, 2016), the court received seventy-nine cases, including eight collective labor suits. What had happened? And how did the court respond?

The judges at the Hintalo Wajirat Wereda Court held contrasting opinions on the cause of the increasing number of labor disputes brought to their court. Judge Mengesha blamed the Chinese employer's abusive labor practices. Expatriate managers failed to adhere to the labor law, especially regarding dismissals and redundancies. "They simply say, 'Go!' This is the only word in English they know. This is how they fire their employees," he explained, adding, "As I told you, the [Ethiopian] Labor Proclamation sides with the laborer. They get compensation and payment for the failure [of the employer] to give notice. The workers can get a lot of money this way."[9] The Ethiopian labor law is widely known to be pro-employee,[10] to the detriment of officials keen to attract foreign investment.

The word "go" surfaced in many recollections of Ethiopian judges who had entertained Chinese labor cases and lawyers who had worked for Chinese enterprises as in-house counsel. The monosyllabic order epitomized the tenuous relationship between Chinese management and Ethiopian workers, who were often fired at a whim by low-level Chinese foremen lacking the mandate to dismiss employees in the first place. The Ethiopian labor law only allows staff in managerial positions to terminate employment agreements.[11] Even so, foremen frequently uttered "Go!" in frustration at the workers under their direction.

In contrast to Judge Mengesha, Judge Kahsay and Judge Mehari held that opportunism on the side of Ethiopian laborers had caused the surge in labor cases. In fact, Judge Kahsay believed workers' calculated maneuvering had been fueled by the decisions of Judge Mengesha: "The first plaintiffs had received a decision in favor of them. The plaintiffs who came to court after this had high expectations."[12] Judge Kahsay later clarified:

> Everyone took legal action once a few people brought suit and began receiving payments. The court looked like a marketplace. The salary of the workers was small. So, these workers sued the company, and their compensation was a lot. Mind you, when a daily laborer institutes a case and gets a decision from sixty thousand up to seventy thousand birr, everyone started to leave their job, whether they had a reason to do so or not. They began spending the day in court. The damages awarded to them by the court were more lucrative than their salaries.[13]

Shortly after Judge Kahsay assumed his post at the Hintalo Wajirat Wereda Court in 2016, things began to change. The company's fate was reversed by Kahsay's rulings, in which the Chinese defendant repeatedly emerged as the winner. How-ever, ruling against Ethiopian plaintiffs was difficult, especially in the beginning. "Everyone in this region is armed. People bring their weapons to court. Sometimes you cannot help but wonder what will happen when you give the judgments I gave, and the plaintiffs expect to win," Judge Kahsay recalled. "What if a plaintiff is really angry about the decision?"[14]

Litigants were required to leave their Kalashnikovs and other firearms at the court gate, where security officers and the police officer on call kept an eye on them. Judge Kahsay, however, denied that public pressure influenced his decisions. He commuted between Mekelle and Adi Gudem, which afforded him some dis-tance from the local community. If he had lived in town, it would have been an entirely different matter.

Reflecting on Chinese labor practices, Judges Mehari and Kahsay questioned the meaning of "Go!" "What they understand as 'discipline' in their country and what they find here is different," Judge Mehari speculated about expatriate managers' expectations. "The Chinese just want to work, and get a rest, and work, and get a rest. They don't want to be fully involved. They must have gotten furious. They fired their workers simply by saying, 'Go!'"[15] The increase in labor cases was, in Judge Mehari's eyes, the result of a confrontation between Chinese work ethics and Ethiopian work-ers' lack of discipline. The statement "They don't want to be fully involved" illustrates the attitude of Chinese managers who saw interactions with the local community, including those in the courtroom, as distracting from the very reason they had come to Ethiopia: to work. In Judge Mehari's eyes, the curt dismissals of Chinese managers were a response to the poor attitude of Ethiopian laborers:

> Workers came to court just because they had heard about earlier decisions. Some had won their cases. Others hoped that the court would decide in favor of them too. However, when a Chinese says "Go!" it does not necessarily mean they are dismissed. They nonetheless opened a file, charging their Chinese employer with unlawful ter-mination of contract. If the company dismisses you, they will call you [to the office] and say that your employment contract will be terminated due to this and this rea-son. . . . "Go, go!" is not enough.[16]

According to Judge Mehari, workers were eager to find a ground to sue manage-ment. Chinese foremen's impatience, which often led them to discharge work-ers with a simple "Go!," "Go, go!," or "Go, go, go!," usually accompanied by irate gestures, provided one such ground. He questioned whether Chinese managers always intended to dismiss their workers in the first place.

Even Judge Mengesha acknowledged that laborers had started taking advantage of the law: "The workers intentionally stopped working and stood around lean-ing on their shovels, waiting for the Chinese to say 'Go!'"[17] Employees leaving the workplace on their own initiative without notifying management are only entitled to their outstanding salary.

Initially, the court observed that the company's acts harmed the workers. It was a little conservative. This encouraged workers to get fired such that they could claim compensation. We, as a court, came to realize this. We started investigating whether the worker was actually dismissed or not.[18]

Judge Mengesha admitted the court was protective of Ethiopian laborers or, in his words, "a little conservative." Note that Judge Mengesha refers to "the court" and talks about "we" as a discursive technique to deny sole responsibility for the accusations leveled against him by his colleagues.

Apart from the interjection "Go!," the silence surrounding the content of the employment agreement was another source of disagreement between judges as much as between management and labor. Most Ethiopian workers were hired by oral agreement and oblivious to the terms of their employment relationship. They had little clue, for instance, about the duration of their employment and the tasks they were expected to carry out. The language barrier further complicated communication between employer and employee.

According to Halefom, a scribe who had written more than fifteen pleadings for workers of Chinese companies during that period, the absence of employment contracts sent the wrong message. It did not give workers the feeling that they were "professionals working in a profession."[19] His statement captures the expatriate managers' lack of respect for employees conveyed by Ethiopian workers in chapter 2. To Halefom, it came as no surprise that Chinese employment practices backfired. "As a manager, you must follow the legal route when a worker is at fault. The Chinese get angry and impatient when workers do something wrong. They simply shout 'Go!' This opens a door for workers to become lazy. They go to court, saying that the company fired them."[20] Halefom construed workers' indolence as a response to managerial whims. Laborers sought recourse to law not just to restore their rights but also to reclaim their dignity.

Bereket and I spoke with Halefom in a tiny restaurant near the Adi Gudem town market. Sporting a 2012 Tigray elections T-shirt under a black jacket,[21] he gulped down a bowl of spaghetti with freshly made tomato sauce while we drank tea. Over the years, Halefom had amassed much experience as a scribe. He had wanted to pursue a university degree in law, but Mekelle University no longer accepted students who, like him, had previously received vocational training. Weldiya University did, but the political climate at the time, marked by growing anti-Tigrayan sentiments, ruined his plans, so he instead signed up for legal training sessions organized by Mekelle Law School for court support staff and administrators.

Labor cases involving Chinese employers and those concerning Ethiopian employers were different, Halefom maintained. The main difference lay in communication or, rather, its lack. Ethiopian employers communicated with their employees. Chinese employers did not, or they did so very little. Employees of local firms knew the terms of their contracts. Their counterparts employed by Chinese enterprises rarely did. Lack of clarity due to the absence of communication became an issue on the construction site and in the courtroom, as we have seen in previous chapters. The court filled the communication gap between Chinese employers and Ethiopian employees. It did so in different ways, depending on the presiding judge.

Chinese managers had their own explanations for what drove laborers to court. "There is no way a Chinese party can win in court," claimed a Chinese engineer who had witnessed the wave of labor cases in Adi Gudem.[22] He concurred that project management had been unable to stop the tide of litigation. "The law is not on our side," he stated matter-of-factly. He believed part of the problem lay with the Ethiopian legal system. To him and most Chinese managers, as we saw in chapter 3, the law and the courts, particularly the lower ones, were biased against them. They favored poor local farmers over well-endowed multinational enterprises. Class biases intersected with racial prejudices, in other words, amounting to what he described as the racial profiling of Chinese nationals.[23]

Chinese enterprise managers tried to steer away from litigation, he explained. Yet this was not an easy task. "You have to be careful. As soon as you get angry, they will sue you in court and request compensation. Carrying out construction projects in Ethiopia is becoming harder by the day."[24] Chinese managers like him felt that they were walking on eggshells. The slightest confrontation with an Ethiopian worker could evolve into a fierce legal battle.

In a moment of self-reflection, the Chinese manager laid blame not only on Ethiopian laborers but also on Chinese foremen. The wave of court cases was partly fueled by a situation where "peasants [*nongmin*] are managing black people [*heiren*]."[25] With "peasants," he referred somewhat indignantly to the aged builders, mostly from rural backgrounds, who served as line managers of Ethiopian laborers ("black people"). Many had rough edges, developed over years of labor on building sites in China. The foremen had previously occupied the bottom rungs of the corporate hierarchy as manual workers. Their management style mirrored practices prevalent in China's domestic building industry, yet corporate hierarchies were reinforced by racial disparities.[26]

Project managers, most of whom were university-educated engineers, went to great lengths to bring these foremen into line.[27] However, this was not easy. Lower-level managers were typically employed by Chinese subcontractors, and higher-level managers, who were younger and less experienced, had little authority over them. There was nothing they could do when they fired workers by shouting "Go!" in the absence of higher-level managers. The lack of compliance by subcontractors caused project management a headache. The issue of legal representation further complicated this. As mentioned, subcontractors often did not have a trade license and therefore lacked a legal personality under Ethiopian law. As a result, Chinese contractors were frequently forced to defend disputes to which they were not a party.

Given the lack of control over subcontractors' employment practices, project managers could not stem the tide of labor cases until an assertive Ethiopian in-house counsel, whom I will call Hagos, took matters into his own hands. "I was sick and tired of labor cases," Hagos admitted in an interview at the Atlas, one of Mekelle's fanciest hotels and one of the last places in town allowed to serve coffee in April 2020, when Covid measures restricted the sale of Ethiopia's most popular beverage.[28] When Hagos joined CCCC, the company was knee-deep in litigation. Each day, he ran from one court to another. He frequently missed hearings, as hearings in one court coincided with those in another.[29] But, thanks to his efforts and those of his colleagues, labor disputes had almost entirely stopped after his first year of service:

> Some years ago, Chinese managers' awareness of Ethiopian law was minimal. They did not care about the law. If they dismissed a worker, they would say "Go!" They dismissed anyone by saying "Go!" Awareness matters. They even failed to consult lawyers. That culture gradually changed. Nowadays, they consult their lawyer on every matter.[30]

Hagos confirmed the learning curve discussed in chapter 3. Regarding what areas his Chinese employer could still improve, he replied curtly, "They should know the Labor Proclamation from *A* to *Z*." Indeed, disputes had not entirely disappeared. However, Hagos tried to intervene before a case went to court.

Hagos represented CCCC in the final labor case, *Fisiha Tekle-Medhin v. CCCC*,[31] decided by the Hintalo Wajirat Wereda Court on October 19, 2018. The construction blaster who instituted the lawsuit claimed that his employer had wrongfully discharged him when the railway project ground to a halt. The court ruled that Fisiha Tekle-Medhin's contract had been terminated unlawfully, granting him nearly 170,000 birr in damages (Fisiha had earned a monthly income of twenty thousand birr). The Chinese witness had admitted in his testimony that Fisiha Tekle-Medhin had not been very disciplined. He displayed a whiff of discontent, suggesting management had sought to fire the explosives worker regardless of the circumstances.

The company filed for an appeal, and the high court in Maychew reversed the decision. It ruled that the dismissal was lawful, leaving Fisiha Tekle-Medhin empty-handed.[32] Judgments not only between the lower and higher courts, but also decisions among judges at the Hintalo Wajirat Wereda Court, regularly diverged. Having sketched the broader context in which disputants sought legal action, I now turn to the cases and their rulings to reveal how judges amplified some voices while silencing others.

MOMENTS OF DISCRETION

Judges enjoy considerable discretion irrespective of the type of case and the level of jurisdiction they represent.[33] As I demonstrated in chapter 4, their discretion is often even more extensive in cross-cultural adjudication. Here, I discuss one lawsuit in detail to illustrate the moments in which judges use discretion and the creative ways in which they do so, thereby tilting the scale in one way or another in Ethiopian–Chinese disputes.

The Ethiopian plaintiff in *Tamru Belay v. CCCC*,[34] a labor case entertained by Judge Yohannes, was employed as a welder by the Chinese contractor or one of its subcontractors. (It is unclear from the judgment who the plaintiff's employer was, illustrating the fuzziness created by the deliberate obfuscation of legal personality.) Tamru Belay hailed from Sidama in southern Ethiopia and had worked on the railway project for barely a month when the police arrested him on suspicion of theft. The officers stormed into his room in the middle of the night after receiving a complaint from a Chinese manager, who alleged that the welder had stolen money from him. The police rejected Tamru's request for bail, and the welder spent more than seven months in custody, during which the police investigated the incident and the prosecutor prepared a charge.

The court, however, set Tamru Belay free on the grounds of insufficient evidence. On January 3, 2017, he was released and returned to his workplace to find that most of his former coworkers and Chinese managers had left. Building activities had been suspended while he was in custody. The Ethiopian security personnel at the Chinese camp, Tamru recalled in his witness testimony, announced that he was dismissed and sent him to a Chinese manager, who gave Tamru a month's salary and requested him to leave.

Tamru Belay went to court on the same day, requesting 99,000 birr in damages for unlawful dismissal. He claimed a severance payment, compensation for unpaid overtime, damages for the employer's failure to give one month's notice, and salary for the months he spent in custody. The Sidama welder, however, soon discovered that the Chinese and Ethiopian witnesses he had listed on his pleading had also left the area. His expatriate managers had returned to China and his coworkers to Hawassa in southern Ethiopia. Judge Yohannes allowed him to search for new witnesses,[35] at which point Tamru Belay put forward himself and a former colleague still based in Hintalo Wajirat.

At this point, Judge Yohannes made a debatable decision. He assigned a defense lawyer to Tamru Belay, justifying his resolve by arguing that the plaintiff spoke minimal Amharic, let alone Tigrigna. He proposed, too, that the plaintiff did not have sufficient legal knowledge or funds to pay for legal advice, referring to Article 37 of the Constitution of the Federal Democratic Republic of Ethiopia, which provides for the right to access to justice.[36] CCCC's lawyer, Hagos, objected to this unconventional move. The court usually allocates defense lawyers to indigent defendants in criminal cases. Defense lawyers are not typically deployed in civil cases, let alone assigned to plaintiffs. Although a criminal suit preceded this case, it concerned a civil one.

Hagos stated there was no legal ground for assigning a defense lawyer in such a case and presented a letter from the public prosecutor's office saying the same. Judge Yohannes nevertheless stood his ground. He proceeded with the case, also rejecting Hagos's second preliminary objection that the six-month limitation period had lapsed. While Tamru Belay sat in custody, he had been unable to institute a case. Hence, the six months did not count.

Due to his limited Amharic proficiency, Tamru Belay's testimony was interpreted from Sidaamu Afoo to Amharic. The court registrar interpreted the statement from Amharic to Tigrigna. (None of the documents in the case file indicates who interpreted from Sidaamu Afoo to Amharic.) The plaintiff's second witness confirmed that Tamru Belay had worked for the defendant's company and that they had commenced work on the same day, March 24, 2016. He also confirmed Tamru's subsequent arrest. The defense witness, a Chinese employee of CCCC, denied that the company had employed the Sidama welder on the stated site 182. As Tamru did not have an employment contract, it was up to Judge Yohannes to define the existence and nature of the employer–employee relationship based on witness testimonies.

Judge Yohannes questioned the credibility of the testimony given by the Chinese witness. By so doing, he strengthened the evidence that CCCC had employed Tamru. He wrote in his judgment:

> The witness who testified that the plaintiff was not an employee of the defendant's company is *a Chinese national. He has a close relationship with the company. He presumably gave his testimony in a way that benefits the defendant's company.* Although the plaintiff cannot prove that he worked on site 182 through a written contract, he did so through witness testimonies. Furthermore, the [criminal] case that was brought against him states that he was accused of theft while working at the Mekelle–Weldiya Railway Construction Project, site 182. We can infer from this that he was arrested while working for the defendant's company.[37]

Judge Yohannes was not the only one to impugn the validity of testimonies from Chinese witnesses. Some judges admitted they gave less weight to Chinese witness accounts, partly because they were translations. However, other judges insisted that the court gave equal importance to testimonies.

Giving voice to the plaintiff while silencing the defendant, Judge Yohannes ruled that CCCC had employed Tamru Belay and unlawfully dismissed him. Because the Sidama welder had not completed his probation period, he was not entitled to compensation for the employer's failure to give notice. However, the judge did award him his salary for the months he spent in custody. As a result, Tamru Belay received 42,900 birr and an additional five hundred birr for expenses and losses.

Throughout the proceedings, there were several moments in which Judge Yohannes could have made different choices favoring the defendant over the plaintiff. He instead chose to amplify the Ethiopian plaintiff's voice. From giving Chinese witness testimonies less weight and classifying Tamru Belay as an employee of CCCC, despite competing testimonies, to the allocation of a defense lawyer and the rejection of the defendant's preliminary objection, which he did not support with legal evidence, Judge Yohannes made decisions that revealed a specific stance and the discretionary power to express it.

LEGAL CONSIDERATIONS

How can we explain the contrasting verdicts given by the four Hintalo Wajirat Wereda Court judges? Unfortunately, there is no easy answer to this question. Judges make myriad decisions throughout legal proceedings—for instance, regarding the issues framed, the facts discerned, the weight given to witness testimonies, and—importantly in cross-cultural disputes—how they fill silences created by structural impasses and linguistic bottlenecks.

Legal considerations mattered whenever judges marshaled their professional discretion. Alongside the ambiguity surrounding the nature of the employer–employee relationship, the contested doctrine of precedent in Ethiopia's court system accounts for the sharp contrasts between court rulings. It partly explains why the Ethiopian plaintiffs won in cases entertained by Judge Mengesha and Judge Yohannes and lost in disputes over which Judge Kahsay and Judge Mehari presided. In the remainder of the chapter, I show that legal considerations often overlap with political orientations and personal experiences.

Legally speaking, the main difference in the judges' respective rulings lay in the classification of the plaintiffs as employed for an indefinite or a definite period. Judges Mengesha and Yohannes defined Ethiopian plaintiffs as permanent employees, provided they had completed probation. They based their decisions on Ethiopia's former *Labor Proclamation No. 377/2003*, which held that employees who successfully finished a probation period of forty-five days were considered in post for an indefinite time, regardless of whether they signed an employment agreement.[38]

In response to complaints from employers, including foreign investors, the legislature extended the probation period to sixty working days in the new *Labor Proclamation No. 1156/2019*, which came into force in 2019. However, there are exceptions to this provision that Judges Mengesha and Yohannes did not consider. Employees hired for piece or seasonal work or as replacement for staff on leave are considered temporary employees and are not entitled to benefits such as severance payment. By law, Chinese management must provide an employment contract within fifteen days of employment, signed by both parties and stating the name and address of the employer, the name, age, address, and work card number of the employee, and the nature of the work. Because they often did not provide such a contract, they could not back up their claim that employees had been employed for piece work or as "daily laborers"—a term they commonly used in court to refer to their Ethiopian employees regardless of status and seniority, perhaps in an attempt to escape any responsibility assigned to employers by the labor law.[39]

As I noted earlier, Ethiopian employees were often uncertain about the terms of their employment agreement. It was ultimately up to the bench to decide whether the plaintiffs had been employed on a permanent or a temporary basis. In all cases, Judge Mengesha and Judge Yohannes categorized plaintiffs as permanent employees, granting them the benefits they requested if the company failed to prove it had lawfully terminated the workers. Indeed, the burden of proof typically lies on the employer in labor cases.

Judge Kahsay, conversely, defined the employer–employee relationship as temporary. Instead of referring to statutory law, he based his judgments on precedents issued by the Federal Supreme Court Cassation Division. The reference to cassation decisions radically altered the outcome of the cases he heard. Judge Kahsay drew on one cassation decision in particular: *Afrikawit Building Contractors Association v. Indris Ali.*[40] The case concerns a class suit in 2008, instituted by a group of carpenters, masons, and timekeepers, who had been made redundant. Their employer was a local construction firm contracted by Wollo University in Kombolcha, Amhara, to construct eight multistory buildings. After three structures had been completed, the contractor dismissed the workers. It had done so unlawfully, the plaintiffs claimed, as none of them had received a notice of termination citing the date and reason for their redundancy.

The lower court in Kombolcha awarded the plaintiffs damages for unlawful dismissal. The construction firm appealed the case twice. Finally, the Federal Supreme Court's cassation bench ruled that the firing was lawful because the construction work was nearing completion—a fact the workers had not denied in their testimonies. It, moreover, classified construction work as being of a temporary nature, with the result that the construction firm was not obliged to give notice of redundancy. Based on this case, Judge Kahsay argued that Ethiopian workers employed by the Chinese were temporary workers and, thus, not entitled to benefits.

Much like Judge Mengesha's decision to construe workers as permanent employees, Judge Kahsay's commitment to categorizing them as temporary employees is debatable. The Federal Supreme Court's ruling on *Afrikawit Construction v. Indris Ali* is disputable for two reasons. First, construction companies, including Chinese firms, also hire permanent employees. Many Ethiopian staff of Chinese enterprises work for their employers for years, as they accompany their employer from one project to another. The cassation decision effectively dismisses their rights as permanent employees when one or the other project is close to completion. Furthermore, the cassation decision gave a binding interpretation not of the law but of the nature of employment in the construction industry. On the other hand, one can also disapprove of Judge Mengesha forgoing cassation decisions altogether. Legally speaking, the cassation court gives *binding* interpretations.

For one, the conflicting judgments given by the judges at the Hintalo Wajirat Wereda Court are symptomatic of the disputed doctrine of precedent and its controversial role in the Ethiopian legal system. Variously referred to as "judicial law," "case law," "judge-made law," or in Latin, *stare decisis* (let the decision stand), precedent is central to common law. A standing decision furnishes the bases for subsequent cases with comparable facts and issues. Yet, in Ethiopia, the principle of precedent has never been fully incorporated. In common law countries, such as the United States and the United Kingdom, precedent is defined as *making* law, whereas in Ethiopia, it is construed as *interpreting* the law. The Cassation Division, in other words, gives binding interpretations of codified law.[41] What is more, only decisions of the Cassation Division of the Federal Supreme Court are binding to all courts in Ethiopia.

The origin of the principle of precedent in Ethiopian legal thought has been debated, contributing to contestations about its implementation. Some scholars have argued that the principle is a legal import promoted by the British in the period after Ethiopia's liberation from Italian occupation. Others believe it may have grown out of imperial Ethiopia's *atsé sir'at*, which loosely translates as "the law of the sovereign," which existed before the introduction of modern codes.[42] In the past, adjudicating disputes and crimes was part of public administration, with the emperor placed at the top of the hierarchy.[43] When he rendered a decision at the Royal Court (*Zufan Chilot*), his ruling counted as the law of the sovereign and could be cited in future cases.[44]

In the wake of the modernization of the Ethiopian justice system in the 1950s, Emperor Haile Selassie I rejected the adoption of the doctrine of precedent. Why he chose to do so has been the subject of debate. According to René David, the French law professor who drafted Ethiopia's Civil Code, the overriding reason the emperor chose Roman-Germanic law was political, driven by "the desire to counter-balance, by an appeal to other sources, an English or Anglo-American influence which they [Ethiopians] feared was becoming excessive."[45] Fearing further infringements of Ethiopian sovereignty, the emperor opted for a legal tradition with which those who exerted most pressure on the country were unfamiliar. Another oft-cited reason for the emperor's decision against the implementation of a common law legal system was the Roman origin of the *Fetha Negast* (the Law of Kings), Ethiopia's oldest body of laws, and the sovereign's wish to remain faithful to tradition. Administrators had long used the principles spelled out in this centuries-old document to dispense justice.[46]

Notwithstanding the emperor's reservations about the doctrine of precedent, *Proclamation No. 195/1962*, in the late imperial period, and *Proclamation No. 40/1993*, enacted by the transitional government at the dawn of the new Federal Democratic Republic of Ethiopia, made decisions of the highest court binding for lower courts on matters of the law. However, court decisions were not disseminated until the late 1990s, and the principle could hardly be applied in practice.[47] Since the Federal Supreme Court began publishing cassation decisions, it has been increasingly incorporated in judgments at all levels of jurisdiction.

The growing importance of cassation decisions has been the subject of heated academic debate in Ethiopia, reflecting long-standing controversies about the advantages and disadvantages of civil and common law. Critics argue that the Federal Supreme Court misuses its law interpretation mandate. Interpretations often include new laws that conflict with domestic or private international laws.[48] Proponents of the growing influence of case law maintain that cassation decisions are flexible and, more importantly, representative of rapidly changing social, economic, and political circumstances.[49] It is, for instance, not surprising that the cassation decision *Afrikawit Construction v. Indris Ali* of 2008[50] was issued in the wake of Ethiopia's construction boom, backed by a growth-driven developmental state.

In practice, judges give unequal weight to cassation decisions, as the contrasting decisions of the judges at the Hintalo Wajirat Wereda Court reveal. Recognizing one another's approaches, judges attributed these to differences in legal interpretation alone. Judge Kahsay backed up his colleague Judge Mengesha: "He decided what he thought was right. Each decision of a judge is the right decision for that judge.[51] He ruled that the workers were entitled to certain payments because he considered them permanent workers. However, in my eyes, they are not." Kahsay remained diplomatic throughout, even though Judge Mengesha's decisions had posed a challenge to him. The plaintiffs had appeared in the courtroom with high expectations, putting him under considerable pressure.

Whereas judges like Kahsay described differences in decisions as a result of their "different interpretation of the law," other factors may have played a role too. I was struck by the overlap between legal considerations, judges' ideological positions, and their personal experiences. It is, however, impossible to draw a causal link between judges' decisions and their standpoints. I nevertheless want to reflect on these extralegal dimensions, as they are essential to understanding the context in which judges give their verdicts.

IDEOLOGICAL CONSIDERATIONS

Whether and to what extent judges are guided by their personal agendas have occupied scholars in law and society for decades. They have advanced various models,[52] including the legal model, in which judges seek to interpret the law as well as possible; the attitudinal model, in which they strive to make good policy; and the strategic model, in which the judiciary considers not only policy but also its broader outcomes.[53] Yet other approaches to judicial decision-making shed light on the economic, sociological, psychological, and cultural dimensions.[54] More recently, scholars have combined different dimensions that are brought to bear on judges' decisions to underline the complementarities between the models.[55]

Few scholars would deny that there is a personal element to judging, just as few would contest that this element is constrained and influenced by distinct professional obligations and jurisprudential schools of thought.[56] Law matters. It certainly did at the benches of the Hintalo Wajirat Wereda Court. Even so, a host of other factors meant the playing field in front of the bench was never fully level.

The labor disputes were tried by the court in Adi Gudem against the backdrop of national debates about labor and its protection against global capital—debates that have become heated since the influx of foreign investors in the 2010s. Critical observers accuse foreign enterprises, many of which are Chinese-run, of paying razor-thin wages. Labor in the construction industry fares slightly better, mainly since many workers have successfully mobilized the law against their employers. To a certain extent, the labor law has served its intended purpose of protecting employees against predatory capital.

By taking their disputes to court, Ethiopian plaintiffs have granted judges a voice in these debates. Owing to the nature of adjudication, judges have been required to take a position. Whereas Judge Mengesha and Judge Yohannes identified with the plight of Ethiopian laborers, accusing Chinese firms of abusive labor practices, Judge Kahsay and Judge Mehari were more sympathetic to Chinese corporations, faulting Ethiopian laborers for their poor work ethic. The rulings of the two pairs of judges matched their political views.

In her work on language and ideology in lower courts in Tucson, Arizona, Susan Philips demonstrates how judges enact political ideas, even though they are reluctant to admit doing so.[57] Ideologies, she argues, are constituted and presented in social practice and transpire in spoken and written law. She distinguishes procedure-oriented judges who adopt a liberal stance from record-oriented judges who take a more conservative approach. The former view themselves as representatives of the state, assuming the role of a guardian for individuals whom they feel need help to acquire due process. The latter eschew the role of protector, believing it is the responsibility of the individual and their lawyer to know and defend their rights.

Ideological differences, grounded in contrasting views of the state's role and its responsibility toward vulnerable groups in society, can also be found among Ethiopian judges. If we adopt the left–right spectrum to measure ideological positions, Judge Mengesha and Judge Yohannes would be firmly placed on the left. In contrast, Judge Kahsay and Judge Mehari would hover right of center. I should pause here to quickly mention that decision-making in Ethiopian courtrooms is equally affected by political views regarding ethnicity and the country's nationalities question,[58] which can overshadow other ideologies. In Adi Gudem, however, the ethnic dimension hardly played a role. Labor disputes pitted Ethiopians ("us") against Chinese ("them") rather than one ethnic group against another. In fact, some of the collective labor cases entertained at the Hintalo Wajirat Wereda Court were filed by workers from different ethnic backgrounds. Ideological differences manifested first and foremost in contrasting ideas about the relationship between Ethiopian labor and Chinese capital—the most salient representative and rendition of global capital.

Ethiopian judges held divergent opinions on whether foreign investors merit preferential treatment beyond the benefits afforded them by the country's investment laws and the Ethiopian legal system more generally. For example, the Investment Proclamation makes foreign enterprises eligible for investment incentives such as tax holidays.[59] Apart from this, the justice system also has built-in advantages for foreign parties. Labor cases aside, other lawsuits with a foreign element, for instance, fall under federal jurisdiction.[60] As a result, for civil cases with equal claims or criminal cases with similar charges, the judges presiding over them have more years of experience under their belt.

Individual judges can choose to make additional concessions within the bounds of their discretionary power. Some judges, for instance, appointed Chinese litigants for the mornings, so they did not have to wait until other hearings had finished and could swiftly return to work after the proceedings. Yet, when asked whether foreign nationals and enterprises received preferential treatment, judges almost unanimously declared that they did not, referring to the maxim "all are equal before the law."[61]

Judge Mehari entertained perhaps the most unconventional ideas among his colleagues. The Ethiopian labor law, he believed, was ill-suited for foreign enterprises. Echoing the idea that the law ought not stand in the way of development, he went so far as to suggest that it might be better for the government to issue a separate proclamation tailored to the needs of foreign companies, effectively writing possibilities for immunity into the law. "The [labor] law is fair," he explained.[62] "However, the law assumes that the employer and the employee are Ethiopian. The labor law does not consider foreign companies." Foreign investors' rights ought to be better protected, Judge Mehari maintained. They ought to enjoy a special status as critical contributors to domestic development and economic growth. At the very least, they should be able to do their job without unnecessary interruptions. "One of the grounds of attracting foreign direct investment is how a country's law protects the investor's rights." He paused. "There are no unfair provisions in the labor law for the foreign investors, but they should not have to spend all of their time in court." Echoing the aggrieved words of Chinese litigants in their requests for immunity, Judge Mehari sympathized with foreign enterprise management and a federal government that attempted to spur development.

Left-leaning judges, in stark contrast, denounced the discourse of "cheap labor" (*rikash gulbet*) used and, as they believed, abused by the Ethiopian government to attract foreign capital.[63] Images of Ethiopia as a lucrative investment frontier were feared to encourage a race to the bottom that would turn cheap labor into slave labor, with workers sacrificing their lives in the name of national development. While some of these judges blamed the government and its investment policies, others accused foreign investors of taking advantage of the country's poverty.

Those who saw a role for the state as a guardian, such as Judge Mengesha, appreciated the Ethiopian labor law and believed it could serve its purpose, if only foreign investors paid it more respect. "Our labor law is better than that of many other countries in the world," Judge Mengesha held with some pride.[64] "The labor law is pro-laborer and protects the rights of laborers to work and get paid. The laborer shall not be fired like an animal." The law punishes employers who disregard labor rights. "If you simply say 'Go!' to a worker, the law forces you to pay about three months' salary and other damages."[65]

PERSONAL CONSIDERATIONS

Personal sentiments toward Ethiopian and Chinese disputants played a role as well. This was particularly true for Judge Mengesha, who confided that he had been harsh with Chinese managers who failed to treat workers with dignity. They had denied him his dignity too. Physically impaired, Judge Mengesha walked with a limp, and he had received denigrating looks from those to whom he referred with the generic category of "the Chinese." "The Chinese view the workers in Tigray as cheap." "Cheap" in this comment meant unworthy of respect. Combining workers' experiences with his own, he asserted: "They think only *they* [the Chinese] are human beings. They do not believe that other people eat and sleep." In Judge Mengesha's eyes, dignity meant respecting different people as humans of equal worth. He used "eating" and "sleeping" as the banal ways in which humans sustain life, shared across differences of race and ethnicity. He repeated a discourse on humanity with the workers we encountered in chapter 2.

The judge empathized with the plaintiffs, partly because of his own experience with discrimination. Indeed, empathy, as the capacity to adopt someone else's perspective, assumed an essential role in Judge Mengesha's decisions. Empathy can, yet does not have to, lead to sympathy.[66] It can be induced in various ways. In their study of the impact of empathy on jurors in US courtrooms, Plumm and Terrance distinguish two forms of empathy: *trait empathy* and *situational empathy*.[67] Trait empathy relies on similar characteristics between the one who empathizes, the observer, and the subject of empathy, the actor. Situational empathy, on the other hand, is predicated on the capacity of the observer to place oneself in the actor's situation. Both types of empathy and the sympathy they can induce influence judicial decision-making. African American judges and jurors, for instance, are more likely to rule liberally on cases with a racial component,[68] partly because they have experienced similar situations of discrimination.[69]

Both trait and situational empathy emerge from Judge Mengesha's rulings. The judge not only shared essential characteristics with the plaintiffs, including nationality, race, and language, but also found himself in a position of being looked down on. He admitted that his sympathy for workers and personal experiences with Chinese managers transpired in his decisions—in the cost orders, not in the judgments, he was quick to stress. In Ethiopia, as elsewhere, an award of costs is at the court's discretion. As a rule, the loser pays the winner's costs. The judge assesses and calculates the amount. The most common cost orders in labor cases decided in Adi Gudem, like elsewhere in Ethiopia, included the reimbursement of transport, accommodation, and meal costs. It did not include the lawyer's fee, as most plaintiffs represented themselves. In all his rulings, Judge Mengesha ordered the Chinese defendant to cover the expenses of the plaintiffs, some of which amounted to a generous two or three thousand birr (actual costs could be as low as four hundred birr).[70] "I expressed my sentiments when it came to cost orders. . . . As for the remainder, I adhered to the law."[71]

Judge Mengesha insisted that he remained within the bounds of the law. He had been strict with corporations due to Ethiopia's laws more than anything else:

> The Chinese hated me. However, I am a person. The law is the one to decide. Not me. In one case, I awarded 137,000 birr to the plaintiff. They despised me for it. But this is the law. I interpreted it accordingly. If I make a mistake, they can go to the appellate court. However, company management complained to the government that I was intentionally tough on them.[72]

Countering allegations made by the Chinese that his rulings were biased, Judge Mengesha de-personified his decisions. As a judge, he merely *interpreted* the law. It is ultimately the law that decides, he asserted. Of course, one can argue that Judge Mengesha, much like the laborers, mobilized the law to serve his purposes, and did so for similar reasons while driven by similar sentiments.

To conclude, judges possessed considerable discretion, which they exercised from their first assessment of a case to the execution of its decision. Judge Yohannes, for instance, exercised his discretion to assign a defense lawyer to the welder from Sidama. Judge Mengesha took the provisions in Labor Proclamation 377/2003 as final and did not consider cassation court decisions on similar issues and facts. By making these choices, they tipped the balance toward Ethiopian plaintiffs. Judge Kahsay, on the other hand, insisted on the precedence of a cassation decision that defined construction workers as temporary employees. Like Judge Mehari, he assumed that workers on Chinese-managed projects exploited the rights generously granted them by the Labor Proclamation. They, in contrast, tipped the scales in favor of Chinese employers.

Despite the biases of its judges, the court brought parties together and facilitated communication between them. Regardless of diverging political orientations and personal experiences, all judges sought to enact their jurisdiction and demanded recalcitrant enterprise managers respect it. While the relationship between the state, Chinese capital, and vulnerable groups was ferociously contested, the question of immunity was not.

POLITICAL AFTERMATH

Given their steep number, the labor cases brought to court in Adi Gudem became a major obstacle to the Chinese contractor and its subcontractors. Company representatives took their concerns to Abay Weldu, then president of Tigray, and the presidents of the Tigray Supreme Court in Mekelle and the High Court in Maychew, pleading for help. The president of the South-Eastern Zone High Court requested the transfer of all labor cases, including pending ones, from Judge Mengesha to Judge Kahsay.

The latter protested. The judge's caseload was already heavy. Yet the high court president offered to assist him. Judge Mengesha remained silent to us on the cases that had been taken from him. He did mention the complaints Chinese management lodged against him and blamed President Abay and the state council for escalating matters. He suspected that Addisalem Balema, one of the TPLF's top leaders with close ties to the Chinese, had exerted pressure on the regional president. Today, Addisalem still enjoys a reputation as a henchman of the Chinese. The police arrested him in December 2020, one month into the Tigray War. He stood trial in Addis Ababa for various crimes, including conspiring with the then-purged vice president of Tigray, Debretsion Gebremichael, and others "to dismantle the constitutional order of the country." The police suggested that Addisalem had approached African Union officials to put pressure on the federal government and, according to the *Ethiopia Observer*, had met with the Chinese Ambassador "to try to create a Chinese–TPLF Communist Party" in the wake of the armed conflict, thereby jeopardizing the government's "law enforcement operation"—as the war effort was known in official discourse at the time.[73]

"The Chinese came to the country to work," Abay Weldu said when he was still in power, reiterating the trope used by Chinese managers to justify claims to immunity. Yet the Tigray Supreme Court president, Judge Mengesha pointed out, did not waver. She suggested that Chinese management appeal a case when they were dissatisfied with its outcome. "Because I was considered to be tough on the Chinese," Judge Mengesha reflected, "they wanted to replace me with another judge. They were not successful. The system does not allow them to do this." Political tug-of-wars in court administrative matters notwithstanding, all judges sought to retain cases and ensure they received a verdict.

The stirring events in Adi Gudem show that what are customarily considered routine cases can transform into political cases once they threaten to disrupt operations or spoil the reputation of the corporation or the Chinese community at large. When this happens, interventions and invitations occur, drawing in a broad range of people and institutions. Rather than demanding court cases be suspended and granting immunity to the foreign defendants, the intervenors in this case opted for a solution that would not directly discredit the plaintiffs and upset the public: the transfer of case files to a judge who would give more favorable verdicts to Chinese corporations. Importantly, their intervention kept the cases in court and ultimately protected local jurisdiction.

Conclusion

"They were gunning for near immunity," recalled an Ethiopian lawyer who participated in the negotiations leading to the 1998 Bilateral Investment Treaty (BIT) between Ethiopia and China, using a military metaphor.[1] "I objected to this. Laborers are not diplomats." The Chinese side feared having to deal with the local judicial system—a fear that was not, as it turned out, unjustified. The lawyer, who resigned from politics not long after completing his assignment in Beijing, dismissed this arrangement as being both impractical and unacceptable. "What if a fight breaks out on a building site in Weldiya? What if local authorities intervene and arrest the people in question? We had to face local realities." If disputes were to arise, they could hardly be settled by diplomatic intervention, especially in far-flung regions like mountainous northern Amhara, where Chinese teams of engineers had constructed a road from Weldiya to Wereta in the 1970s and 1980s.

The Chinese delegation yielded to Ethiopian objections at the negotiating table. Not all African countries had been as assertive as Ethiopia, the lawyer noted later in our conversation. He took neighboring South Sudan as an example. Chinese security forces there had guarded the construction of a pipeline and patrolled a vast area around it, meaning South Sudan had effectively invited a foreign army onto its soil. A comparable request for the Chinese-funded railway project from Addis Ababa to Djibouti was taken off the table immediately. "Why?" I asked. "It'd be unthinkable in this country," he said. "Remember, Ethiopia was never colonized."[2]

Ethiopia proudly withstood colonization during and after the European scramble for Africa in the nineteenth century. It had resisted interventions and refused invitations. Why should a country that had never been colonized make concessions to its sovereignty now? Referring to past experiences to explain and justify present-day sentiments and decisions, the lawyer alluded to Ethiopia's victory against the Italian army at Adwa in 1896.

Still in effect today, the BIT between Ethiopia and China reveals the relative equality between the parties who signed it in Beijing in 1998. The treaty, Won Kidane argues, reflects China's transformation from being the largest recipient of foreign direct investment (FDI) to one of the primary senders of FDI—a metamorphosis that happened before it could update its BIT.[3] China's second-generation treaties, of which Ethiopia's is one, were drafted to impose the least possible restrictions on the host state. They preserve the latter's decisional autonomy, for instance, regarding the lawfulness of expropriation and respect its domestic legal system, allowing a resort to arbitration only in the final instance.[4]

Whether the egalitarian nature of the treaty was the result of the assertiveness of the Ethiopian side or of China's still-nascent market economy and its lack of political clout at the time is open to debate. The lawyer, however, underscored Ethiopian agency. "The Chinese you see here on the street did not come of their own accord," he explained, dispelling a common assumption that the Chinese invited themselves. "We invited them."[5] Portraying the Chinese as guests who had been welcomed strictly on the host's terms, the lawyer explained how he and his colleagues in Beijing had handpicked the Chinese enterprises that would come to carry out the first projects in Ethiopia.

Ethiopian opposition to the idea of immunity proposed in the negotiations in the 1990s has not prevented Chinese enterprise managers from raising the issue ever since they began to face lawsuits. They substantiate these informal and extra-legal requests for exemption from legal process and prosecution by referring to the premise that, in certain situations, social aims outweigh the value of imposing liability. *Immunity on Trial* has shown that the nature of such social aims and the question of whether they are met are contested. Ethiopian critics recast these aims as business incentives, calling into question the presumed largesse of Chinese corporations and their expatriate managers. By questioning whether Chinese activities amount to social benefits in the first place, they dispute the right to immunity. Expatriate executives, in contrast, underscored the benevolence of initiatives that, they propounded, hardly made financial sense.[6] They incurred losses on most infrastructure projects in Ethiopia, yet they continued building roads, railways, industrial parks, and dams, installing electricity lines and fiber-optic cables, and creating employment, enabling knowledge exchange, and opening local business opportunities. In their eyes, they *did* meet social aims that would outweigh the value of imposing liability.

The tussle over immunity, or the principle that justified it, was heated. It cut to the heart of a question that has long been debated in Ethiopia: Should the government make concessions to sovereignty to attract foreign currency?

This book opens the possibility of conceiving of immunity more broadly as exemptions from rules and regulations that are not just anchored in and sanctioned by international law or agreed upon in commercial contracts between a state and a creditor or corporation. Immunity is more often generated on the ground, where it emerges in contestations between those who *fight, exact, grant,* or *weigh* it. In the context described in this book, these four positions were taken by members of local communities who sought to hold corporations liable, corporate executives who justified claims to immunity, government officials who ceded authority or turned a blind eye to unlawful practices, and Ethiopian judges who weighed arguments for and against immunity, torn as they were between serving justice and preventing demotion, and between determination and unease.

Of course, the boundaries that separate these four groups and their positions are not definitive. An Ethiopian fruit-grower may choose to support a Chinese corporation because the road it is building will help her transport her produce more easily; a Chinese manager may support the cause of Ethiopian workers out of sympathy or ideological conviction; a government official may back the local workforce out of commiseration or because her neighbor's son works as an excavator operator for the company; and a judge may extend immunity without asking questions. The four groups, however, map roughly onto the realities I observed.

The judiciary arguably gained the most leverage in the tussle over immunity, thanks to the Ethiopian plaintiffs who have en masse brought Chinese corporations to court. Indeed, contestations over immunity should be understood against the background of a surge in litigation against Chinese firms since they first entered Ethiopia in the late 1990s. The bench seeks to retain disputes, preventing corporations or their government allies from taking them out of court. Recall the judge in Sheraro who flatly ignored appeals by state functionaries to close a contentious collective labor case. In the courtroom, he rebuked attempts by the Chinese project manager and his deputy to disrupt the court proceedings through raising their voices, arguing, and playing the language card.

By moderating mutinous voices, demanding a degree of comportment, and instilling court etiquette, judges disciplined foreign litigants and, by so doing, solidified their jurisdiction. Indeed, the bench requires an audience to assert its jurisdiction. Ensnaring an audience that contests its power is a powerful way to establish jurisdictional authority and extend its reach. Of course, listening to and agreeing with what is being said in court are two different things, yet performed listening is sufficient for the law to be effective. The jurisdictional disputes between assertive judges and contrarian litigants affirmed the authority of the former and reinforced judicial sovereignty.

NEGOTIATING IMMUNITY BEYOND ETHIOPIA

To what extent are questions of sovereignty and concerns about immunity addressed in other parts of Africa and beyond? Are debates about immunity unique to Ethiopia, or do they resonate more broadly? Does Ethiopia remain a frequently cited exception on the continent because it was never colonized? Several African countries have witnessed waves of domestic litigation against Chinese corporations, including neighboring Kenya. A small random sample of thirty-five cases drawn from the Kenya Law Cases Database shows that the disputing parties, the claims, the issues, and the outcomes of cases instituted against Chinese firms in Kenya are remarkably similar to those in Ethiopia. A cursory comparison, then, propounds the broader relevance of the events described in this book and the questions they raise.

The problem of communication and its lack comes to the fore even more in Kenyan labor cases than in Ethiopia. It seems many workers sue their Chinese employer for violating Article 41 of Kenya's Employment Act,[7] which requires employers to notify employees of their dismissal in advance and arrange a hearing with them. The labor law compels employers to do so in a language the employee understands and allows them the chance to respond. The judgments of Kenyan labor suits suggest that workers, like their counterparts in Ethiopia, are often left in the dark as to why they were dismissed. In Kenya, as much as in Ethiopia, language barriers and structural impasses seem to jeopardize communication and impede dialogue. There, too, it looks as though the judge is tasked with closing the communication gap.

This happened in a lawsuit filed by Lawrence Karani Njagi, who sued China Railway Engineering Group No. 10 for unlawful dismissal in 2017.[8] Njagi, a Kenyan builder who had worked on a road project at Mau Summit, northwest of Nairobi, was laid off after two years of service in a manner he described as "demeaning, illegal, embarrassing, and punitive," adding that the behavior of his Chinese supervisor "should not be encouraged in [a] civilized society."[9] The plaintiff stated that he did not receive notice of termination and was unaware of why he was dismissed,[10] accusing his Chinese employer of violating various provisions of the Employment Act, including articles 41 and 45, the latter of which requires employers to provide a valid reason for dismissal.[11] He also referred to the right of employment under the country's constitution and proposed that age discrimination was at play (the plaintiff was forty at the time of his dismissal). Njagi was represented by Oumo & Co. Advocates, a firm based in Nakuru, the city closest to the project site.

The Chinese company failed to attend court, and the judge, like his Ethiopian counterparts, decided to continue proceedings without the defendant. He ruled that the dismissal was "wrongful, unfair and unlawful" and granted the plaintiff a relief of 186,767 Kenyan shillings (about 1,800 US dollars),[12] including compensation for the failure to give notice (26,681 shillings) and six months' salary as compensation for unlawful termination of employment (160,086 shillings). Moreover, he ordered the respondent to pay litigation costs (sixty thousand shillings).[13]

The claim in *Lawrence Karani Njagi v. China Railway Engineering Group No. 10* is akin to those made by workers in Ethiopia, much like the award. The Kenyan plaintiff mentioned his line manager's disrespect toward him, describing his attitude as degrading and unlawful ("demeaning, illegal, embarrassing and punitive"). Conveying indignation, Njagi's words resonate with those uttered by Ethiopian laborers and their accusations that big companies ought to know better and treat them in a way expected in a "civilized society." The Kenyan builder might have experienced his manager's attitude as a threat to his dignity in much the same way as experienced by Ethiopian laborers on Chinese-managed building sites in their country. Note that Njagi's four ireful adjectives evoke a combination of status and emotional harm on the one hand and, on the other, legal transgression, linking dignity to rights and the violation of dignity to the violation of rights.

Unlike their Ethiopian counterparts, however, Njagi and other Kenyan workers in the sample were represented by legal professionals from local firms. Whereas cases heard in Kenya and Ethiopia are remarkably similar, there are a few differences. In Kenya, trade unions, such as the Building and Construction Workers Union and the Union of Road Contractors and Civil Engineering Workers,[14] seem to assume a more prominent role, encouraging workers to take their disputes to court or suing corporations themselves. As such, they position themselves as critical mediators of Kenyan–Chinese legal encounters, more so than their Ethiopian counterparts.

The Kenyan sample also includes a handful of cases initiated by Chinese firms or cases in which both parties were Chinese. This suggests that Chinese companies in Kenya have undergone a learning curve similar to their counterparts in Ethiopia. The most notorious of these cases was the bitter dispute between China Wu Yi and Edermann Property, an enterprise incorporated in Kenya but directed by a Chinese national.[15] The Kenyan media lapped up the lawsuit: "Chinese Firms Lock Horns in Kenyan Courts" ran a headline in the *Daily Nation*, one of Kenya's most widely read newspapers.[16]

The legal battle between the two construction firms concerned a loan agreement, revolving around a supplementary agreement Edermann later described as "invalid and a sham" and to which it claimed not to be a party.[17] China Wu Yi accused Edermann of failing to fully settle a loan of one billion shillings. It went to court to obtain the outstanding portion of the loan—300 million shillings—on top of a penalty of 50 million shillings for breach of contract. The state-owned firm had advanced one million shillings to Edermann to construct the Great Wall Apartment Project in Mlolongo, off the Nairobi–Mombasa Highway. Edermann, however, denied the debt, professing to have paid the 920 million shillings it claimed had been agreed on. It also filed an application to the high court, seeking to strike out China Wu Yi's lawsuit, accusing the state-owned firm of noncompliance with Kenyan law and questioning the legal status of its representative, Hui Liu. The plaintiff argued for a lifting of the corporate veil of the first defendant, Edermann Property Limited, holding its managing directors—the second and third defendants—responsible for embezzling the loan's outstanding portion.

China Wu Yi v. Edermann Property illustrates China Wu Yi's trust in the Kenyan High Court. At least, the company deemed the Kenyan court capable of solving its dispute with Edermann. It could also have turned to the Chinese embassy or higher officials to mediate the dispute, yet perhaps they were seen to be less neutral. The high-profile legal battle, which must have provoked amusement among Kenyan observers, exemplifies the extent to which Chinese parties have started taking African courts seriously.

Although I cannot tell whether the judgments in my Kenyan sample were enforced, the judiciary there, like its Ethiopian counterpart, seems to have been successful in retaining disputes involving Chinese parties and ruling on them. The judgments, however, do not betray whether Kenyan judges equally faced claims for immunity. Often made informally or outside the courtroom, these claims leave no trace in case files, let alone judgments. Only further empirical research can establish whether this is the case. I should also note that not all African countries have witnessed waves of litigation against Chinese corporations. In some countries, the unions or government institutions contain, diffuse, or solve disputes.[18] In other places, the police or the military suppress conflicts or the courts do not enjoy the degree of legitimacy they do in Ethiopia and Kenya.[19] The courts lean on the support of litigants who entrust them with their disputes to enact their jurisdiction. Even so, it is fair to say that concerns about immunity and, more broadly, sovereignty resonate across Africa. Why is this the case?

THE AFRICAN QUESTION OF SOVEREIGNTY

Sovereignty, both as an ideology and a political principle, has been central to postcolonial Africa.[20] When upheld through international recognition, sovereignty guarantees juridical statehood, political authority, and national security. It is therefore not surprising that newly independent African governments embraced the very sovereignty regime that had once been used to subordinate them.[21] Upon its establishment in 1963, the Organization of African Unity confirmed inherited colonial boundaries and framed territory as the principal space for exercising sovereignty and self-determination. The charter drawn up in Addis Ababa that year reinforced the equality of member states, affirming sovereignty and territorial integrity.[22]

In practice, African governments often had to negotiate de facto sovereignty, confronting external interventions while also extending invitations to secure their autonomy. Formal recognition is one thing; the actual authority to govern without external interference is another. As this book illustrates, true jurisdictional control and sovereignty in action are harder to achieve.

Economic pressures posed, and continue to pose, the greatest threats to sovereignty. From the period immediately following liberation to the present day, transnational corporations and financial institutions have challenged African autonomy. In the 1980s, the doctrine of foreign sovereign immunity began to erode with the advent of structural adjustment programs and the extension of the judicial reach of global powers.[23] The now codified commercial exception to sovereign immunity enabled predominantly wealthier countries to sue poorer ones in national courts, for instance, over loan defaults. These changes, along with loan conditions demanding democratization and governance reforms, were experienced as affronts to sovereignty.[24]

What has been dubbed the Chinese Century has produced new forms of dependence.[25] China, too, has simultaneously strengthened African sovereignty through aid, investment, and infrastructure construction, while also jeopardizing it.[26] The latest fears over the loss of sovereignty are compounded by the alleged debt-trap diplomacy, in which the Chinese government is accused of burdening poor nations with unsustainable loans. Whether inflated or not,[27] these accusations have rekindled popular concerns about sovereignty. In an opinion piece titled "Why China Remains the Greatest Threat to Kenya's Sovereignty," Kenyan lawyer Makau Mutua accused China of neocolonialism: "I was shocked to learn that Chinese nationals are running the SGR [Standard Gauge Railway from Nairobi to Mombasa], including collecting tickets and sales. Is Kenya an independent country, or not?"[28] Similar sentiments have been expressed about the Addis Ababa–Djibouti railway in Ethiopia. Yet, blame is often directed at African governments for failing to negotiate better terms.[29]

Sovereignty debates across Africa thus reflect the paradox of sovereignty: Since independence, many states have had to concede aspects of sovereignty to consolidate it.[30] Yet states, as anthropologists remind us, consist of a multitude of actors with different positions, interests, and goals.[31] While some state actors may willingly compromise state immunity, others seek to protect it. These competing positions, interests, and goals are visible in Ethiopia, where part of the judiciary—especially in the regions—takes a determined stance, making an emphatic statement against federal executive organs that they believe have gone too far in extending invitations to foreign firms. They have put up clear "no trespassing" signs in an attempt to strengthen their jurisdiction and, by doing so, restore sovereignty. As such, they provide a counterweight to the expanding judicial territory of global powers, including China.

LOCAL COURTS AS GLOBAL ACTORS

Ethiopia's domestic courts have become a critical stage for contestations over immunity and sovereignty. *Immunity on Trial* has shown that the judiciary has been effective in entertaining and, equally importantly, retaining lawsuits involving international corporations, despite concerted efforts by foreign enterprises, embassies, state officials, and other third parties to lift disputes out of court and, at times, have them solved through diplomatic negotiation. By ensnaring multinational corporations in their jurisdiction, Ethiopian judges have become adjudicators of de facto international disputes. What explains the relative potency of the courts in enacting their jurisdiction and becoming global actors in the process?

Even though they are state institutions, local courts in Ethiopia remain at a critical geographic and social distance from the political center in Addis Ababa, affording judges a marked degree of independence. The fact that local plaintiffs and occasionally Chinese disputants entrust them with their disputes suggests that they enjoy appreciable legitimacy.

The courts' success in retaining disputes can also be explained by the number of courts and the number of cases filed against Chinese corporations. All wereda districts in Ethiopia, rural or urban, have a court. Tigray alone, for instance, had 284 courts in 2020.[32] (The number fluctuates depending on the merging of existing administrative units and the creation of new ones.) On top of this, the sheer number of lawsuits heard in the wereda courts, the high courts, and the supreme courts at the state and federal levels makes interventions in all cases by corporations, the state, or both unfeasible. Last, the geographic dispersion of Chinese activities equally complicates administrative meddling. Interventions and invitations are for these reasons restricted to a handful of cases in which the reputation of the Chinese community is at stake or those that are entertained in the federal first instance, high, and supreme courts in Addis Ababa close to the political center.

The answer to why the judiciary has been relatively successful in asserting its jurisdiction and has become a global actor as a result lies, moreover, in the courts' communicative function in cross-cultural dispute resolution. In Ethiopian–Chinese interactions, they have opened a critical avenue for communicating demands, disgruntlement, and critique that cannot be voiced outside the court due to language barriers and structural impasses generated by steep corporate hierarchies, racial divisions, and socioeconomic disparities—all factors that impede communication. Parties often did not voice words to prevent the loss of face or,[33] worse, the loss of their job, client, or business partner.[34] The bench, however, can close the communication gap and, by so doing, assign rights and responsibilities. The communicative function of the court boosts its discretionary power to shape the subjectivities of the parties and the relationship between them.

Yet what explains judges' grit and strength of character in enacting their jurisdiction against interventions by multinational corporations and invitations by state officials? As concerned Ethiopian citizens, judges participated in national debates about the place of global capital and the treatment of international corporations. They, too, asked whether foreign firms deserved concessions, exemptions, or incentives and, if so, at what cost. Confronted with at times bold requests and blunt demands from enterprise managers to be exonerated from legal process and prosecution, judges were forced to take a firm stance. Many embraced the opportunity to make a mark by enacting their jurisdiction and asserting sovereignty. A few shunned it and opted for compromise. Most, however, sought to protect their integrity as a judge, the probity of the court, and ultimately the sovereignty of the nation.

This is not to say that there are no limits to jurisdictional reach. Even if the judiciary is relatively successful in asserting its jurisdiction against corporate interventions and government invitations, it occasionally hits a wall. A judge in the Supreme Court of Amhara presided over a lawsuit in which a Chinese company, commissioned by Ethiopian Electric Power to install electricity lines, damaged Ethio Telecom's broadband internet cables during the construction work.[35] As the financial loss was significant, the Ethiopian telecommunications provider sought indemnification. The Chinese firm, however, did not have assets in Ethiopia. The Export–Import Bank of China funded the project, transferring the finances directly into the contractor's Chinese bank account. Furthermore, the company had rented its equipment and vehicles, so had no tangible assets that the court could confiscate. Usually there is the option to request the client—in this case, Ethiopian Electric Power—deduct money from its regular payments to the contractor. This was not possible either, as the money had never left China.

The judge was forced to close the case. He sent the file to the Ministry of Foreign Affairs, hoping it would convince the company to pay. The lack of bargaining power on the side of the court reflected Ethiopia's lack of bargaining power in the international arena. "We cannot order a foreign country to execute our decisions," the judge regretted. This episode drives home the extent to which global power disparities compromise the legal process, including in domestic litigation.

In short, the location of the court, the nationality of the judges, and that of the parties to a lawsuit can determine the outcome. This holds true for cases in which reputation is at stake. Criminal cases like those of Benli Li, on which the court ruled in absentia, or of Binzheng Zhang, which never reached the court, signal the limits of jurisdiction of countries like Ethiopia. Expatriates and corporations from powerful nations pose an existential threat to its national jurisdiction. Given its entrenched involvement in the Ethiopian economy, China is the most prominent example, but it is not alone. European, American, Turkish, Israeli, Indian, and Saudi firms have all, at one time or another, tried to escape liability in Ethiopia by drawing on a plethora of resources, excuses, and tactics.[36]

The judge from the Amhara Supreme Court still got wound up by the compensation case involving Ethio Telecom, laying partial blame on the Ethiopian government. "The government wants to attract FDI, but it expects the judicial system to treat investors differently," he explained. "When they come here, foreign investors shall be informed that they will be treated on equal terms with Ethiopian investors. If they [federal officials] want to attract investors, they should do so in other ways!" This statement captures the tension between the legal and the executive organs of government over the question of immunity. The judge and his colleagues at the regional supreme court contested the concessions granted to foreign corporations by the government through what were euphemistically known as "incentives." The unlucky outcome for Ethio Telecom in this compensation dispute illustrates that the long executive arm of the state was often the court's main nemesis in debates about and tussles over immunity.

Fundamentally, the jurisdictional bickering between judges, litigants, and government officials was symbolically and politically charged. It revolved around debates about the independence of the legal system and the strength of national sovereignty as much as around the status of foreign nationals and the management of foreign capital. The fragility of domestic jurisdictions indexed the fragility of sovereign control. By extension, the consolidation of Ethiopia's national jurisdiction represented the consolidation of its sovereignty writ large. Disputes over immunity, then, were critical to affirming and safeguarding sovereignty.

ACKNOWLEDGMENTS

One day before I left Ethiopia in December 2020, I managed to reach one of the judges I had met in Tigray earlier that year.

"It was the first time in my life I saw people dying in front of my eyes," he told me, still shaken. A month earlier, the Ethiopian National Defence Force (NDF) had encircled Mekelle, leaving its residents in trepidation. He had fled the city for a small town in central Tigray, where he was posted as a judge.

Two days after the capture of Mekelle on November 17, he was having coffee outdoors with two friends when Eritrean troops stormed into town, shooting at everyone who attempted to flee for safety. Terrified, the three friends ran to the mountains. They hid in a rock-hewn church, one of many in the region, where they stayed for more than two weeks, until fate struck. One of the judge's friends was bitten by a snake and died.

Desperate, the two remaining men eventually ventured out, each going their own way, the judge in the flip-flops he had worn while drinking coffee on that fateful day. After walking for what felt like hours, he was spotted by NDF soldiers in a vehicle, all of whom were Ethiopians. They searched him while he made up a white lie that possibly saved his life. He told the soldiers he was a teacher. The servicemen took him to Mekelle, his hometown, where he arrived on December 18. I spoke to him the following day as he, still in shock, described what had happened.

In December 2020, I left a country at war for a country in pandemic lockdown to start what was perhaps the most challenging year of my life. Throughout 2021, I saw a place I had come to know so intimately transform into a war zone. Daily, I woke up and went to bed to images of gang-raped women, orphaned children, mutilated men, and executed soldiers. I thought of all the people I had met in 2020 across Tigray, wondering and worrying about their whereabouts and well-being.

Many judges, prosecutors, and lawyers joined the fighting. Some lost their lives, while others were displaced. The Tigray justice system was one of the many casualties of the war. Numerous courts were destroyed or looted, with court files burned and damaged.[1] "Before the conflict, the court was in relatively good shape. People sought our expertise," recalls Tsegai Berhane Ghebretekle, who became president of the Tigray Supreme Court in September 2023 and is leading efforts to rebuild the region's judicial infrastructure.[2] He regrets that, in the aftermath of the war, many people have been left without access to justice or have lost trust in the legal system.[3] As this book goes to press, political tensions persist and violence continues to flare up in Tigray, Amhara, and elsewhere in Ethiopia.

I cannot begin to express my gratitude to the many people I met in Ethiopia during field research, most of whom go by pseudonyms in this book. All have been patient and giving. In Tigray, Bereket Asmelash, Kidanu Tekle, and Abrha Tsegay made a heavy year light and enjoyable. Without them, my research would never have been possible. Kahsay Giday, then head of Mekelle University Law School, supported me with enthusiasm. Fana Hagos, former president of the Tigray Supreme Court and a gifted legal scholar herself, gave the project her blessing and graciously facilitated it. Kedir Abdel-Khadir, president of the Central Zone High Court of Tigray (Abiy Addi Bench), went out of his way to arrange interviews and facilitate archival research. I am also indebted to the judges, registrars, and court support staff of the Mekelle High Court, the Hadenet Wereda Court, the Hintalo Wajirat Wereda Court, the Werkamba Wereda Court, and the Tankua Abergele Wereda Court.

Amid a divisive political climate, Yohannes Hailemariam provided a rare and invaluable connection between Mekelle and Bahir Dar.

In Amhara, I am grateful for the generous and gracious support of Zewdu Mengesha. My hosts, Negist, Tiruye, and Kalkidan, made my stay comfortable and pleasant. Abiye Kassahun, then president of the Amhara Supreme Court, facilitated research in the court, the city, and far beyond. I also thank the judges, registrars, and court support staff of the Amhara Supreme Court, the Bahir Dar and Surroundings High Court, the Bahir Dar and Surroundings Wereda Court, the Bahir Dar City Wereda Court, the East Gojjam High Court, and the North Achefer Wereda Court. When Zewdu and I explained that we were interested in lawsuits involving Chinese parties, registrars often looked overwhelmed. I vividly remember one registrar at the Amhara Supreme Court staring at us, exclaiming, "But there are so many!" while drawing a mountain with his arms. Although eager to provide guidance, he did not know where to start. He, together with others, reminded me of the importance of this project.

I also thank the staff of the Bahir Dar City Bureau for Labour and Social Affairs, who shared gut-wrenching stories of workers they had assisted in the past. Thanks moreover to President Shimilis of the East Gojjam High Court and Biniam Yohannes, who gave kind guidance and critical support in Debre Markos.

Geke, Tamrat, Qidis, Semay, Tejitu, and Temesgen provided a soft landing and a home full of warmth and creativity on return trips to Addis Ababa. Teklemuz Gebreselassie offered a vital helping hand in the capital. I am also indebted to the Federal Supreme Court research department, especially Asrat Mamuye, who helped me dig out unpublished cassation decisions.

I also thank my friends and interlocutors within the Chinese community in Ethiopia for their continued trust, support, and companionship over a decade that saw the geopolitical mood harden.

My 2020 research was conducted as part of the European Research Council–funded China, Law, and Development project at the University of Oxford (grant no. 803763).

I thank Matthew Erie for bringing me on board and for his attentive support. I am also grateful to my former colleagues Irna Hofman and Do Hai Ha. Sharing an office with the project administrator, Vicky Hayman, was a real pleasure.

This book was in many ways conceived during my doctoral research in Ethiopia in 2011 and 2012, when a spike in litigation surprised me as much as the Chinese managers with whom I worked. I returned to Ethiopia in 2017 to try to find out why Ethiopians of all walks of life sue Chinese firms and what the courts do for them. This field research was enabled by the Leverhulme Trust (ECF-2015-696) and, in 2019, by a British Academy/ Leverhulme Small Grant (SRG1819-190625). During my 2019 research trip, the support of Sitelbenat Hassen, then dean of Dire Dawa University's College of Law, and Gizachew Girma, lecturer at Dire Dawa University and founder of the Access to Justice Project there, was indispensable.

The China Centre writing group, including Pamela Hunt and Gordon Barrett, Coraline Jortay, Aoife Cantrill, Annabella Mei Massey, Beth Smith Rosser, Giulia Falato, and others who joined over the years, offered the peer support and companionship vital to seeing a book project through to the end. We moved online when most of us went on to greener pastures and have continued writing together from a distance.

During lockdown in 2021, I shared a virtual office space with Graeme Ward. His dry humor and listening ear made the daily writing process less lonely.

In 2022, I joined the Baldy Center at the University at Buffalo for a one-year fellowship. Samantha Barbas, Mekonnen Firew Ayano, Caroline Funk, and Amanda Benzin kindly accommodated my stay. Tian Xu, Yige Dong, Yan Liu, and Irus Braverman made cold and icy Buffalo a warm and welcome home.

I have been fortunate to find informal mentors in David Engel and Lynette Chua. They brought a wonderful group of young scholars together in Singapore and have generously supported us over the years. At the Asian Law and Society workshops they organized at the National University of Singapore, Kwai Hang Ng and Mary Gallagher provided a critical sounding board for early ideas. Rosie Harding and Ayako Hirata commented on a paper that became the foundation of this book.

Over the years, many colleagues and friends read one or more chapters and provided thoughtful comments: Mekonnen Firew Ayano, Darren Byler, Mingwei Huang, Sida Liu, David Matyas, Till Mostowlansky, Pál Nyíri, Fernanda Pirie, Cheryl Mei-ting Schmitz, Graeme Smith, Freek van der Vet, and Ina Zharkevich.

Maria Repnikova, my brilliant, driven, and inspiring writing companion, continued to push and pull on my thinking as this project took shape.

At Oxford, the book benefited greatly from the lunchtime seminar organized by David Pratten. I thank him and other colleagues who attended the workshop, including Elizabeth Ewart, Inge Daniels, David Gellner, Dominic Martin, José María Valenzuela, and Jingsi Wang for their thoughtful feedback. This book was also nurtured by stimulating conversations with smart friends. I thank Annelien Bouland, Jin-ho Chung, Ding Fei, Shilla Lee, Fernanda Pirie, Willy Sier, Amanuel Tesfaye, Hannah Theaker, Denise van der Kamp, Biao Xiang, Chigusa Yamaura, Ina Zharkevich, Ruiyi Zhu, and my colleagues of the Northeast Africa Forum: Jason Mosley, Biruk Terrefe, Angela Raven Roberts, and many others.

I also gained much from the critical and constructive engagement of workshop and conference participants at the University of Toronto, Yale University, the University of Edinburgh, the University of Bayreuth, the University of Liège, and the London School of Economics and Political Science. I thank Tim Oakes, Vivien Chang, Benedito Machava, Sandhya Fuchs, Tom McNamara, Jana Hönke, Yifan Yang, Sophie Andreetta, Sara Dezalay, and Yuezhou Yang for inviting me to share my work. Special thanks to Christopher Lee for his advice to appreciate African agency, even if it is forced into tight corners; to Tobias Kelly, who made me realize that state functionaries can be the main nemesis of the court; and to Elisa Gambino for her encouragement to dig deeper.

I had the privilege and pleasure of working with Maura Roessner at the University of California Press. Her infectious enthusiasm and superb professionalism made the publication process smooth and enjoyable. Thank you to Nora Becker and Sam Warren for being fantastic editorial assistants. I am also grateful to Jan Borrie and Hannah Varacalli for the fabulous copyediting and to the Bodleian Libraries and Martin Davis for the generous assistance with rendering the maps. To the three anonymous reviewers for the press, thank you for helping me see what I had written in a clearer light while pointing out the project's weaknesses and drawing out its strengths.

Finally, it is with great joy that I thank my family, without whom this project would have never come to fruition. I am especially grateful to my parents for their gentle and unpressured interest in the progress of this book.

I met my partner, Max, when the manuscript of this book was beginning to gather dust on my shelf. He gently encouraged me to pick it up again, continue where I had—disheartened—left off, and see it through to its completion. I am truly blessed to have him in my life.

APPENDIX

ETHIOPIAN LAWS CITED

Arbitration and Conciliation Working Procedure, Proclamation No. 1237/2021
Civil Code of Ethiopia, Proclamation No. 165/1960
Civil Procedure Code of Ethiopia, Proclamation No. 52/1965
Constitution of the Federal Democratic Republic of Ethiopia, Proclamation No. 1/1995
Criminal Code of the Federal Democratic Republic of Ethiopia, Proclamation No. 242/2004
Criminal Procedure Code of Ethiopia, Proclamation No. 185/1961
Federal Advocacy Service Licensing and Registration Proclamation No. 199/2000
Federal Advocacy Service Licensing and Administration Proclamation No. 1249/2021
Federal Courts Proclamation No. 25/1996
Federal Courts Proclamation No. 1234/2021
Investment Proclamation No. 1180/2020
Labour Proclamation No. 377/2003
Labour Proclamation No. 1156/2019

ETHIOPIAN CASES CITED

Abadir Abdulsemed and Tesfahun Abibual v. Konso Yabelo Asphalt Road Construction Company, Federal Supreme Court, Case No. 132133, 2009 [Gregorian calendar 2017].
Afrikawit Building Contractors Association v. Indris Ali, Federal Supreme Court, Cassation Decision No. 42075, Volume 8, 2001 [Gregorian calendar, 2008].
Amhara Regional State v. Li Benli, Amhara Supreme Court, Case No. 2015812, 2010 [Gregorian calendar, 2018].
Biniyam Geremew v. China Road and Bridge Corporation, Federal Supreme Court, Case No. 20416, 2000 [Gregorian calendar, 2007].

CCCC v. Ashenafi Hailemariam, Federal Supreme Court, Cassation Decision No. 136572, 2009 [Gregorian calendar, 2017].

CCCC v. Fisiha Tekle-Medhin, South Eastern Zone High Court (Tigray), Case No. 11734, 2011 [Gregorian calendar, 2018].

CCECC (Mieso-Dewele Railway Project Company) v. Tewodros Weldeyesus, Federal Supreme Court, Cassation Decision No. 176552, 2012 [Gregorian calendar, 2020].

Fisiha Tekle-Medhin v. CCCC, Hintalo Wajirat Wereda Court, Case No. 07603, 2011 [Gregorian calendar, 2018].

Fisiha Tekle-Medhin v. CCCC, Tigray Supreme Court, Case No. 111429, 2011 [Gregorian calendar, 2018].

Mulugeta Gebremedhin/Milano Hotel v. Huawei Technologies Ethiopia, Tigray Supreme Court, Case No. 75201, 2009 [Gregorian calendar, 2017].

Professor Reda Tekle-Haymanot v. Semeneh Tefera, Federal Supreme Court, Cassation Decision No. 45984, Volume 9, 2002 [Gregorian calendar, 2010].

Tamru Belay v. CCCC, Hintalo Wajirat Wereda Court, Case No. 06358, 2009 [Gregorian calendar, 2017].

Weldehib Gebre-Hiwet v. CCCC, Hintalo Wajirat Wereda Court, Case No. 05544, 2008 [Gregorian calendar, 2016].

KENYAN CASES CITED

Abigael Jepkosgei Yator and Ann Cheruto v. China Hanan [sic] International Co. Ltd., Employment and Labour Relations Court of Kenya at Eldoret, Case No. 136, 2018

China Wu Yi v. Edermann Property, Ze Yun Yang, and Jing Zhang, High Court at Nairobi, Civil Case No. 362, 2012

Joseph Aura v. China Jiangxi International (K) Limited, Employment and Labour Relations Court of Kenya at Kericho, Case No. 267, 2015

Kenya Union of Road Contractors and Civil Engineering Workers v. China Railway No. 5 Engineering Group, Employment and Labour Relations Court at Nairobi, Case No. E233, 2022

Lawrence Karani Njagi v. China Railway Engineering Group No. 10, Employment and Labour Relations Court of Kenya at Kericho, Case No. 27, 2017

FOREIGN LAW

Foreign Sovereign Immunities Act (FSIA), United States, 1976
State Immunity Act, United Kingdom, 1978
Employment Act, Kenya, 2007

INTERNATIONAL AGREEMENTS, TREATIES, AND CONVENTIONS

Anglo-Ethiopian Agreement, 1942
Anglo-Ethiopian Agreement, 1944
Bilateral Investment Treaty between China and Ethiopia, 1998
New York Arbitration Convention on the Recognition and Enforcement of Foreign Arbitral Awards, New York, 1958
OAU (Organization of African Unity) Charter, 1963

INTRODUCTION

1. The information is drawn from the case file of *Amhara Regional State v. Li Benli*, Amhara Supreme Court, Case No. 2015812, 2010 [Gregorian calendar, 2018].

2. The prosecutor charged Li with violating Article 354.3 of Ethiopia's *Criminal Code*, regarding homicide by negligence "where the criminal has negligently caused the death of two or more persons or where he has deliberately infringed express rules and regulations disregarding that such consequences may follow or even where he has put himself in a state of irresponsibility by taking drugs or alcohol."

3. *Amhara Regional State v. Li Benli*, Amhara Supreme Court, Case No. 2015812, 2010 [Gregorian calendar, 2018].

4. I do not know this for certain. I assume this to be the case because it happened in two dozen similar cases I recorded during fieldwork in Ethiopia. Serving as patrons, Chinese state firms in Africa often step in to prevent prosecution. See Yang, "Following the State-Owned Enterprises."

5. There are two reasons Li could have been denied bail: First, the prosecution demanded what the Ethiopian *Criminal Code* and *Criminal Procedure Code* describe as "rigorous imprisonment," in which case bail is not allowed; second, the bail applicant, Li, was not likely to comply with the conditions laid out in the bail bond. A federal court judge explained to me that he did not allow bail to foreign nationals for this reason. See Ethiopia's *Criminal Procedure Code*, Chapter 3 ("Bail"), Art. 63 and 67.

6. *Merriam-Webster Dictionary*, "Immunity." Roberto Esposito draws an interesting analogy between medical immunity and political immunity. See Esposito, *Immunitas*, and "Community, Immunity, and Biopolitics."

7. Many scholars have written about the principle of diplomatic immunity and its challenges. See, among others, Brown, "Diplomatic Immunity"; Ross, "Rethinking Diplomatic Immunity"; Vark, "Personal Inviolability and Diplomatic Immunity in Respect of Serious

Crimes." For a discussion of immunity in the Ethiopian context, see Gerbi, "Immunities and Privileges of UN Agencies in Ethiopia"; Tirfesa, "The Right of Access to Justice and Diplomatic Immunity in Ethiopia."

8. As an international legal doctrine, foreign sovereign immunity protects states from being sued in the courts of other countries. Since the 1970s, laws such as the 1976 US Foreign Sovereign Immunities Act (FSIA) and the 1978 UK State Immunity Act have established the commercial exception to the principle of sovereign immunity, allowing states to be sued in the courts of other countries when they engage in private commercial transactions.

9. Potts, *Judicial Territory*.

10. Potts, *Judicial Territory*; Yoon, "When the Sovereign Contracts." I will elaborate on these popular debates in the next chapter.

11. Schmitt, *Political Theology*.

12. Hobbes, *Leviathan*; Agamben, in *Homo Sacer*, also paints the sovereign as absolute.

13. Pang Laikwan makes a similar argument in her analysis of the logics of Chinese sovereignty, showing that sovereignty cannot be complete; see Pang, *One and All*.

14. See, among others, Bryant and Hatay, *Sovereignty Suspended*; Darian-Smith, *Bridging Divides*; Dzenovska, "Good Enough Sovereign, Or on Land as Property and Territory in Latvia."

15. See, among others, Cattelino, *High Stakes*; Chalfin, *Neoliberal Frontiers*; Dennison, "Entangled Sovereignties."

16. Ong, *Neoliberalism as Exception*, and "Graduated Sovereignty in South-East Asia."

17. See, among others, Pavel, *Divided Sovereignty*; Roitman, *Fiscal Disobedience*.

18. See, among others, Hansen, "Sovereignty in a Minor Key"; Hansen and Stepputat, "Sovereignty Revisited"; Fei, "Flexible Sovereignty and Contested Legality."

19. Humphrey, "Sovereignty."

20. Humphrey, "Sovereignty"; Simpson, *Mohawk Interruptus*.

21. Interview with judge, Bahir Dar, Amhara, October 24, 2020.

22. Interview with judge, Shire, Tigray, July 24, 2020.

23. Interview with judge, Dire Dawa, May 20, 2020.

24. Immunity would be a legally established exemption from legal process and prosecution.

25. The most important bilateral agreement is the 1998 Bilateral Investment Treaty Agreement Between Ethiopia and China, which does not contain immunity clauses. Nor are Chinese litigants considered diplomats or UN workers.

26. Mauss, *The Gift*.

27. Mauss, *The Gift*.

28. Conversation with legal scholar, Mekelle, September 2, 2020.

29. Late Prime Minister Meles Zenawi goes by "Meles" in Ethiopia. "Zenawi" is his father's name.

30. Dorsett and McVeigh, *Jurisdiction*, 4.

31. Other scholars also refer to the etymology of jurisdiction, as analyzed by Émile Benveniste in *Dictionary of Indo-European Language and Society*. Also see Douzinas, "The Metaphysics of Jurisdiction," 3; Kaushal, "The Politics of Jurisdiction," 761; Richland, "Jurisdiction," 212.

32. Richland, "Hopi Tradition as Jurisdiction," 209.

33. Richland, "Hopi Tradition as Jurisdiction," 207; see also Richland, "Jurisdiction."

34. Here I take inspiration from Danilyn Rutherford, who suggested that sovereignty and sovereign power require an audience; see *Laughing at Leviathan.*

35. Mariana Valverde writes about the invisibility of jurisdictions. The technicalities of jurisdictions conceal its political nature. See Valverde, "Jurisdiction and Scale."

36. Benton, *Law and Colonial Cultures,* 10; see also Saksena, "Jousting over Jurisdiction"; Kahn, *Islands of Sovereignty.*

37. Jonas, *The Battle of Adwa;* Zewde, *A History of Modern Ethiopia.*

38. Furtado and Smith, "Ethiopia."

39. Several scholars address the question of Ethiopian agency in the country's partnership with China. See Cheru, "Emerging Southern Powers and New Forms of South–South Cooperation"; Chiyemura, "The Winds of Change in Africa–China Relations?"; Chiyemura, Gambino, and Zajontz, "Infrastructure and the Politics of State Agency"; Driessen, "Pidgin Play"; Lauria, "Chinese Financing in Ethiopia's Infrastructure Sector"; Oqubay, *Made in Africa;* Tesfaye, *China in Ethiopia.*

40. The EPRDF was made up of four political parties: the Tigray People's Liberation Front (TPLF), the Oromo People's Democratic Party (OPDP), the Amhara National Democratic Movement (ANDM), and the Southern Ethiopian People's Democratic Movement (SEPDM).

41. See, among others, Ayano, "Rural Land Registration in Ethiopia: Myths and Realities"; Lyons, "Closing the Transition"; Vaughan, "Revolutionary Democratic State-Building."

42. For instance, they suspended aid during the war between Ethiopia and Eritrea (1998–2000) and after the controversial 2005 elections. See Furtado and Smith, "Ethiopia."

43. Stiglitz, *Globalization and Its Discontents;* see also Feyissa, "Aid Negotiation." Feyissa shows how aid and its delivery were negotiated.

44. Within the agricultural sector, the bone of contention was whether land and fertilizer distribution should be privatized; see Stiglitz, *Globalization and Its Discontents.*

45. Furtado and Smith, "Ethiopia."

46. Clapham, "The Ethiopian Developmental State"; Fourie, "China's Example for Meles' Ethiopia"; Ziso, "The Political Economy of the Chinese Model in Ethiopia."

47. Driessen, *Tales of Hope, Tastes of Bitterness,* and "Chinese Workers in Ethiopia Caught Between Remaining and Returning"; Goodfellow and Huang, "Contingent Infrastructure and the Dilution of 'Chineseness'"; Lauria, "Chinese Financing in Ethiopia's Infrastructure Sector"; Yalew and Guo, "China's Belt and Road Initiative."

48. On China's involvement in high technology and telecommunications, see Fei, Samatar, and Liao, "Chinese–African Encounters in High-Tech Sectors"; Fei, "Chinese Telecommunications Companies in Ethiopia"; Gagliardone, *The Politics of Technology in Africa,* and *China and the African Internet;* Jalata, "Development Assistance from the South"; Workneh, "Chinese Multinationals in the Ethiopian Telecommunication Sector."

49. See, among others, Bräutigam and Tang, "African Shenzhen"; Chen, "The Dynamics of Chinese Private Outward Foreign Direct Investment in Ethiopia"; Fei and Liao, "Chinese Eastern Industrial Zone in Ethiopia"; Oqubay, *Made in Africa;* Oya and Schaefer, "The Politics of Labour Relations in Global Production Networks"; Tang, *Coevolutionary Pragmatism.*

50. Cook, Lu, Tugendhat, and Alemu, "Chinese Migrants in Africa"; Huang, "Rwanda Market in Addis Ababa"; Van Boekel, Schutjens, and Zoomers, "Can the Dragon Make the Lion Breathe Fire?"

51. See, among others, Buelli, "The Hands Off Ethiopia Campaign, Racial Solidarities and Intercolonial Antifascism in South Asia"; Gebrekidan, "In Defense of Ethiopia"; Fronczak, "Local People's Global Politics."

52. Fisher, "#HandsOffEthiopia."

53. Strauss, "The Past in the Present." Scholars working on China in Africa and beyond have questioned whether the nonintervention paradigm has been upheld in practice; see, for instance, Alden and Large, "On Becoming a Norms Maker"; Gonzalez-Vicente, "The Limits to China's Non-Interference Foreign Policy"; Hodzi, *The End of China's Non-Intervention Policy in Africa*; Li, *China's New World Order*; Mumuni, "China's Non-Intervention Policy in Africa."

54. Taylor, *Africa Rising?*

55. I was told about this incident in a conversation with a former judge and current university lecturer, Mekelle, January 27, 2020.

56. Meles Zenawi was president between 1991 and 1995, after which he became prime minister. He remained in office until his death in 2012.

57. Richland, "Dignity as (Self-)Determination"; Fisher, "In Search of Dignified Work."

58. These sentiments were sometimes captured by the popular notion of *Ethiopiawinet* ("Ethiopianness"). See, for instance, Chanie and Ishiyama, "Political Transition and the Rise of Amhara Nationalism in Ethiopia"; Geremew, "The Tragedy of Colonialism in a Non-Colonised Society." It should be noted that some perceive the idea and ideal of Ethiopiawinet as dominated by Amhara culture, disregarding the multinational character of the country. See Ishiyama and Basnet, "Ethnic Versus National Identity in Ethiopia." Proponents of Ethiopiawinet, however, suggest the concept is inclusive and can be taken as representing a pan-African sentiment; see Muchie, "Revisiting Ethiopiawinet!"

59. Hans Steinmüller argues that sovereignty involves not only practices of violence but also practices of care directed toward a community. Meles Zenawi's gesture can be interpreted as an expression of care that contributes to the formation of a moral community. Like dignity, sovereignty is inherently collective, grounded in the creation of a shared moral community. See Steinmüller, "Sovereignty as Care."

60. Di Nunzio, "Work, Development, and Refusal in Urban Ethiopia," and *The Art of Living*.

61. Interview with welder and mechanic, Bahir Dar, November 26, 2020.

62. Hoben, "Social Stratification in Traditional Amhara Society"; Kenaw, "The Rite of 'Footwashing' at *Abinet* Schools and Its Ethics of Humility"; Malara and Boylston, "Vertical Love."

63. Cicero, *On Duties*.

64. Kant, *Groundwork for the Metaphysics of Morals*.

65. Grossman and Trubina, "Dignity in Urban Geography"; Miller, "Reconsidering Dignity Relationally"; Forst, "The Ground of Critique."

66. Fanon, *Black Skin, White Masks*, and *The Wretched of the Earth*; Baldwin, *Collected Essays*; see also Bromell, "Democratic Indignation"; Acevedo, "Reclaiming Black Dignity."

67. Pérez, "Toward a Life with Dignity," 508; see also Pérez, *The Right to Dignity*; Di Nunzio, *The Act of Living*.

68. Krasner, *Sovereignty*.

69. Krasner, *Sovereignty*; see also Gardner, *Sovereignty Without Power*.

70. Ethiopia has also attracted investment and involvement from Turkish, Saudi Arabian, and Indian actors. Its infrastructure projects have been funded by the African Development Bank, the Organization of the Petroleum Exporting Countries, and other third parties. See, among others, Hailu, "Foreign Direct Investment (FDI) Outlook in Ethiopia"; Whitfield, Staritz, and Morris, "Global Value Chains, Industrial Policy and Economic Upgrading in Ethiopia's Apparel Sector"; Cheru, "Emerging Southern Powers and New Forms of South–South Cooperation."

71. Eric Lewis Beverley argues that supranational organizations and economic alliances often serve as instruments for advancing claims to territorial sovereignty. See Beverley, "Introduction." Whether foreign involvement and investment erode or bolster state sovereignty in Ethiopia and beyond has been a topic of debate. Tsegaye Moreda and Tom Lavers, for instance, show the Ethiopian government has harnessed agricultural investments to extend its reach in the lowland peripheries, thus expanding national sovereignty. See Lavers, "Agricultural Investment in Ethiopia"; Moreda, "Large-Scale Land Acquisitions, State Authority and Indigenous Local Communities." The use of external forces and actors to strengthen one's position resonates with Bayart's concept of "extraversion." See Bayart, *The State in Africa*.

72. The precise number of cases is, however, hard to pin down. Many court cases are heard in rural regions where Chinese enterprises carry out road, railway, electricity, telecommunication, and water supply projects, which can stretch across hundreds of miles, crossing several local and regional jurisdictions.

73. Cattelino, *High Stakes*; Dennison, "Entangled Sovereignties"; Simpson, *Mohawk Interruptus*.

74. Dennison, "Entangled Sovereignties," 684.

75. Mulugeta, *The Everyday State in Africa*, and "Everyday Conceptions of the State in Ethiopia." See also Howard, "Stable Jobs, Precarious Lives."

76. Johnson, "The Mechanics of Sovereignty"; see also Maurer, "Cyberspatial Sovereignties."

77. Darian-Smith, *Laws and Societies in Global Contexts*, 10; see also Darian-Smith and McCarty, *The Global Turn*.

78. Sara Dezaley and Sharon Weill organized a stimulating double panel on the topic for the 2022 Annual Meeting of the Law and Society Association in Lisbon.

79. Darian-Smith builds on the work of Franz von Benda-Beckmann and Keebet von Benda-Beckmann; see, for instance, their edited volume *Rules of Law and Laws of Ruling*.

80. Darian-Smith, *Laws and Societies in Global Contexts*; Darian-Smith and McCarty, *The Global Turn*.

81. Weill, "Transnational Jihadism and the Role of Criminal Judges."

82. See, among others, Cotula, Weng, Ma, and Ren, *China-Africa Investment Treaties*; Erie, "Chinese Law and Development"; Kidane, *China-Africa Dispute Settlement*, and "China's Bilateral Investment Treaties with African States in Comparative Context"; Łągiewska, "International Dispute Resolution of BRI-Related Cases."

83. Zhu, "Arbitration as the Best Option for the Settlement of China-African Trade and Investment Disputes."

84. Erie, "The Soft Power of Chinese Law," and "The New Legal Hubs"; Kanokanga, "The China-Africa Joint Arbitration Centre (CAJAC)"; Kidane, *China-Africa Dispute Settlement*.

85. Addis Ababa Chamber of Commerce and Sectoral Associations Arbitration Institute in full.

86. This estimate is based on my own small survey.

87. *Convention on the Recognition and Enforcement of Foreign Arbitral Awards* in full.

88. *Arbitration and Conciliation Working Procedure Proclamation* No. 1237/2021.

89. Zhu, "Arbitration as the Best Option for the Settlement of China-African Trade and Investment Disputes."

90. My work is inspired by studies that explore how geopolitics manifests and is embodied in everyday settings. See, among others, Lu, "Emplacing Capital"; An, Zhang, and Wang, "The Everyday Chinese Framing of Africa."

91. Schmitz, "Significant Others."

92. Sheridan, "'If You Greet Them, They Ignore You,'" 244.

93. Schmitz, "Kufala!," and "Making Friends, Building Roads."

94. See, among others, Adunbi, *Enclaves of Exception*; Appel, *The Licit Life of Capitalism*; Sawyer, *The Small Matter of Suing Chevron*.

95. Appel, *The Licit Life of Capitalism*. Appel uses the term "modularity" to describe the process; see "Offshore Work." Igor Rogelja discusses similar dynamics regarding Chinese involvement in the Balkans; see Rogelja, "Concrete and Coal."

96. Others show the limits of these attempts at disentangling. See, for instance, Adunbi, *Enclaves of Exception*; Kirsch, *Mining Capitalism*; Welker, *Enacting the Corporation*. Some scholars have looked at how kinship ties corporate activities to local communities. See, for instance, Destrée, "'We Work for the Devil'"; Shever, "Neoliberal Associations."

97. Bill Maurer describes the legal and economic dimensions of the offshore. See Maurer, "Cyberspatial Sovereignties," and "Due Diligence and 'Reasonable Man,' Offshore."

98. Sawyer, "Disabling Corporate Sovereignty in a Transnational Lawsuit," and *The Small Matter of Suing Chevron*.

99. See Driessen, *Tales of Hope, Tastes of Bitterness*, chapter 2, for more information on legal and illegal subcontracting arrangements and, more generally, the organizational structure of Chinese corporations in the road construction sector. Comparable practices exist in other parts of Africa. Jie Wang and Josh Stenberg, for instance, write about such illegal practices in Libya under Gadhafi, where subcontracting on government contracts was forbidden altogether. See Wang and Stenberg, "Localizing Chinese Migrants in Africa," 79.

100. My findings partly challenge Marc Galanter's. See Galanter, "Why the Haves Come Out Ahead."

101. Maurer, "Re-Regulating Offshore Finance."

102. On the impact of the pandemic on the lives of Chinese migrants in Ethiopia, see Fei, "Transnational Mobility and Precarity in the Shadow of Pandemics."

103. Von Pezold and Driessen, "Made in China, Fashioned in Africa."

104. Mekonnen Firew Ayano provides an insightful analysis of the debate about the postponement of the elections and the leading role of Ethiopian elite lawyers in it. See Ayano, "Lawyering on the Eve of a Civil War."

105. The Tigray War started on November 4, 2020, and officially ended upon the signing of the Pretoria Agreement on November 2, 2022. However, hostilities continue. Despite being one of the deadliest conflicts in the past decades, the war received scant international attention. Teklehaymanot G. Weldemichel argues that, apart from factors like race and

Ethiopia's geopolitically peripheral status, the Ethiopian government has been responsible for creating what he calls a "zone of invisibility" around the Tigray War. See Weldemichel, "Tigray War." For other scholarly accounts on the war, see Plaut and Vaughan, *Understanding Ethiopia's Tigray War*; Gardner, *The Abiy Project*. Erlich's *Greater Tigray and the Mysterious Magnetism of Ethiopia* and Berhe's *Laying the Past to Rest* provide critical insight into the historical context in which the conflict in Tigray unfolded.

106. See, among others, Driessen, "The African Bill," and "Migrating for the Bank."

107. All errors are my own.

108. Alone or together with Bereket or Zewdu, I interviewed thirty-eight judges, thirty lawyers, fourteen prosecutors, eight court support staff, five police officers, eight liaison officers cum facilitators who dealt with court cases and had acquainted themselves to various degrees with the law, and thirty-five Ethiopian and Chinese litigants.

109. Article 4 (Criminal Jurisdiction) of the *Federal Courts Proclamation* No. 25/1996 states that the federal courts have jurisdiction over offenses committed by and against foreign nationals. Article 5 (Civil Jurisdiction) indicates that "cases to which a foreign national is a party" are heard by the federal courts (Art. 5.4).

110. Tura, "Uniform Application of Law in Ethiopia." See also Abdo, "Review of Decisions of State Courts over State Matters by the Federal Supreme Court." Ethiopia's dual court system was introduced in the transition period (1991–94) and consolidated under the 1995 Constitution of the Federal Democratic Republic of Ethiopia. See Fiseha, "Separation of Powers and Its Implications for the Judiciary in Ethiopia."

111. In case of appeal, the first case would be brought to the cassation bench of the Amhara Supreme Court, the second to the Amhara Supreme Court, and the third to the East Gojjam High Court.

112. Guesh, *Inakhedkha M'tsbay*, 9.

113. Guesh, *Inakhedkha M'tsbay*, 9.

114. Guesh, *Inakhedkha M'tsbay*, 9.

115. Telephone conversation with Bereket Asmelash on December 28, 2020.

116. Yan and Sautman, "China, Ethiopia and the Significance of the Belt and Road Initiative."

117. Fei, "Transnational Mobility and Precarity in the Shadow of Pandemics."

1. SOVEREIGNTY AND CONTESTED CLAIMS OF IMMUNITY

1. Letter by Solomon Gebeyhu Gelew, criminal case coordinator of the zonal prosecutor's office to the North Achefer Police Office, No. 00303, November 30, 2009. Given common errors in transliteration of Chinese names into Amharic, Binzheng Zhang may not be the exact name.

2. Interview with former judge based at Liben, Bahir Dar, October 31, 2020.

3. The Blue Party (Semayawi Party) would later merge with Ethiopian Citizens for Social Justice (EZEMA).

4. Run by the Ethiopian diaspora, Ethiopian Satellite Television assumed a critical role in the spread of information among opponents of the EPRDF government and the dissemination of news about the brutalities of government forces, becoming the "voice and eyes" of protestors in Amhara and beyond. See Makahamadze and Fikade, "Popular Protests in the

Amhara Region and Political Reforms in Ethiopia, 2016–2018." As Mastewal Bitew shows, the Amhara diaspora played a critical role in fueling Amhara identity sentiment both within Ethiopia and abroad, prompting a shift from pan-Ethiopianism to Amhara nationalism; see Bitew, "Transnational Amhara Nationalism."

5. Several scholars have written about the close diplomatic partnership between Ethiopia and China and between the EPRDF and the Chinese Communist Party. See, for instance, Cabestan, "China and Ethiopia"; Tesfaye, *China in Ethiopia*.

6. See, among others, Moges, "Shaping Amhara Nationalism for a Better Ethiopia"; Tazebew, "Amhara Nationalism"; Tesfaye, "The Birth of Amhara Nationalism."

7. Makahamadze and Fikade, "Popular Protests in the Amhara Region and Political Reforms in Ethiopia, 2016–2018."

8. Conveying the spirit of resistance and unity, the name "Woyane" was first used during the Woyane Rebellion, also known as the First Woyane, in which Tigrayans countered Emperor Haile Selassie's violent attempts at centralization in 1943. The Second Woyane refers to the Ethiopian Civil War, in which the TPLF fought against the Derg regime (1974–91). The Tigray War (2020–22) has been named the Third Woyane.

9. These were largely foreign-run horticulture farms growing flowers for export, such as the Dutch Esmeralda Farms. See *Al Jazeera*, "'Foreign Firms Attacked' as Ethiopia Protests Continue."

10. In the subsequent two years, this and other incidents led to radical government reforms. See Desta, Dori, and Mihretu, *Ethiopia in the Wake of Political Reforms*.

11. It abandoned the Addis Ababa Master Plan—the controversial plan for the capital city's expansion onto surrounding Oromo lands—and took responsibility for the political crisis.

12. I learned this from interviews with a former judge based at Liben, Barhir Dar, October 31, 2020, and a police officer in Liben, December 9, 2020.

13. Many judges mentioned Chinese claims for immunity and the arguments about development assistance and investment they put forward in support of these claims.

14. Clapham, "Sovereignty and the Third World State"; Scholler, *The Special Court of Ethiopia*; Spencer, *Ethiopia at Bay*.

15. Levine, *Wax and Gold*.

16. Marsden, *The Barefoot Emperor*; Zewde, *A History of Modern Ethiopia*, and "Concessions and Concession-Hunters in Post-Adwa Ethiopia."

17. Pankhurst, "Menilek and the Utilisation of Foreign Skills in Ethiopia."

18. Pankhurst, "Menilek and the Utilisation of Foreign Skills in Ethiopia."

19. Jonas, *The Battle of Adwa*.

20. Pankhurst, "Menilek and the Utilisation of Foreign Skills in Ethiopia," 46.

21. Pankhurst, "Menilek and the Utilisation of Foreign Skills in Ethiopia," 51–52.

22. UK Foreign Office, Diplomatic correspondence 401/10, Thomas Hohler, June 28, 1907.

23. UK Foreign Office, Diplomatic correspondence 401/8, John Lane Harrington, August 6, 1905.

24. Scholler, *The Special Court of Ethiopia*.

25. Perham, *The Government of Ethiopia*.

26. Sedler, "The Chilot Jurisdiction of the Emperor of Ethiopia."

27. Pankhurst, "Menilek and the Utilisation of Foreign Skills in Ethiopia."

28. UK Foreign Office, Diplomatic correspondence 401/10, Thomas Hohler, October 2, 1907.

29. Brown, "The Precarious Life and Slow Death of the Mixed Courts of Egypt"; Brinton, "The Mixed Courts of Egypt"; Hoyle, *Mixed Courts of Egypt*.

30. Scholler, *The Special Court of Ethiopia*.

31. See correspondence in United States Foreign Relations, "Ethiopia: Proposed Revision of Basic Treaty Governing Ethiopian Relations with Foreign Powers," Volume II, 1931, 217–36.

32. The case is described by Scholler, *The Special Court of Ethiopia*, 86–87.

33. Perham, *The Government of Ethiopia*.

34. Feyissa, "European Extraterritoriality in Semicolonial Ethiopia"; Ruskola, *Legal Orientalism*.

35. The Minister in Ethiopia (Southard) to the Secretary of State, Letter No. 746, Addis Ababa, June 17, 1931, 884.512 Consumption/19, *Foreign Relations*, 1931, Volume II, 223.

36. See diplomatic correspondence in the 1930s, such as United States Foreign Relations, "Ethiopia: Proposed Revision of Basic Treaty Governing Ethiopian Relations with Foreign Powers," Volume II, 1931, 217–36.

37. Fanta, "The British on the Ethiopian Bench"; Feyissa, "European Extraterritoriality in Semicolonial Ethiopia."

38. British War Cabinet, *Minutes 9(41)*, January and February 1941, 45.

39. Cited in Fanta, "The British on the Ethiopian Bench," 71.

40. Feyissa, "European Extraterritoriality in Semicolonial Ethiopia"; Vestal, "Consequences of the British Occupation of Ethiopia During World War II."

41. Feyissa, "European Extraterritoriality in Semicolonial Ethiopia."

42. 1944 Anglo-Ethiopian Agreement, Art. 4, cited in Perham, *The Government of Ethiopia*, 475.

43. Perham, *The Government of Ethiopia*.

44. Fanta, "The British on the Ethiopian Bench."

45. Fanta, "The British on the Ethiopian Bench," 68.

46. Feyissa, "European Extraterritoriality in Semicolonial Ethiopia."

47. Weldesellassie, "The Prosecution of the Derg Criminals in Ethiopia."

48. Agegnehu, "Some Thoughts on the Organization of Legal Practice in Ethiopia."

49. *Federal Advocacy Service Licensing and Registration Proclamation No. 199/2000*.

50. *Federal Advocacy Service Licensing and Administration Proclamation No. 1249/2021*, Arts 6.1a and 8.

51. This new form of dependence has been discussed by, among others, Adem, *Africa's Quest for Modernity*; Tarrósy, "China's Belt and Road Initiative in Africa, Debt Risk and New Dependency"; and Taylor and Zajontz, "In a Fix." For comprehensive overviews of Ethiopia–China relations, see Adem, *Africa's Quest for Modernity*; Mulualem, *Africa–China Relations*; and Tesfaye, *China in Ethiopia*.

52. Chinese state-owned companies have been at the forefront of China's economic internationalization since the "going out" policy, announced as a national strategy in 2000. See, among others, Leutert, *China's State-Owned Enterprises*; Xu, "Chinese State-Owned Enterprises in Africa"; Zhang, "The Aid-Contracting Nexus." In Africa, provincial SOEs

play an important role alongside national SOEs; see Lam, *China's State Owned Enterprises in West Africa*; Shi and Hoebink, "From Chengdu to Kampala."

53. See, among others, Driessen, *Tales of Hope, Tastes of Bitterness*; Fei, "The Compound Labor Regime of Chinese Construction Projects in Ethiopia"; Goodfellow and Huang, "Contingent Infrastructure and the Dilution of 'Chineseness'"; Lauria, "Chinese Financing in Ethiopia's Infrastructure Sector."

54. Lauria, "Chinese Financing in Ethiopia's Infrastructure Sector."

55. See, among others, Bräutigam, Tang, and Xia, "What Kind of Chinese 'Geese' Are Flying to Africa?"; Fei and Liao, "Chinese Eastern Industrial Zone in Ethiopia"; Oqubay, *Made in Africa*; Tang, *Coevolutionary Pragmatism*.

56. Driessen, *Tales of Hope, Tastes of Bitterness*.

57. Interview with Ethiopian trader, Addis Ababa, July 7, 2017, partly quoted in Driessen, "Laughing About Corruption in Ethiopian–Chinese Encounters," 914.

58. This figure is taken from the Chinese Loans to Africa Database, run by the Boston University Global Development Policy Center. While the total amount stands at 14.5 billion US dollars, the number of loans is sixty-six as of 2025.

59. Fourie, "China's Example for Meles' Ethiopia."

60. Clapham, "The Ethiopian Developmental State"; Lavers, *Ethiopia's "Developmental State."*

61. *Constitution of the Federal Democratic Republic of Ethiopia*, Art. 39.1 states: "Every Nation, Nationality and People in Ethiopia has an unconditional right to self-determination, including the right to secession."

62. See, for instance, Aalen, *The Politics of Ethnicity in Ethiopia*; Donham, *Marxist Modern*; Turton (ed.), *Ethnic Federalism*; Zeleke, *Ethiopia in Theory*.

63. Borago, "What Is the Point in Amhara Nationalism?" On ethnic federalism and the challenges and criticism it faced, see Amare, *Ethnic Federalism in Ethiopia*; Fessha, *Ethnic Diversity and Federalism*; Gedamu, *The Politics of Contemporary Ethiopia*; Kefale, *Federalism and Ethnic Conflict in Ethiopia*.

64. Clapham, "The Ethiopian Developmental State"; Lavers, *Ethiopia's "Developmental State."*

65. Oqubay, *Made in Africa*.

66. Lavers, *Ethiopia's "Developmental State."*

67. United Nations Conference on Trade and Development, *World Investment Report 2022*.

68. Much has been written about China's overseas SEZs and FTZs. See, among others, Adunbi, *Enclaves of Exception*; Mohan, "Beyond the Enclave"; Nyíri, "Enclaves of Improvement." For Ethiopia's SEZs, see, among others, Bräutigam and Tang, "African Shenzhen"; Fei and Liao, "Chinese Eastern Industrial Zone in Ethiopia"; Giannecchini and Taylor, "The Eastern Industrial Zone in Ethiopia"; Tang, "Lessons from East Asia."

69. Tian, "Private Security Companies."

70. Gonzalez-Vicente, "Varieties of Capital and Predistribution"; Rogelja, "Concrete and Coal."

71. Here I take inspiration from Gonzalez-Vicente, "Make Development Great Again?"

72. Adunbi, *Enclaves of Exception*.

73. Ong, *Neoliberalism as Exception*.

74. Rogelja, "Concrete and Coal"; Gonzalez-Vicente, "Make Development Great Again?" Owing to the support they enjoy from the central government, Chinese state firms have been effective and efficient in insulating themselves from local jurisdictions. This is not to say that the interests of state firms and the diplomatic branches of government always align. As Min Ye illustrates, due to fragmentation, the state organs that deal with China's external relations, the Ministry of Foreign Affairs and the Ministry of Commerce, have little sway over corporations that report to the State Assets Supervision and Administration Council (SASAC) and are subject to the power of the National Development and Reform Commission (NDRC). See Ye, *The Belt Road and Beyond*, 10. See also Zhang and Smith, "China's Foreign Aid System."

75. See, among others, Bräutigam and Tang, "African Shenzhen"; Fei and Liao, "Chinese Eastern Industrial Zone."

76. Adunbi, *Enclaves of Exception*.

77. Adunbi, *Enclaves of Exception*, 76.

78. Erie, "The Soft Power of Chinese Law."

79. Potts, *Judicial Territory*.

80. *Buyer Credit Loan Agreement for the Kenya Mombasa–Nairobi Standard Gauge Railway Project*, signed between the Export–Import Bank of China and the government of the Republic of Kenya, Contract No. 1410302052014210766, 2014 [hereinafter *China–Kenya Buyer Credit Loan Agreement*]; *Preferential Buyer Credit Loan Agreement for the Kenya Mombasa–Nairobi Standard Gauge Railway Project*, signed between the government of the Republic of Kenya and the Export–Import Bank of China, Contract No. 1420303052014210788, 2014 [hereinafter *China–Kenya Preferential Buyer Credit Loan Agreement*].

81. *China–Kenya Buyer Credit Loan Agreement*, Article 15.5, states: "Furthermore, pursuant to the provisions of the Government Proceedings Act, Chapter 40 of the Laws of Kenya (the 'Government Proceedings Act'), this Agreement had the transactions contemplated thereby constitute commercial activities (rather than Governmental or public activities) of Kenya Government which is subject to private commercial law with respect thereto and Kenya Government shall waive any immunity in relation to this Agreement, subject to the provisions applicable to the Government of Kenya under the Government Proceedings Act."

82. *China–Kenya Buyer Credit Loan Agreement*, Art. 15.1.

83. *China–Kenya Buyer Credit Loan Agreement*, Art. 15.5.

84. Kimari, "'Under Construction'"; Taylor, "Kenya's New Lunatic Express." Chinese law governs many loan agreements signed between the Export–Import Bank of China and African governments. See *Financial Times*, "China Applies Brakes to Africa Lending." I have not been able to access loan agreements signed by the bank with the Ethiopian government and do not know whether these contain a comparable governing law clause.

85. *The Guardian* (Nigeria), "China-Backed Railway Agreement Puts Kenya's Sovereignty at Risk"; Okoth, "SGR Pact with China a Risk to Kenyan Sovereignty, Assets."

86. I have recorded two dozen cases in which a Chinese national was pardoned for homicide—in most cases, homicide by negligence.

87. Interview with former judge at Liben, Bahir Dar, October 31, 2020. This entire section draws on this interview.

88. For details on the history of the Tana Beles project, see Fantini et al., "Salini."

89. The project was renamed from Tana-Beles to Beles Multipurpose Project to mark the start of a new phase of construction; see Fantini et al., "Salini."

90. *Criminal Code of the Federal Democratic Republic of Ethiopia*, Art. 534.

91. Although workers generally spoke positively of Salini when drawing comparisons with Chinese enterprises, they could also be critical of the Italian firm in other situations.

92. Interview with the Chief of Police, Liben, December 9, 2020.

93. Interview with the victim's mother and grandfather, Liben, December 9, 2020.

94. Interview with federal court judge formerly based in Dire Dawa, Mekelle, May 20, 2020.

95. Interview with state public prosecutor, Bahir Dar, October 26, 2020.

96. Interview with state public prosecutor, Bahir Dar, October 26, 2020.

97. Interview with state public prosecutor, Bahir Dar, October 26, 2020.

98. Judges, prosecutors, and lawyers mentioned incidents in which the Ministry of Foreign Affairs intervened, usually by way of a cryptic instruction or order by telephone.

2. THE ETHIOPIAN PLAINTIFFS: "EVEN THE LAW SAW IT AND SMILED"

1. Interview with crane operator, Bahir Dar, November 24, 2020.

2. Interview with crane operator, Bahir Dar, November 24, 2020.

3. Interview with crane operator, Bahir Dar, November 24, 2020; see also interview with welder and mechanic, Bahir Dar, November 26, 2020; and interview with interpreter, Mekelle, June 16, 2020.

4. Di Nunzio, *The Act of Living*; Mains, *Hope Is Cut*.

5. Robinson, *Black Marxism*. For recent ethnographies on racial capitalism, see, among others, Amrute, *Encoding Race, Encoding Class*; Appel, *The Licit Life of Capitalism*; Byler, *Terror Capitalism*; Hendriks, *Rainforest Capitalism*; Huang, *Reconfiguring Racial Capitalism*.

6. For insightful studies on how Chinese engagement in Africa builds on and perpetuates structures of inequality and dynamics of dispossession, see Huang, *Reconfiguring Racial Capitalism*; Kimari and Ernstson, "Imperial Remains and Imperial Invitations"; Zhang, "Burn to Harvest, Burn to Sabotage."

7. Ke-Schutte, *Angloscene*; Sheridan, "The Semiotics of Heiren (黑人)."

8. Franquesa, *Power Struggles*.

9. The dynamics between Ethiopian laborers and Chinese managers described in this chapter strongly resonate with those identified by Robert Wyrod and Kimberlee Chang in Uganda. See Wyrod and Chang, "Tensions in Sino-African Labour Relations."

10. Bernadette Atuahene explores the process of dehumanization in "dignity takings," state-driven appropriations of property that are accompanied by the dehumanization and infantilization of its owners; see *We Want What's Ours*, and "Dignity Takings and Dignity Restoration."

11. Graeber, *Toward an Anthropological Theory of Value*.

12. Tadiar, *Remaindered Life*.

13. Richland, "Dignity as (Self-)Determination"; Atuahene, *We Want What's Ours*, and "Dignity Takings and Dignity Restoration."

14. Di Nunzio, *The Act of Living*.

15. Mains, *Under Construction*, and "Blackouts and Progress."

16. Many socio-legal scholars have written about the transformation of disputes when or after they are brought to court. See, among others, Ewick and Silbey, *The Common Place of Law*; Merry, *Getting Justice and Getting Even*.

17. Ethiopian real wages have hit a historic low in recent years, which was partly the reason for a wave of strikes that has affected Ethiopia's manufacturing and horticulture sectors since 2017 and contributed to the growing assertiveness of the Confederation of Ethiopian Trade Unions, as documented by Samuel Andreas Admasie in "Amid Political Recalibrations." More recently, the war and ongoing ethnic strife have had a significant impact on the trade union movement. See Admasie, "Trade Union Resurgence in Ethiopia."

18. Interview with crane operator, Bahir Dar, November 24, 2020.

19. Interview with HR manager and facilitator, Mekelle, June 26, 2020.

20. Compare with similar situations in other African contexts; see, among others, Liu, "(Mis)communicating Through Conflicts"; Schmitz, "Kufala!"; Sheridan, "'If You Greet Them, They Ignore You'"; Wu, *Affective Encounters*.

21. Driessen, "Pidgin Play." For contact languages that emerged on Chinese construction sites in other parts of Africa, see Haruyama, "Shortcut English"; Franceschini, "'You Walawala Too Much!'"

22. Schmitz, "Kufala!"

23. Wu, *Affective Encounters*.

24. Interview with HR manager and facilitator, Mekelle, June 26, 2020.

25. Interview with HR manager and facilitator, Mekelle, June 26, 2020.

26. Interview with HR manager and facilitator, Mekelle, June 26, 2020.

27. Interview with HR manager and facilitator, Mekelle, June 26, 2020.

28. Many scholars have written about the notion of face, or *mianzi*, in China. See, for instance, Kipnis, "The Language of Gifts"; Smart, "Gifts, Bribes, and Guanxi"; Yang, *Gifts, Favors, and Banquets*; Yan, *The Flow of Gifts*.

29. Interview with crane operator, Bahir Dar, November 24, 2020.

30. Pankhurst, "Introduction."

31. Mains, *Hope Is Cut*; also see Di Nunzio, *The Act of Living*, for insight into the relationship between status and employment or income generation in urban Ethiopia.

32. Mains, *Hope Is Cut*, chapter 4. On the significance of *yilugnta*, see also Heinonen, *Youth Gangs and Street Children*.

33. Interview with interpreter, Mekelle, June 16, 2020.

34. Interview with interpreter, Mekelle, June 16, 2020.

35. Interview with welder and mechanic, Bahir Dar, November 26, 2020.

36. Interview with welder and mechanic, Bahir Dar, November 26, 2020.

37. Interview with welder and mechanic, Bahir Dar, November 26, 2020.

38. Hoben, "Social Stratification in Traditional Amhara Society"; Kenaw, "The Rite of 'Footwashing' at *Abinet* Schools and Its Ethics of Humility"; Malara and Boylston, "Vertical Love."

39. Wu, *Affective Encounters*.

40. As Malara and Boylston argue, hierarchical power in Ethiopian Orthodox society is not merely a coercive force. As a moral good—if ambiguously so—it coexists with and depends on asymmetrical understandings of love and care. See Malara and Boylston, "Vertical Love."

41. Sheridan, "'If You Greet Them, They Ignore You.'"

42. Interview with interpreter, Mekelle, June 16, 2020.

43. Interview with interpreter, Mekelle, June 16, 2020.

44. Interview with interpreter, Mekelle, June 16, 2020.

45. Interview with interpreter, Mekelle, June 16, 2020.

46. Mains and Mulat, "The Ethiopian Developmental State and Struggles over the Reproduction of Young Migrant Women's Labor at the Hawassa Industrial Park."

47. Interview with welder and mechanic, Bahir Dar, November 26, 2020.

48. Several ethnographic studies of Chinese involvement in Africa describe contestations over salaries and, more generally, conflictual relations between Chinese supervisors and African employees; see, for instance, Bunkenborg, Nielsen, and Pederson, *Collaborative Damage*; Lee, "Raw Encounters"; Giese and Thiel, "The Vulnerable Other"; Gukurume, "Chinese Migrants and the Politics of Everyday Life in Zimbabwe"; Nielsen, "Roadside Inventions." Even though wages are contested and considered low, they are not significantly different from those paid by local companies, as shown by Oya and Schaefer in "Do Chinese Firms in Africa Pay Lower Wages?"

49. Several detailed studies show the complexities of begging and its connotations in Ethiopia, including Abebe, "Begging as a Livelihood Pathway of Street Children in Addis Ababa"; Di Nunzio, *The Act of Living*; Heinonen, *Youth Gangs and Street Children*.

50. Interview with three staff members of the Bureau for Labor and Social Affairs, Bahir Dar, November 5, 2020.

51. Interview with three staff members of the Bureau for Labor and Social Affairs, Bahir Dar, November 5, 2020.

52. Waldron, "How Law Protects Dignity."

53. Mitta, "Labor Rights, Working Conditions, and Workers' Power in the Emerging Textile and Apparel Industries in Ethiopia"; Oya and Schaefer, "The Politics of Labour Relations in Global Production Networks."

54. Hardy and Hauge, "Labour Challenges in Ethiopia's Textile and Leather Industries"; Mains and Mulat, "The Ethiopian Developmental State and Struggles over the Reproduction of Young Migrant Women's Labor at the Hawassa Industrial Park."

55. Chu and Fafchamps, "Labor Conflict Within Foreign, Domestic, and Chinese-Owned Manufacturing Firms in Ethiopia"; Huang, Huang, and Mai, "China-Africa Encounter and Worker Resistance."

56. Andreetta, "The Symbolic Power of the State: Inheritance Disputes and Litigants' Judicial Trajectories in Cotonou."

57. See, for instance, Workneh, "From State Repression to Fear of Non-State Actors," and Moges, "Ethiopian Journalism from Self-Censoring to Silence." In her fascinating study on China's soft power in Ethiopia, Maria Repnikova discusses Chinese involvement in the country's media sector; see Repnikova, *Competing for Soft Power*.

58. Galanter, "Why the Haves Come Out Ahead."

59. This stems partially from what Michele Statz terms "judicial intimacy" in the context of rural Wisconsin and Minnesota, where judges share, or can directly relate to, the hardships of poor litigants; see "On Shared Suffering."

60. The cassation decisions that appear in these annual volumes are only a fraction of the number entertained by this court, and this is not necessarily the first case appealed to the court.

61. *Biniyam Geremew v. China Road and Bridge Corporation*, Federal Supreme Court, Case No. 20416, 2000 [Gregorian calendar, 2007].

62. In its judgment, it stated: "The plaintiff has the right to obtain all the payments listed in the Labor Law. When we say that a worker has a right under the Labor Law, it is not erroneous to allow the applicant to amend their pleading when this amendment is necessary for rendering a just decision. A pleading is not only altered or amended to clarify the issues of the claim, but also to give a fair decision." *Biniyam Geremew v. China Road and Bridge Corporation*, Federal Supreme Court, Case No. 20416, 2000 [Gregorian calendar, 2007].

63. Interview with interpreter, Mekelle, June 16, 2020.

64. The workers were unclear about the nature of the mistake their Chinese supervisor had made.

65. Interview with interpreter, Mekelle, June 16, 2020.

66. Interview with interpreter, Mekelle, June 16, 2020.

67. Interview with interpreter, Mekelle, June 16, 2020.

68. Interview with welder and mechanic, Bahir Dar, November 26, 2020.

69. Interview with welder and mechanic, Bahir Dar, November 26, 2020.

70. Interview with welder and mechanic, Bahir Dar, November 26, 2020; interview with crane operator, Bahir Dar, November 24, 2020.

71. Lazarus-Black, "Why Women Take Men to Magistrate's Court: Caribbean Kinship Ideology and Law."

72. Verheul, *Performing Power in Zimbabwe*.

73. *Abadir Abdulsemed and Tesfahun Abibual v. Konso Yabelo Asphalt Road Construction Company*, Federal Supreme Court, Case No. 132133, 2009 [Gregorian calendar, 2017].

74. *Abadir Abdulsemed and Tesfahun Abibual v. Konso Yabelo Asphalt Road Construction Company*, Federal Supreme Court, Case No. 132133, 2009 [Gregorian calendar, 2017].

75. *Abadir Abdulsemed and Tesfahun Abibual v. Konso Yabelo Asphalt Road Construction Company*, Federal Supreme Court, Case No. 132133, 2009 [Gregorian calendar, 2017].

76. Interview with former crane operator, Bahir Dar, November 24, 2020.

77. Lund, *Nine-Tenths of the Law*, 4.

78. McCann, *Rights at Work*.

79. Mulugeta, *The Everyday State in Africa*.

80. The Chinese firms that feature in the top ten are China Communications Construction Group (CCCC), Power Construction Corporation of China (PowerChina), China State Construction Engineering Corporation (CSCEC), and China Railway Construction Corporation (CRCC). They are all state firms.

81. Lonsdale, "Agency in Tight Corners."

3. THE CHINESE DEFENDANTS: "THE LAW IS ON THEIR SIDE"

1. Chinese male netizen, June 6, 2015.

2. Several missionaries and scholars of Ethiopia mention the litigiousness of Ethiopians, most notably Levine, *Wax and Gold*.

3. Whether Ethiopian critics would agree with this statement is a different question. Successive Ethiopian governments have been criticized for their poor democratic record.

4. Conversation with Chinese deputy project manager, Lower Omo Valley, South Ethiopia Regional State, July 27, 2017.

5. Conversation with Chinese engineer, Addis Ababa, June 25, 2019.

6. Petitioning entails going past basic-level institutions to request higher-level bodies of government hear grievances and resolve them; see, among others, O'Brien and Li, *Rightful Resistance in Rural China*. In contemporary China, the most common form of petitioning are appeals to higher authorities through "letters and visits" (*xinfang*) brought to bureaus at all levels and all types of government institutions, including the courts. The practice reflects the ability of higher-placed officials to personally intervene and solve disputes, irrespective of legal norms; see Minzner, "Xinfang." Uncomfortable with the adversarial style of China's modern legal system, citizens may prefer petitioning to litigation, even though it has not proven very effective; see Zhang, "*Zhongguoren zai xingzheng jiefen zhong weihe pianhao xinfang?* [Why do Chinese prefer to settle disputes through petitioning?]."

7. Conversation with Chinese draftsman and Chinese materials engineer, Addis Ababa, June 27, 2019.

8. Lee and Zhang, "The Power of Instability"; Li, Liu, and O'Brien, "Petitioning Beijing."

9. Interview with Chinese project manager, Addis Ababa, August 20, 2019.

10. See, among others, Chen and Li, "How Will Technology Change the Face of Chinese Justice?"; Gao, "*Rengong zhineng shidai de zhongguo sifa* [Chinese justice in the era of artificial intelligence]"; Papagianneas, "Towards Smarter and Fairer Justice?"; Wu and Chen, "*Lun zhihui fayuan de jianyi* [On the construction of smart courts]."

11. Stern et al., "Automating Fairness?"; Zheng, "China's Grand Design of People's Smart Courts."

12. Wang, "*Sifa dashuju yu rengongzheneng jishu yingyong de fengxian ji lunli guizhi* [The dangers and ethical regulation of using judicial big data and artificial intelligence technology]"; Wu and Chen, "*Lun zhihui fayuan de jianyi* [On the construction of smart courts]."

13. See, among others, Ayano, "Lawyering on the Eve of a Civil War"; Massoud, *Law's Fragile State*; Dezalay, "The African Challenge and Its Aftermath," "Lawyers in Africa," and *Lawyering Imperial Encounters*.

14. See, among others, Arce and Long, "Reconfiguring Modernity and Development from an Anthropological Perspective"; Ferguson, *The Anti-Politics Machine*; Escobar, *Encountering Development*.

15. Cheng and Liu, "Temporality and the Geopolitical Enframing of Chinese International Development Thinking." Han Cheng has traced the rise of development thinking and development studies as a discipline in China; see Cheng and Liu, "Disciplinary Geopolitics and the Rise of International Development Studies in China." (This work is primarily based on Han Cheng's PhD dissertation.)

16. Conversation with Chinese deputy project manager, Lower Omo Valley, South Ethiopia Regional State, July 27, 2017.

17. This development thinking is inspired by the idea of the separation of powers, which, as Martin Shapiro argues, exists more as an ideal than a practice; see Shapiro, *Courts*.

18. For narratives of suffering or eating bitterness in Africa, see Driessen, *Tales of Hope, Tastes of Bitterness*, chapter 7; Hanisch, *Searching for Sweetness*; Lee, *The Specter of Global China*. In her monograph *Searching for Sweetness*, Sarah Hanisch helpfully sets off narratives of suffering among Chinese female migrants in Lesotho against their hopes, dreams, and search for sweetness.

19. Interview with Chinese interpreter and deputy manager, Mehoni, Tigray, March 8, 2012.

20. Sheridan, "Weak Passports and Bad Behavior."

21. Interview with Chinese engineer, Addis Ababa, July 14, 2019.

22. Dobler, "Chinese Shops and the Formation of a Chinese Expatriate Community in Namibia"; Schmitz, "Making Friends, Building Roads"; Schmitz, "Significant Others."

23. Sheridan, "Weak Passports and Bad Behavior."

24. The project manager's narrative resonates with a broader sense of victimization felt among Chinese communities across Africa. For an insightful analysis of these dynamics, see Huang, *Reconfiguring Racial Capitalism*, chapter 5.

25. Interview with Chinese project manager, Addis Ababa, July 7, 2019.

26. Sheridan, "Weak Passports and Bad Behavior," 138. Several scholars discuss the vulnerability of Chinese migrants in Africa, mostly at the hands of local police, customs officers, and other state functionaries. See, among others, An, "Narrating China-Africa Relations"; Dobler, "Chinese Shops and the Formation of a Chinese Expatriate Community in Namibia"; Giese and Thiel, "The Vulnerable Other"; Haugen and Carling, "On the Edge of the Chinese Diaspora"; Lam, "Chinese Adaptations"; Wang, "'Hurdles' or 'Lubricants'"; Xiao, "In the Shadow of the State"; Zi, *Iron Sharpens Iron*.

27. Interview with judge, Bahir Dar, October 23, 2020.

28. Interview with judge, Bahir Dar, October 23, 2020.

29. Interview with judge, Bahir Dar, October 23, 2020.

30. Interview with judge, Bahir Dar, October 23, 2020.

31. Conversation with Chinese engineer, Lower Omo Valley, South Ethiopia Regional State, July 27, 2017.

32. Yeh, *Taming Tibet*; see also Yeh and Wharton, "Going West, Going Out."

33. Ewick and Silbey, *The Common Place of Law*.

34. Interview with former Ethiopian interpreter based in Debre Markos, Amhara, December 15, 2020.

35. Chinese translations of Ethiopian laws already circulated when I first conducted field research in Ethiopia in 2011. Some Chinese business associations may also provide translations of local laws. These associations often set up information-sharing platforms for migrants that can also be used to disseminate legal information; see Li and Shi, "Home Away from Home." Civil association leaders, also branded as *qiaoling* in China's official discourse, are critical mediators that assist newcomers in the diaspora to navigate the local regulatory environment, at times by circumventing the law; see Chen, "Harden the Hardline, Soften the Softline," and "Harnessing the Sending State."

36. Interview with former Ethiopian in-house council based in Abala Mekelle, June 9, 2020.

37. Driessen, "Trails of Trustworthiness Between Ethiopian Lawyers and Chinese Clients."

38. Interviews with in-house counsel, Arba Minch, May 16 and 20, 2020.

39. *CCCC v. Ashenafi Hailemariam*, Federal Supreme Court, Cassation Decision No. 136572, 2009 [Gregorian calendar, 2017].

40. The Zone 2 High Court rejected the appeal based on Article 337 of Ethiopia's Civil Procedure Code: "Where the appellant states in his memorandum of appeal that he bases his appeal entirely on the record of the original hearing and does not apply for permission

to call additional evidence, the Appellate Court may, after fixing a day for hearing the appellant or his pleader and hearing him accordingly on that day, dismiss such appeal without calling on the respondent to appear, if it thinks fit and agrees with the judgment appealed from."

41. Interview with two Chinese engineers, January 19, 2020.

42. *CCECC (Mieso-Dewele Railway Project Company) v. Tewodros Demse Weldeyesus*, Federal Supreme Court, Cassation Decision No. 176552, 2012 [Gregorian calendar, 2020].

43. The cassation judgment does not mention the nature and gravity of the injury incurred by the plaintiff.

44. Ethiopian Civil Code, Art. 2081.

45. Unfamiliarity with judicial procedure is not restricted to Chinese actors in Ethiopia. He and Feng identify a general unfamiliarity with procedural justice in China; see He and Feng, "Unfamiliarity and Procedural Justice."

46. Interview with lawyer based in Addis Ababa, August 4, 2020.

47. Conversation with Chinese engineer, Mehoni, Tigray, March 14, 2012.

48. Interview with two Chinese engineers, Addis Ababa, January 19, 2020.

49. Yang, *Gifts, Favors, and Banquets*, 121.

50. Chang, "Affect, Trust and Friendship"; see also Schmitz, "Kufala!"; Sheridan, "'If You Greet Them, They Ignore You.'"

51. Some studies highlight the skill with which Chinese company managers build connections with African elites, as well as the importance of these relationships as companies deepen their internationalisation; see, among others, Gambino and Franceschini, "Flexible Embeddedness"; Lam, *Chinese State-Owned Enterprises in West Africa*; Mohan and Lampert, "Negotiating China."

52. Conversation with two Chinese engineers, Addis Ababa, January 19, 2020.

53. Wu, *Affective Encounters*.

54. WeChat conversation with Chinese project manager, January 20, 2020.

55. WeChat conversation with Chinese project manager, January 20, 2020.

56. Galanter, "Why the Haves Come Out Ahead."

57. For more details and interesting discussions on the domestic and international politics surrounding GERD, see, among others, Endaylalu and Arsano, "Grand Ethiopian Renaissance Dam Project Controversies"; Gebreluel, "Ethiopia's Grand Renaissance Dam"; Lavers, *Dams, Power, and the Politics of Ethiopia's Renaissance*; Verhoeven, "The Grand Ethiopian Renaissance Dam."

58. Welker, *Enacting the Corporation*; Shever, "Engendering the Company."

59. Interview with lawyer based in Addis Ababa, July 13, 2020.

60. Interview with facilitator, Lower Omo Valley, South Ethiopia Regional State, August 8, 2017.

61. Interview with lawyer, Mekelle, April 25, 2020.

62. Interview with lawyer, Mekelle, April 25, 2020.

63. Interview with Chinese project manager, Addis Ababa, July 7, 2019.

64. Interview with lawyer, Mekelle, June 9, 2020.

65. Interview with lawyer, Mekelle, June 9, 2020.

66. Interview with lawyer, Mekelle, June 9, 2020.

67. Interview with Chinese project manager, Addis Ababa, July 7, 2019.

68. See also Driessen, "Trials of Trustworthiness Among Ethiopian Lawyers and Chinese Clients," 278.

4. IMMUNITY THROUGH INEQUALITY

1. David Engel draws attention to the communicative function of the court in "The Oven Bird's Song."

2. Interview with hotel manager, Mekelle, August 11, 2020.

3. China's two telecommunication giants, Huawei Technologies and Zhongxing Tele-communications Equipment, both benefited from Beijing's foreign policy shift in the late 1990s and the introduction of export credits and preferential loans to support Chinese businesses overseas. See Liu, "Africa and China," 77. Huawei first entered the African telecommunications market in 1998 when it began operations in Kenya. See Gagliardone, *China, Africa, and the Future of the Internet*, and *The Politics of Technology in Africa*.

4. *Hotel Rental Agreement Between Huawei Technologies and Mulugeta Gebremedhin Kahsay (Milano Hotel)*, 2014 [hereinafter *Rental Agreement*].

5. *Rental Agreement*, Art. 12.1: "The Lessee has the liberty to reduce/add the quantity of leased room and lease term, to terminate the agreement or to renew the agreement. However, the Lessee shall inform with a written notification 30 days in advance, and then the rental fee (including bedrooms, offices, kitchen and restaurant) shall remain the same as agreed above in this agreement."

6. *Rental Agreement*, Art. 3.8: "The prices listed above shall keep the same during the two years of the agreement period. If there is an extension of the agreement more than the specified period, the prices shall also remain the same."

7. *Rental Agreement*, Art. 4.5: "If the Lessor is not able to follow the Lessor's obligation, the Lessee has the liberty to refuse to pay the remaining 10% of last payment cycle's total amount when the Lessee pays the next cycle payment or when the agreement comes to an end." *Rental Agreement*, Art. 7.10: "The Lessor shall be responsible to keep the Lessee's leased areas safe and free from any theft. The lessor shall compensate for any loss suffered by Huawei or its employees taken place inside its premises."

8. *Rental Agreement*, Art. 12.2: "The Lessor can terminate the agreement by giving 60-days-notice in writing."

9. *Rental Agreement*, Art. 12.1 (see above).

10. *Rental Agreement*, Art. 7.1: "The lessor shall supply water service 24 hours every day, and the duration for water outage shall not be more than half day during one payment cycle (six months); unless it's due to force majeure." *Rental Agreement*, Art. 7.2, requires the same for electricity supply, Article 7.3 for internet provision, and Art 7.5 for hot water supply.

11. Ke-Schutte, *Angloscene*.

12. Interview with hotel manager, Mekelle, August 11, 2020.

13. Driessen, *Tales of Hope, Tastes of Bitterness*.

14. Interview with hotel manager, Mekelle, August 11, 2020.

15. Schmitz, "Kufala!"; Wu, *Affective Encounters*.

16. Schmitz, "Kufala!"

17. Schmitz, "Kufala!," 477.

18. Franceschini, "'You Walawala Too Much!'"

19. Interview with hotel manager, Mekelle, August 11, 2020.

20. Interview with hotel manager, Mekelle, August 11, 2020.

21. Interview with hotel manager, Mekelle, August 11, 2020.

22. Interview with hotel manager, Mekelle, August 11, 2020.

23. Wu, *Affective Encounters*, 165–66.

24. See, among many others, Engel, *Code and Custom in a Thai Provincial Court*; Felstiner, Abel, and Sarat, "The Emergence and Transformation of Disputes"; Merry, *Getting Justice, Getting Even*; Nader and Todd, *The Disputing Process*.

25. Merry and Silbey, "What Do Plaintiffs Want?," 153.

26. The court is allowed to do so, according to *Civil Procedure Code*, Art. 70 ("Defendant failing to appear").

27. Letter drawn up by Huawei's lawyer in response to the decision of the court to entertain the case in absence of his client, July 21, 2015 [hereinafter Letter by Huawei's lawyer]. The letter was included in the case file.

28. Letter by Huawei's lawyer.

29. Letter by Huawei's lawyer.

30. Interview with Huawei's lawyer, Mekelle, August 1, 2020.

31. Interview with Huawei's lawyer, Mekelle, August 1, 2020.

32. Interview with hotel manager, Mekelle, August 11, 2020.

33. Interview with Milano's lawyer, Mekelle, July 29, 2020.

34. Interview with Milano's lawyer, Mekelle, July 29, 2020.

35. Interview with Huawei's lawyer, Mekelle, August 1, 2020.

36. Interview with hotel manager, Mekelle, August 11, 2020.

37. *Mulugeta Gebremedhin/Milano Hotel v. Huawei Technologies Ethiopia*, Tigray Supreme Court, Case no. 75201, 2009 [Gregorian Calendar, 2017] [hereinafter *Milano Hotel v. Huawei Technologies*].

38. *Milano Hotel v. Huawei Technologies*.

39. *Milano Hotel v. Huawei Technologies*, 9.

40. Interview with hotel manager, Mekelle, August 11, 2020.

41. Interview with former judge, Mekelle, June 27, 2020.

42. Interview with former judge, Mekelle, June 27, 2020.

43. Interview with hotel manager, Mekelle, August 11, 2020.

44. Interview with hotel manager, Mekelle, August 11, 2020.

45. Interview with hotel manager, Mekelle, August 11, 2020.

46. Interview with lawyer based in Addis Ababa, August 4, 2020.

47. Interview with lawyer based in Addis Ababa, August 4, 2020.

48. I reconstructed the events based on interviews with China Wu Yi's lawyer, Mekelle, July 25, 2020, and the lawyer of the Ethiopian subcontractor, Mekelle, June 18, 2020.

49. Interview with China Wu Yi's lawyer, Mekelle, July 25, 2020.

50. Interview with China Wu Yi's lawyer, Mekelle, July 25, 2020.

51. Schmitt, *Political Theology*; Agamben, in *Homo Sacer*.

52. Interview with lawyer of Ethiopian subcontractor, Mekelle, June 18, 2020.

53. Schmitz, "Kufala!"

54. See Macaulay, "Non-Contractual Relations in Business." For discussions of the role of contracts in the Chinese context, see Duan, "The Role of Formal Contracts with Weak Legal Enforcement"; Hsu, "Capitalism Without Contracts Versus Capitalists Without Capitalism."

55. Engel, "The Oven Bird's Song." In his earlier work, David Engel also touches on the communicative function of the court when he describes the role of the "missing *phuyai*" in the Thai legal system; see *Code and Custom in a Thai Provincial Court*.

5. ENACTING JURISDICTION, REENACTING SOVEREIGNTY

1. Interview with former judge, Mekelle, August 24, 2020.

2. The second lot of the project was awarded to Hunan Huanda. See Geda and Meskel, "Impact of China–Africa Investment Relations."

3. This entire section is based on an interview with a former judge, Mekelle, August 24, 2020.

4. Driessen, "Trials of Trustworthiness Between Ethiopian Lawyers and Chinese Clients"; Li, "'Going Out' and Going In-House."

5. Many judges mentioned these practices.

6. Ayano, "Decolonizing Legal Influence"; Driessen, "Trials of Trustworthiness Between Ethiopian Lawyers and Chinese Clients." Mekonnen Firew Ayano shows how the growing Chinese presence in Ethiopia has radically changed the legal profession in Ethiopia by offering career opportunities to newly minted lawyers.

7. Interview with former judge, Mekelle, August 24, 2020.

8. Interview with former judge, Mekelle, August 24, 2020.

9. Foucault, *Discipline and Punish*.

10. Clarke, "Missed Manners in Courtroom Decorum," 962.

11. Conley and O'Barr, *Just Words*.

12. Clarke, "Missed Manners in Courtroom Decorum."

13. Interview with judge, Bahir Dar, October 28, 2020.

14. Interview with judge, Bahir Dar, October 28, 2020.

15. Interview with judge based in Shire, Mekelle, July 24, 2020.

16. Interview with judge based in Shire, Mekelle, July 24, 2020.

17. Interview with judge, Bahir Dar, October 24, 2020.

18. Ng and He, *Embedded Courts*; Ng and He, "The Institutional and Cultural Logics of Legal Commensuration."

19. See, among others, Fu, "Putting China's Judiciary into Perspective"; Fu and Cullen, "From Mediatory to Adjudicatory Justice"; Lubman, *Bird in a Cage*.

20. Interview with judge based in Shire, Mekelle, July 24, 2020.

21. Interview with judge based in Shire, Mekelle, July 24, 2020.

22. Driessen, 2020.

23. Stone Peters, "Legal Performance Good and Bad"; Flower, "Doing Loyalty."

24. Anteneh, "Contempt of Court."

25. Interview with judge and court president, Mekelle, August 4, 2020.

26. Interview with judge, Mekelle, August 8, 2020.

27. See also Driessen, *Tales of Hope, Tastes of Bitterness*, chapter 5.

28. Henderson, "The Dialogue of Heart and Head"; Levenson, "Courtroom Demeanor."

29. Bandes, "Remorse, Demeanor, and the Consequences of Misinterpretation."

30. Anteneh, "Contempt of Court."

31. *Criminal Code of Ethiopia*, Art. 449.1a.

32. *Criminal Code of Ethiopia*, Art. 449.1b.

33. *Civil Procedure Code of Ethiopia*, Art. 480.

34. Interview with former judge, Mekelle, August 24, 2020.

35. Seppänen, "Chinese Legal Development Assistance."

36. Clarke, "What's Law Got to Do with It?"

37. Interview with former judge, Mekelle, August 24, 2020.

38. Interview with judge based in Shire, Mekelle, July 24, 2020.

39. Interview with judge based in Shire, Mekelle, July 24, 2020.

40. Interview with lawyer and former judge, Mekelle, June 27, 2020.

41. Interview with lawyer and former judge, Mekelle, June 27, 2020.

42. Interview with judge, Bahir Dar, October 28, 2020.

43. Interview with lawyer and former judge, Mekelle, June 27, 2020.

44. This practice should be understood in the context of legal services practices in China. The Chinese legal system is characterized by what Sida Liu calls a "symbiotic exchange" between the state and the market; see Liu, "Lawyers, State Officials and Significant Others." Chinese lawyers often try to build bridges between the state and the market through reciprocal relations with judges; see also Ng and He, *Embedded Courts*, and Michelson, "Lawyers, Political Embeddedness, and Institutional Continuity in China's Transition from Socialism."

45. Interview with lawyer and former judge, Mekelle, June 27, 2020.

46. Interview with lawyer and former judge, Mekelle, June 27, 2020.

47. Interview with judge, Bahir Dar, October 28, 2020.

48. Interview with judge, Bahir Dar, October 28, 2020.

49. Judges can impose a prison sentence of up to one year for this crime. See *Criminal Code of Ethiopia*, Art. 449, on contempt of court.

50. Interview with judge, Bahir Dar, October 28, 2020.

51. Driessen, *Tales of Hope, Tastes of Bitterness*, chapter 3.

52. Interview with judge, Bahir Dar, October 28, 2020.

53. See, for instance, interview with judge based in Shire, Mekelle, July 24, 2020; interview with judge at Aba'ala, Mekelle, June 20, 2020.

54. Interview with judge, Bahir Dar, October 23, 2020.

55. Interview with judge, Bahir Dar, October 23, 2020.

56. Bandes, "Remorse, Demeanor, and the Consequences of Misinterpretation."

57. Interview with judge, Bahir Dar, October 23, 2020.

58. Interview with judge and court president, Mekelle, August 8, 2020.

59. Interview with judge, Mekelle, June 5, 2020.

60. Interview with judge, Mekelle, June 5, 2020.

6. DIMMING SOME VOICES, AMPLIFYING OTHERS

1. The Southern Nations, Nationalities, and Peoples' Region was dissolved in 2023 and divided into the four regions of Sidama, Central Ethiopia, South West Ethiopia, and South Ethiopia.

2. The number of labor cases and the compressed period in which they were instituted were striking, though not unique. The Hintalo Wajirat Wereda Court is just one of the three lower courts seated in Hintalo Wajirat Wereda, not to mention the courts in neighboring districts. The railway tracks cut across several districts in the states of Amhara, Afar, and Tigray.

3. Gillman, "What's Law Got to Do with It?"; Posner, *How Judges Think*.

4. Rosen, *The Anthropology of Justice*.

5. Conversation with a Chinese engineer, Addis Ababa, June 25, 2019.

6. Donald Trump, in *Al Jazeera English*, "Trump Says Egypt May 'Blow Up' Ethiopia Dam."

7. Conversation with Chinese liaison officer, Mekelle, March 17, 2020.

8. *Weldehib Gebre-Hiwet v. CCCC*, Hintalo Wajirat Wereda Court, Case No. 05544, 2008 [Gregorian calendar, 2016].

9. Interview with judge, August 8, 2020.

10. These complaints are leveled against the former *Labour Proclamation No. 377/2003* and the current *Labour Proclamation No. 1156/2019*.

11. According to *Labour Proclamation No. 1156/2019*, Art. 2.10, a managerial employee "means an employee who, by law or delegation of the employer, is vested with powers to lay down and execute management policies, and depending on the type of activities of the undertaking, with or without the aforementioned powers an employee who is vested with the power to hire, transfer, suspend, layoff, dismiss or assign employees, and includes a legal service head who recommend measures to be taken by the employer regarding such managerial issues, using his independent judgment, in the interest of the employer."

12. Interview with former judge, Mekelle, Tigray, August 15, 2020.

13. Interview with former judge, Mekelle, Tigray, August 15, 2020.

14. Interview with former judge, Mekelle, Tigray, August 15, 2020.

15. Interview with judge, Mekelle, Tigray, May 4, 2020.

16. Interview with judge, Mekelle, Tigray, May 4, 2020.

17. Interview with judge, August 8, 2020.

18. Interview with judge, August 8, 2020.

19. Interview with scribe, Adi Gudem, Tigray, August 18, 2020.

20. Interview with scribe, Adi Gudem, Tigray, August 18, 2020.

21. The year 2012 refers to the Ethiopian calendar. The controversial elections were held on September 9, 2020, Gregorian calendar.

22. Interview with Chinese manager, Lower Omo Valley, South Ethiopia Regional State, July 24, 2017.

23. Cf. Sheridan, "Weak Passports and Bad Behavior."

24. Interview with Chinese manager, Lower Omo Valley, South Ethiopia Regional State, July 30, 2017.

25. Interview with Chinese manager, Lower Omo Valley, South Ethiopia Regional State, July 30, 2017.

26. Abusive labor practices were also rampant among Chinese staff in private subcontracting companies. See Driessen, *Tales of Hope, Tastes of Bitterness* for the Ethiopian case; for other African and Asian contexts, see, among others, Chen, "Sovereign Debt in the Making," Chen and Liukkunen, "Enclave Governance and Transnational Labour Law," Franceschini, "As Far Apart as Earth and Sky," and Halegua and Ban, "Labour Protections for Overseas Chinese Workers."

27. I describe these dynamics in *Tales of Hope, Tastes of Bitterness*, chapters 2 and 3.

28. Interview with in-house counsel, Mekelle, Tigray, April 7, 2020.

29. Interview with in-house counsel, Mekelle, Tigray, April 7, 2020.

30. Interview with in-house counsel, Mekelle, Tigray, April 7, 2020.

31. *Fisiha Tekle-Medhin v. CCCC*, Hintalo Wajirat Wereda Court, Case No. 07603, 2011 [Gregorian calendar, 2018].

32. *CCCC v. Fisiha Tekle-Medhin*, South-Eastern Zone High Court (Tigray), Case No. 11734, 2011 [Gregorian calendar, 2018]. The Tigray Supreme Court upheld this decision, *Fisiha Tekle-Medhin v. CCCC*, Tigray Supreme Court, Case No. 111429, 2011 [Gregorian calendar, 2018].

33. Anleu and Mack, *Performing Judicial Authority in the Lower Courts*.

34. *Tamru Belay v. CCCC*, Hintalo Wajirat Wereda Court, Case No. 06358, 2009 [Gregorian calendar, 2017].

35. The judge referred to the case *Professor Reda Tekle-Haymanot v. Semeneh Tefera*, Federal Supreme Court, Cassation Decision No. 45984, Volume 9, 2002 [Gregorian calendar, 2010].

36. *Constitution of the Federal Democratic Republic of Ethiopia*, 1995 [hereinafter 'Constitution'], Art. 37.

37. This is an excerpt from the judgment with emphasis added by the author; see *Tamru Belay v. CCCC*, Hintalo Wajirat Wereda Court, Case No. 06358, 2009 [Gregorian calendar, 2017].

38. *Labour Proclamation No. 377/2003*, Art. 11.

39. *Labour Proclamation No. 1156/2019*, Art. 4, 5, 6, and 7.

40. *Afrikawit Building Contractors Association v. Indris Ali*, Federal Supreme Court, Cassation Decision No. 42075, Volume 8, 2001 [Gregorian calendar, 2008].

41. See *Constitution*, Art. 80, and the *Federal Courts Proclamation No. 1234/2021*.

42. Jembere, *An Introduction to the Legal History of Ethiopia, 1434–1974*.

43. Fiseha, "Separation of Powers and Its Implications for the Judiciary in Ethiopia."

44. Tura, "Uniform Application of Law in Ethiopia."

45. David, "Civil Code for Ethiopia," 192.

46. David, "Civil Code for Ethiopia"; Vanderlinden, "Civil Law and Common Law Influences on the Developing Law of Ethiopia."

47. Two attempts were made to compile past decisions, by Emperor Menelik II in 1908 and by Emperor Haile Selassie I in the 1950s. The first compilation was made to enhance predictability of the legal system, the second to assist the drafters of the country's new codes; see Abdo, *Legal History*.

48. Setegn, "Legislative Inaction and Judicial Legislation under the Ethiopian Private International Law Regime"; Berega, "Decisions of the Ethiopian Federal Supreme Court Cassation Division." The principle of cassation over cassation, in which the Cassation Division of the Federal Supreme Court can reverse decisions of the Cassation Bench of the State Supreme Courts, has been even more fiercely debated, as it is argued to contradict the spirit of the constitution, which delegates state matters to states and federal matters to the federation. See Abdo, "Review of Decisions of State Courts over State Matters by the Federal Supreme Court"; Afesha, "Judicial Power Decentralization in Ethiopia: Practical Limitations and Implications on Self-governance of Regional States."

49. Tura, "Uniform Application of Law in Ethiopia."

50. *Afrikawit Building Contractors Association v. Indris Ali*, Federal Supreme Court, Cassation Decision No. 42075, Volume 8, 2001 [Gregorian calendar, 2008].

51. Interview with former judge, Mekelle, Tigray, August 15, 2020.

52. Posner, *The Problems of Jurisprudence*; Segal and Speath, *The Supreme Court and the Attitudinal Model*.

53. Baum, *Judges and Their Audiences*.

54. Posner, *How Judges Think*; Rosen, *The Anthropology of Justice*.

55. Kapiszewski, "Tactical Balancing: High Court Decision Making on Politically Crucial Cases"; Tamanaha, *Beyond the Formalist–Realist Divide*.

56. Gillman, "What's Law Got to Do with It?," 466.

57. Phillips, *Ideology in the Language of Judges*.

58. Ethiopia's nationalities question has been raised since the 1960s. It asks whether and to what extent different ethnic groups, referred to as "nationalities" in Ethiopia, should be granted (a certain degree of) self-rule. See Wagaw, "Emerging Issues of Ethiopian Nationalities"; Gebissa, "National Integration Through Political Marginalization"; Zeleke, *Ethiopia in Theory*.

59. *Investment Proclamation No. 1180/2020*, part 6.

60. *Federal Courts Proclamation No. 25/1996*, Art. 4 and 5, and *Federal Courts Proclamation No. 1234/2021*, Art. 4 and 5.

61. This was brought up, for instance, in an interview with a judge, Mekelle, July 24, 2020, and in an interview with a judge in Afar, July 5, 2020. Many other judges mentioned this maxim in different words.

62. Interview with judge, Mekelle, Tigray, May 4, 2020.

63. For more context on the cheap labor debate, see Admasie, "Amid Political Recalibrations"; Mains and Robel, "Reproducing Women's Labor in an Ethiopian Industrial Park"; Tesema, "Despotism on the Shop Floor," and "Unjust Manufacturing."

64. Interview with judge, August 8, 2020.

65. Interview with judge, August 8, 2020.

66. Bandes, "Empathetic Judging and the Rule of Law."

67. Plumm and Terrance, "Battered Women Who Kill."

68. See, for instance, Chew and Kelley, "Myth of the Color-Blind Judge"; Cox and Miles, "Documenting Discrimination"; Levinson and Young, "Different Shades of Bias."

69. Glynn and Sen, "Identifying Judicial Empathy"; Moyer and Haire, "Trailblazers and Those That Followed."

70. This is my estimation. Workers typically shared accommodation, and living costs were the main costs.

71. Interview with judge, August 8, 2020.

72. Interview with judge, August 8, 2020.

73. *Ethiopia Observer*, "Addisalem Balema Appears in Court."

CONCLUSION

1. Conversation with lawyer, Addis Ababa, January 15, 2020.

2. Conversation with lawyer, Addis Ababa, January 15, 2020.

3. Kidane, "The Legal Framework for the Protection of Foreign Direct Investment in China," and "China's Bilateral Investment Treaties with African States in Comparative Context."

4. Kidane, "The Legal Framework for the Protection of Foreign Direct Investment in China," and "China's Bilateral Investment Treaties with African States in Comparative Context."

5. Conversation with lawyer, Addis Ababa, January 15, 2020.

6. Driessen, *Tales of Hope, Tastes of Bitterness*.

7. *Laws of Kenya: Employment Act* (Chapter 226), Art. 41.

8. *Lawrence Karani Njagi v. China Railway Engineering Group No. 10*, Employment and Labour Relations Court of Kenya at Kericho, Case no. 27, 2017.

9. *Lawrence Karani Njagi v. China Railway Engineering Group No. 10*, Employment and Labour Relations Court of Kenya at Kericho, Case no. 27, 2017.

10. Other examples are *Joseph Aura v. China Jiangxi International (K) Limited*, Employment and Labour Relations Court of Kenya at Kericho, Case no. 267, 2015; *Abigael Jepkosgei Yator and Ann Cheruto v. China Hanan [sic] International Co. Ltd.*, Employment and Labour Relations Court of Kenya at Eldoret, Case no. 136, 2018.

11. *Employment Act* (Chapter 226), Art. 45.

12. One US dollar was worth, on average, 101.62 Kenyan shillings in 2017.

13. *Lawrence Karani Njagi v. China Railway Engineering Group No. 10*, Employment and Labour Relations Court of Kenya at Kericho, Case no. 27, 2017.

14. One example is *Kenya Union of Road Contractors and Civil Engineering Workers v. China Railway No. 5 Engineering Group*, Employment and Labour Relations Court at Nairobi, Case E233, 2022.

15. *China Wu Yi v. Edermann Property, Ze Yun Yang, and Jing Zhang*, High Court at Nairobi, Civil case 362, 2012.

16. *Daily Nation*, "Chinese Firms Lock Horns in Kenyan Courts over Sh350 Million Dispute."

17. *China Wu Yi v. Edermann Property, Ze Yun Yang, and Jing Zhang*, High Court at Nairobi, Civil case 362, 2012.

18. I learned this from colleagues working in Ghana and Mozambique, who drew on anecdotal evidence.

19. In Zimbabwe, for instance, few cases are reported to the police or brought to courts because Chinese actors are connected to senior police officials and politicians with the power to interfere; see Gukurume, "Chinese Migrants and the Politics of Everyday Life in Zimbabwe."

20. Clapham, "Sovereignty and the Third World."

21. Seymour, "Sovereignty, Territory and Authority."

22. *OAU Charter*.

23. Potts, *Law, Capital, and the Expansion of American Empire*; Yoon, "When the Sovereign Contracts."

24. Clapham, "Sovereignty and the Third World," and *Africa and the International System*.

25. Mbembe, *Out of the Dark Night*, chapter 1.

26. Central to articulating and exercising sovereignty, infrastructure is a key mediator of sovereignty; see Terrefe and Verhoeven, "The Road (Not) Taken." In Ethiopia, Chinese involvement in the construction industry boosted the legitimacy of the EPRDF government and continues to enhance the image of the current government under Abiy Ahmed. As both material and discursive projects, infrastructures have allowed successive Ethiopian governments to project the ideals of solidarity and cohesion amid upheaval. See Hagmann and Korf, "Agamben in the Ogaden"; Mains, *Under Construction*; Terrefe, "Infrastructures of Renaissance," and "Urban Layers of Political Rupture."

27. Bräutigam, "A Critical Look at Chinese 'Debt-Trap Diplomacy'"; Carmody, "Dependence Not Debt-Trap Diplomacy"; Singh, "The Myth of "Dept-Trap Diplomacy," and Realities of Chinese Development Finance."

28. Mutua, "Why China Remains Greatest Threat to Kenya's Sovereignty."

29. Kimari, "'Under Construction.'"

30. See, among others, Bayart, *The State in Africa*; Gardner, *Sovereignty Without Power*; Lavers, "Agricultural Investment in Ethiopia."

31. For Ethiopia, see Chinigò, *Everyday Practices of State Building in Ethiopia*; Mulugeta, *The Everyday State in Africa*. For Africa more generally, see Bierschenk and Olivier de Sardan, *States at Work*; Chalfin, *Neoliberal Frontiers*. For anthropological studies of the state beyond Africa, see, among others, Mathur, *Paper Tiger*; Gupta, *Red Tape*.

32. Interview with lawyer and former judge, Mekelle, June 27, 2020.

33. Wu, *Affective Encounters*.

34. Schmitz, "Kufala!"

35. Interview with judge, Bahir Dar, October 23, 2020.

36. I came across a range of cases concerning other foreign nationals, including nationals from the listed countries.

ACKNOWLEDGMENTS

1. United Nations Development Program Ethiopia, "Reviving the Formal Justice System for Peace and Stability."

2. Ghebretekle, "Message of the President."

3. Ghebretekle, "Message of the President."

Aalen, Lovise. *The Politics of Ethnicity in Ethiopia: Actors, Power and Mobilisation Under Ethnic Federalism*. Leiden: Brill, 2011.

Abdo, Muradu. *Legal History: Part I A Teaching Material for the Undergraduate Course in Legal History in Ethiopian Law Schools*. Addis Ababa: Addis Ababa University, 2009.

———. "Review of Decisions of State Courts over State Matters by the Federal Supreme Court." *Mizan Law Review* 1, no. 1 (2007): 60–74.

Abebe, Tatek. "Begging as a Livelihood Pathway of Street Children in Addis Ababa." *Forum for Development Studies* 36, no. 2 (2009): 275–300.

Acevedo, John Felipe. "Reclaiming Black Dignity." *Texas Law Review* 99 (2020): 1–9.

Adem, Seifudein. *Africa's Quest for Modernity: Lessons from Japan and China*. New York: Springer, 2023.

Admasie, Samuel Andreas. "Amid Political Recalibrations: Strike Wave Hits Ethiopia." *Labor and Society* 21 (2018): 431–35.

———. "Trade Union Resurgence in Ethiopia." *Global Labour Journal* 13, no. 2 (2022): 171–86.

Adunbi, Omolade. *Enclaves of Exception: Special Economic Zones and Extractive Practices in Nigeria*. Bloomington: Indiana University Press, 2022.

Afesha, Nigussie. "Judicial Power Decentralization in Ethiopia: Practical Limitations and Implications on Self-governance of Regional States." *Mizan Law Review* 13, no. 3 (2019): 363–83.

Agamben, Giorgio. *Homo Sacer: Sovereign Power and Bare Life*. Palo Alto, CA: Stanford University Press, 1998.

Agegnehu, Tameru Wondim. "Some Thoughts on the Organization of Legal Practice in Ethiopia." *Mizan Law Review* 11, no. 1 (2017): 229–38.

Alden, Chris, and Daniel Large. "On Becoming a Norms Maker: Chinese Foreign Policy, Norms Evolution and the Challenges of Security in Africa." *The China Quarterly* 221 (2015): 123–42.

Amare, Mulatu. *Ethnic Federalism in Ethiopia: Challenges and Prospects*. Saarbrucken: Lambert, 2014.

Amrute, Sareeta. *Encoding Race, Encoding Class: Indian IT Workers in Berlin*. Durham, NC: Duke University Press, 2016.

An, Ning. "Narrating China-Africa Relations: Perspectives from New Chinese Immigrants in Zimbabwe." *South Africa Geographical Journal* 106, no. 3 (2024): 249–67.

An, Ning, Jiayin Zhang, and Min Wang. "The Everyday Chinese Framing of Africa: A Perspective of Tourism-Geopolitical Encounter." *Geopolitics* 28, no. 4 (2023): 1422–41.

Andreetta, Sophie. "The Symbolic Power of the State: Inheritance Disputes and Litigants' Judicial Trajectories in Cotonou." *Political and Legal Anthropology Review* 43, no. 1 (2020): 5–20.

Anleu, Sharyn Roach, and Kathy Mack. *Performing Judicial Authority in the Lower Courts*. London: Macmillan, 2017.

Appel, Hannah. "Offshore Work: Oil, Modularity, and the How of Capitalism in Equatorial Guinea." *American Ethnologist* 39, no. 4 (2012): 692–709.

———. *The Licit Life of Capitalism: US Oil in Equatorial Guinea*. Durham, NC: Duke University Press, 2019.

Arce, Alberto, and Norman Long. "Reconfiguring Modernity and Development from an Anthropological Perspective." In *Anthropology, Development and Modernities*, edited by Alberto Arce and Norman Long, 1–31. London: Routledge, 2000.

Atuahene, Bernadette. "Dignity Takings and Dignity Restoration: Creating a New Theoretical Framework for Understanding Involuntary Property Loss and the Remedies Requires." *Law & Social Inquiry* 41, no. 4 (2016): 796–823.

———. *We Want What's Ours: Learning from South Africa's Land Restitution Program*. Oxford: Oxford University Press.

Ayano, Mekonnen Firew. "Decolonizing Legal Influence: China's Role in the Changing Landscape of the Ethiopian Legal Profession, 2000–2018." *Notre Dame Journal of International & Comparative Law* 13, no. 1 (2023): 1–50.

———. "Lawyering on the Eve of a Civil War: The Role of Law and Lawyers in Ethiopia's Civil War, 2018–2024." *Dickinson Law Review* 120, no. 2 (2025), forthcoming.

———. "Rural Land Registration in Ethiopia: Myths and Realities." *Law & Society Review* 52, no. 4 (2018): 1060–97.

Baldwin, James. *Collected Essays*. Ypsilanti, MI: Library of America. 1998.

Bandes, Susan. "Empathetic Judging and the Rule of Law." *Cardozo Law Review De Novo* (2009): 133–48.

———. "Remorse, Demeanor, and the Consequences of Misinterpretation." *Journal of Law, Religion and State* 3 (2014): 170–99.

Baum, Lawrence. *Judges and Their Audiences: A Perspective on Judicial Behavior*. Princeton, NJ: Princeton University Press, 2009.

Bayart, Jean-François. *The State in Africa: The Politics of the Belly*. Harlow: Longman, 1993.

Benda-Beckmann, Franz, Keebet von Benda-Beckmann, and Julia Eckert (eds.). *Rules of Law and Laws of Ruling: On the Governance of Law*. London: Routledge, 2013.

Benton, Lauren. *Law and Colonial Cultures: Legal Regimes in World History, 1400–1900*. Cambridge: Cambridge University Press, 2002.

Benveniste, Émile. *Dictionary of Indo-European Concepts and Society*. London: HAU, 2016.

Berega, Yirgalem Germu. "Decisions of the Ethiopian Federal Supreme Court Cassation Division: Imprescriptible Invalidation of Contract of Land Sale." *International Journal of Law and Public Administration* 1, no. 2 (2018): 58–64.

Berhe, Mulugeta Gebrehiwot. *Laying the Past to Rest: The EPRDF and the Challenges of Ethiopian State-Building.* Hurst, 2020.

Beverley, Eric Lewis. "Introduction: Rethinking Sovereignty, Colonial Empires, and Nation-States in South Asia and Beyond." *Comparative Studies of South Asia, Africa and the Middle East* 40, no. 3 (2020): 407–20.

Bierschenk, Thomas, and Jean-Pierre Olivier de Sardan (eds.). *States at Work: Dynamics of African Bureaucracies.* Leiden: Brill, 2014.

Bitew, Mastewal. "Transnational Amhara Nationalism: From Discourse Transformation to Placemaking in Ethiopia." *African Identities*. DOI: https://doi.org/10.1080/14725843.2025.2548900.

Borago, Teshome M. "What Is the Point in Amhara Nationalism?" *Ethiopia Insight*, December 10, 2018.

Bräutigam, Deborah. "A Critical Look at Chinese 'Debt-Trap Diplomacy': The Rise of a Meme." *Area Development and Policy* 5, no. 1 (2020): 1–14.

Bräutigam, Deborah, and Xiaoyang Tang. "African Shenzhen: China's Special Economic Zones in Africa." *Journal of Modern African Studies* 49, no. 1 (2011): 27–54.

Bräutigam, Deborah, Xiaoyang Tang, and Ying Xia. "What Kind of Chinese 'Geese' Are Flying to Africa? Evidence from Chinese Manufacturing Firms." *Journal of African Economies* 27, no. 1 (2018): 29–51.

Brinton, Jasper. "The Mixed Courts of Egypt." *American Journal of International Law* 20, no. 4 (1926): 670–88.

Bromell, Nick. "Democratic Indignation: Black American Thought and the Politics of Dignity." *Political Theory* 41, no. 2 (2013): 285–311.

Brown, Jonathan. "Diplomatic Immunity: State Practice Under the Vienna Convention on Diplomatic Relations." *International and Comparative Law Quarterly* 37 (1988): 53–88.

Brown, Nathan J. "The Precarious Life and Slow Death of the Mixed Courts of Egypt." *International Journal of Middle East Studies* 25, no. 1 (1993): 33–52.

Bryant, Rebecca, and Mete Hatay. *Sovereignty Suspended: Building the So-Called State.* Philadelphia: University of Pennsylvania Press, 2020.

Buelli, Arlena. "The Hands Off Ethiopia Campaign, Racial Solidarities and Intercolonial Antifascism in South Asia (1935–36)." *Journal of Global History* 18, no. 1 (2023): 47–67.

Bunkenborg, Mikkel, Morten Nielsen, and Morten Axel Pedersen. *Collaborative Damage: An Experimental Ethnography of Chinese Globalization.* Ithaca, NY: Cornell University Press, 2022.

Byler, Darren. *Terror Capitalism: Uyghur Dispossession and Masculinity in a Chinese City.* Durham, NC: Duke University Press, 2022.

Cabestan, Jean-Pierre. "China and Ethiopia: Authoritarian Affinities and Economic Cooperation." Translated by N. Jayaram. *China Perspectives* 4, 92 (2012): 53–62.

Carmody, Pádraig. "Dependence Not Debt-Trap Diplomacy." *Area Development and Policy* 5, no. 1 (2020): 23–31.

Cattelino, Jessica. *High Stakes: Florida Seminole Gaming and Sovereignty.* Durham, NC: Duke University Press, 2008.

Chalfin, Brenda. *Neoliberal Frontiers: An Ethnography of Sovereignty in West Africa.* Chicago: University of Chicago Press, 2010.

Chang, Janny. "Affect, Trust and Friendship: A Case Study of Chinese and Zambian Relationships at the Workplace." *International Journal of Business Anthropology* 4, no. 1 (2013): 38–61.

Chanie, Bantanyehu Shiferaw, and John Ishiyama. "Political Transition and the Rise of Amhara Nationalism in Ethiopia." *Journal of Asian and African Studies* 56, no. 5 (2021): 1036–50.

Chen, Benjamin Minhao, and Zhiyu Li. "How Will Technology Change the Face of Chinese Justice?" *Columbia Journal of Asian Law* 34, no. 1 (2020): 1–58.

Chen, Wanjing Kelly. "Harden the Hardline, Soften the Softline: Unravelling China's *Qiaoling*-Centred Diaspora Governance in Laos." *The China Quarterly* 250 (2022): 397–416.

———. "Harnessing the Sending State: Pragmatic Improvisations and Negotiated Memberships of the Chinese Diaspora in Laos." *Political Geography* 89 (2021), 102425.

———. "Sovereign Debt in the Making: Financial Entanglements and Labor Politics Along the Belt and Road in Laos." *Economic Geography* 96, no. 4 (2020): 295–314.

Chen, Weiwei. "The Dynamics of Chinese Private Outward Foreign Direct Investment in Ethiopia: A Comparison of the Light Manufacturing Industry and the Construction Materials Industry." PhD diss., SOAS University of London, 2021.

Chen, Yifeng, and Ulla Liukkunen. "Enclave Governance and Transnational Labour Law—A Case Study of Chinese Workers on Strike in Africa." *Nordic Journal of International Law* 88 (2019): 558–86.

Cheng, Han, and Weidong Liu. "Disciplinary Geopolitics and the Rise of International Development Studies in China." *Political Geography* 89 (2021), 102452.

———. "Temporality and the Geopolitical Enframing of Chinese International Development Thinking." *Geopolitics* 28, no. 5 (2023): 1942–66.

Cheru, Fantu. "Emerging Southern Powers and New Forms of South-South Cooperation: Ethiopia's Strategic Engagement with China and India." *Third World Quarterly* 37, no. 4 (2016): 592–610.

Chew, Pat K., and Robert E. Kelley. "Myth of the Color-Blind Judge: An Empirical Analysis of Racial Harassment Cases." *Washington University Law Review* 86, no. 5 (2009): 1117–66.

Chinigò, Davide. *Everyday Practices of State Building in Ethiopia: Power, Scale, Performativity.* Oxford: Oxford University Press, 2022.

Chiyemura, Frangton. "The Winds of Change in Africa-China Relations? Contextualising African Agency in Ethiopia-China Engagement in Wind Energy Infrastructure Financing and Development." PhD diss., The Open University, 2019.

Chiyemura, Frangton, Elisa Gambino, and Tim Zajontz. "Infrastructure and the Politics of African State Agency: Shaping the Belt and Road Initiative in East Africa." *Chinese Political Science Review* 8 (2023): 105–31.

Chu, James, and Marcel Fafchamps. "Labor Conflict Within Foreign, Domestic, and Chinese-Owned Manufacturing Firms in Ethiopia." *World Development* 159/106037 (2022): 1–18.

Cicero (Marcus Tullius). *On Duties.* Translated by Walter Miller. London: Loeb, 1989.

Clapham, Christopher. *Africa and the International System: The Politics of State Survival.* Cambridge: Cambridge University Press, 1996.

——. "Sovereignty and the Third World State." *Political Studies* 47, no. 3 (1999): 522–37.

——. "The Ethiopian Developmental State." *Third World Quarterly* 39, no. 6 (2018): 1151–65.

Clarke, Catherine Thérèse. "Missed Manners in Courtroom Decorum." *Maryland Law Review* 50, no. 4 (1991): 945–1026.

Clarke, Donald C. "What's Law Got to Do with It? Legal Institutions and Economic Reform in China." *UCLA Pacific Basin Law Journal* 10, no. 1 (1991): 1–76.

Conley, John M., and William M. O'Barr. *Just Words: Law, Language, and Power.* Chicago: Chicago University Press, 1998.

Cook, Seth, Jixia Lu, Henry Tugendhat, and Dawit Alemu. "Chinese Migrants in Africa: Facts and Fictions from the Agri-Food Sector in Ethiopia and Ghana." *World Development* 81 (2016): 61–70.

Cotula, Lorenzo, Xiaoxue Weng, Qianru Ma, and Peng Ren. *China-Africa Investment Treaties: Do They Work?* London: International Institute for Environment and Development, 2016.

Cox, Adam B., and Thomas J. Miles. "Documenting Discrimination." *Columbia Law Review Sidebar* 108 (2008): 31–38.

Darian-Smith, Eve. *Bridging Divides: The Channel Tunnel and English Legal Identity in the New Europe.* Berkeley: University of California Press, 1999.

——. *Laws and Societies in Global Contexts: Contemporary Approaches.* Cambridge: Cambridge University Press, 2013.

Darian-Smith, Eve, and Philip C. McCarty. *The Global Turn: Theories, Research Designs, and Methods for Global Studies.* Berkeley: University of California Press, 2017.

David, René. 1962. "Civil Code for Ethiopia: Considerations on the Codification of the Civil Law in African Countries." *Tulane Law Review* 37, no. 2 (1962): 187–204.

Dennison, Jean, "Entangled Sovereignties: The Osage Nation's Interconnections with Governmental and Corporate Authorities." *American Ethnologist* 44, no. 4 (2017): 684–96.

Desta, Geboya Melaku, Feyissa Dereje Dori, and Esmelealem Mamo Mihretu. *Ethiopia in the Wake of Political Reforms.* Addis Ababa: Tsehai, 2020.

Destrée, Pauline. "'We Work for the Devil': Oil Extraction, Kinship and the Fantasy of Time on the Offshore Frontier." *Critique of Anthropology* 43, no. 1 (2023): 24–43.

Dezalay, Sara. *Lawyering Imperial Encounters: Negotiating Africa's Relationship with the World Economy.* Cambridge: Cambridge University Press, 2025.

——. "Lawyers in Africa: Brokers of the State, Intermediaries of Globalization." *Indiana Journal of Global Legal Studies* 25, no. 2 (2018): 639–70.

——. "The African Challenge and Its Aftermath: Colonial Legacies and the (Re)making of the International Legal Order." In *The Palgrave Handbook of International Political Theory*, vol. 1, edited by Howard Williams, David Boucher, Peter Sutch, David Reidy, and Alexandros Koutsoukis, 265–81. London: Macmillan, 2023.

Di Nunzio, Marco. *The Act of Living: Street Life, Marginality, and Development in Urban Ethiopia.* Ithaca, NY: Cornell University Press, 2019.

——. "Work, Development, and Refusal in Urban Ethiopia." *American Ethnologist* 49, no. 3 (2022): 401–12.

DiCarlo, Jessica, and Meredith DeBoom. "Six Paths of Global China: A Genealogy of a Contested Geographical Imaginary." *Dialogues in Human Geography.* DOI: https://doi.org/10.1177/20438206251345563.

Dobler, Gregor. "Chinese Shops and the Formation of a Chinese Expatriate Community in Namibia." *The China Quarterly* 199 (2009): 707–25.

Donham, Donald L. *Marxist Modern: An Ethnographic History of the Ethiopian Revolution*. Berkeley: University of California Press, 1999.

Dorsett, Shaunnagh, and Shaun McVeigh. *Jurisdiction*. London: Routledge, 2012.

Douzinas, Costas. "The Metaphysics of Jurisdiction." In *Jurisprudence of Jurisdiction*, edited by Shaun McVeigh, 21–32. London: Routledge, 2007.

Driessen, Miriam. "Chinese Workers in Ethiopia Caught between Remaining and Returning." *Pacific Affairs* 94, no. 2 (2021): 329–46.

———. "Laughing About Corruption in Ethiopian-Chinese Encounters." *American Anthropologist* 121, no. 4 (2019): 911–22.

———. "Migrating for the Bank: Housing and Chinese Labour Migration to Ethiopia." *The China Quarterly* 221 (2015): 143–60.

———. "Pidgin Play: Linguistic Subversion on Chinese-Run Construction Sites in Ethiopia." *African Affairs* 119/476 (2020): 432–51.

———. *Tales of Hope, Tastes of Bitterness: Chinese Road Builders in Ethiopia*. Hong Kong: Hong Kong University Press, 2019.

———. "The African Bill: Chinese Struggles with Development Assistance." *Anthropology Today* 31, no. 1 (2015): 3–7.

———. "Trials of Trustworthiness Between Ethiopian Lawyers and Chinese Clients." *Political and Legal Anthropology Review* 45, no. 2 (2022): 274–89.

Duan, Mingming. "The Role of Formal Contracts with Weak Legal Enforcement: A Study in the Chinese Context." *Strategic Organization* 10, no. 2 (2012): 158–86.

Dzenovska, Dace. "Good Enough Sovereignty, or on Land as Property and Territory in Latvia." *History and Anthropology* 35, no. 3 (2024): 415–33.

Endaylalu, Gashaw Ayferam, and Yacob Arsano. "Grand Ethiopian Renaissance Dam Project Controversies: Understanding the Role of Worldviews and Nexus." *African Anthropologist* 22, no. 2 (2024): 215–47.

Engel, David M. *Code and Custom in a Thai Provincial Court: The Interaction of Formal and Informal Systems of Justice*. Tucson: University of Arizona Press, 1978.

———. "The Oven Bird's Song: Insiders, Outsiders, and Personal Injuries in an American Community." *Law & Society Review* 18, no. 4 (1984): 551–82.

Erie, Matthew S. "Chinese Law and Development." *Harvard International Law Journal* 62, no. 1 (2021): 51–115.

———. "The New Legal Hubs: The Emergent Landscape of International Commercial Dispute Resolution." *Virginia Journal of International Law* 60, no. 2 (2020): 224–98.

———. "The Soft Power of Chinese Law." *Columbia Journal of Transnational Law* 61, no. 1 (2023): 1–66.

Erlich, Haggai. *Greater Tigray and the Mysterious Magnetism of Ethiopia*. London: Hurst, 2023.

Escobar, Arturo. *Encountering Development: The Making and Unmaking of the Third World*. Princeton, NJ: Princeton University Press, 2001.

Esposito, Roberto. "Community, Immunity, Biopolitics." *Angelaki: Journal of the Theoretical Humanities* 18, no. 3 (2013): 83–90.

———. *Immunitas: The Protection and Negation of Life*. Cambridge: Polity, 2011.

Ewick, Patricia, and Susan S. Silbey. *The Common Place of Law: Stories from Everyday Life*. Chicago: Chicago University Press, 1998.

Fanon, Frantz. *Black Skin, White Masks*. London: Penguin, 2021.

———. *The Wretched of the Earth*. London: Penguin, 2001.

Fanta, Esubalew Belay. "The British on the Ethiopian Bench: 1942–1944." *Northeast African Studies* 16, no. 2 (2016): 67–96.

Fantini, Emanuele, Luca Puddu, Edegilign Hailu Woldegebrael, and Tom Lavers. "Salini: An Ethio-Italian Story." In *Dams, Power, and the Politics of Ethiopia's Renaissance*, by Tom Lavers. Oxford: Oxford University Press, 2024, 118–37.

Fei, Ding. "The Compound Labor Regime of Chinese Construction Projects in Ethiopia." *Geoforum* 177 (2020): 13–23.

———. "Transnational Mobility and Precarity in the Shadow of Pandemics: Chinese Migrants in Africa." *Journal of Ethnic and Migration Studies*, DOI: https://doi.org/10.1080/1369183X.2024.2417968.

———. "Flexible Sovereignty and Contested Legality: The Overseas Employment and Legal Struggles of Chinese Workers." *EPD: Society and Space*, DOI: https://doi.org/10.1177/02637758241288101.

Fei, Ding, Abdi Ismail Samatar, and Chuan Liao. "Chinese–African Encounters in High-Tech Sectors: Comparative Investigation of Chinese Workplace Regimes in Ethiopia." *Development Policy Review* 36, no. 1 (2018): 455–75.

Fei, Ding, and Chuan Liao. "Chinese Eastern Industrial Zone in Ethiopia: Unpacking the Enclave." *Third World Quarterly* 41, no. 4 (2020): 623–44.

Fei, Ding, Motolani Peltola, and Shuo Zhang. "Unpacking the Competitive Relations Among Chinese Business Actors in Africa." *Eurasian Geography and Economics* 66, no. 2 (2025): 247–78.

Felstiner, William L. F., Richard L. Abel, and Austin Sarat. "The Emergence and Transformation of Disputes: Naming, Blaming, Claiming . . ." *Law & Society Review* 15, no. 3–4 (1980–81): 631–54.

Ferguson, James. *The Anti-Politics Machine: 'Development,' Depoliticization, and Bureaucratic Power in Lesotho*. Minneapolis: University of Minnesota Press, 1994.

Fessha, Yonatan Tesfaye. *Ethnic Diversity and Federalism: Constitution Making in South Africa and Ethiopia*. London: Routledge, 2011.

Feyissa, Dereje. "Aid Negotiation: The Uneasy 'Partnership' Between EPRDF and the Donors." *Journal of Eastern African Studies* 5, no. 4 (2011): 788–817.

Feyissa, Hailegabriel G. "European Extraterritoriality in Semicolonial Ethiopia." *Melbourne Journal of International Law* 17, no. 1 (2016): 107–34.

Fiseha, Assefa. "Separation of Powers and Its Implications for the Judiciary in Ethiopia." *Journal of Eastern African Studies* 5, no. 4 (2011): 702–15.

Fisher, Jonathan. "#HandsOffEthiopia: 'Partiality,' Polarization and Ethiopia's Tigray Conflict." *Global Responsibility to Protect* 14 (2022): 28–32.

Fisher, Josh. "In Search of Dignified Work: Gender and the Work Ethic in the Crucible of Fair Trade Production." *American Ethnologist* 45, no. 1 (2018): 74–86.

Flower, Lisa. "Doing Loyalty: Defense Lawyers' Subtle Dramas in the Courtroom." *Journal of Contemporary Ethnography* 47, no. 2 (2018): 226–54.

Forst, Rainer. "The Ground of Critique: On the Concept of Human Dignity in Social Orders of Justification." *Philosophy and Social Criticism* 37, no. 9 (2011): 965–76.

Foucault, Michel. *Discipline and Punish: The Birth of the Prison*. London: Penguin, 1977.

Fourie, Elsje. "China's Example for Meles' Ethiopia: When Development 'Models' Land." *Modern African Studies* 53, no. 3 (2015): 289–316.

Franceschini, Costanza. "'You Walawala Too Much': Chinglish Interactions Between Chinese and Ghanaian Construction Workers." *Antropologia* 9, no. 3 (2021): 153–71.

Franceschini, Ivan. "As Far Apart as Earth and Sky: A Survey of Chinese and Cambodian Construction Workers in Sihanoukville." *Critical Asian Studies* 52, no. 4 (2020): 512–29.

Franceschini, Ivan, and Nicholas Loubere. *Global China as Method*. Cambridge: Cambridge University Press, 2022.

Franquesa, Jaume. *Power Struggles: Dignity, Value, and the Renewable Energy Frontier in Spain*. Bloomington: Indiana University Press, 2018.

Fronczak, Joseph. "Local People's Global Politics: A Transnational History of the Hands Off Ethiopia Movement of 1935." *Diplomatic History* 39, no. 2 (2015): 245–74.

Fu, Hualing. "Putting China's Judiciary into Perspective: Is It Independent, Competent, and Fair?" In *Beyond Common Knowledge: Empirical Approaches to the Rule of Law*, edited by Erik G. Jensen and Thomas C. Heller, 193–219. Stanford, CA: Stanford University Press, 2003.

Fu, Hualing, and Richard Cullen. "From Mediatory to Adjudicatory Justice: The Limits of Civil Justice Reform in China." In *Chinese Justice: Civil Dispute Resolution in Contemporary China*, edited by Margaret Y. K. Woo and Mary E. Gallagher, 25–57. New York: Cambridge University Press, 2011.

Furtado, Xavier, and James W. Smith. "Ethiopia: Aid, Ownership, and Sovereignty." GEG Working Paper no. 28, Global Economic Governance Programme, University of Oxford, 2007.

Gagliardone, Iginio. *China, Africa, and the Future of the Internet: New Media, New Politics*. London: Zed Books, 2019.

———. *The Politics of Technology in Africa: Communication, Development, and Nation-Building in Ethiopia*. Cambridge: Cambridge University Press, 2016.

Galanter, Marc. "Why the Haves Come Out Ahead: Speculations on the Limits of Legal Change." *Law & Society Review* 9, no. 1 (1974): 95–160.

Gambino, Elisa, and Costanza Franceschini. "Flexible Embeddedness: How Chinese Lead Firms Internationalise in Africa." *Review of International Political Economy*. DOI: https://doi.org/10.1080/09692290.2025.2538187.

Gao, Xueqiang. "*Rengong zhineng shidai de zhongguo sifa* [Chinese justice in the era of artificial intelligence]." *Falü Shiyong* [*Journal of Law Application*] 1 (2019): 58–64.

Gardner, Leigh. *Sovereignty Without Power: Liberia in the Age of Empires, 1822–1980*. Cambridge: Cambridge University Press, 2022.

Gardner, Tom. *The Abiy Project: God, Power and War in the New Ethiopia*. London: Hurst, 2024.

Gebissa, Ezekiel. "National Integration Through Political Marginalization: Contradictions of Nation-Building in Ethiopia." *Northeast African Studies* 21, no. 2 (2021): 151–81.

Gebrekidan, Fikru. "In Defense of Ethiopia: A Comparative Assessment of Caribbean and African American Anti-Fascist Protests, 1935–1941." *Northeast African Studies* 2, no. 1 (1995): 145–73.

Gebreluel, Goitom. "Ethiopia's Grand Renaissance Dam: Ending Africa's Oldest Geopolitical Rivalry?" *The Washington Quarterly* 37, no. 2 (2014): 25–37.

Geda, Alemayehu, and Atenafu G. Meskel. "Impact of China–Africa Investment Relations: Case Study of Ethiopia." Working Paper, Department of Economics, Addis Ababa University, 2010.

Gedamu, Yohannes. *The Politics of Contemporary Ethiopia: Ethnic Federalism and Authoritarian Survival.* London: Routledge, 2021.

Gemeda, Anteneh Geremew, "Contempt of Court: The Interpretative Practice in East Gojjam Courts, Ethiopia." *Elixir Law* 133 (2019): 53529–38.

Gerbi, Yohannes Tessema. "Immunities and Privileges of UN Agencies in Ethiopia: Problems and Possible Remedies." *International Journal of Ethiopian Legal Studies* 3, no. 1 (2018): 1–27.

Geremew, Birhanu Bitew. "The Tragedy of Colonialism in a Non-Colonised Society: Italy's Historical Narratives and the Amhara Genocide in Ethiopia." *Journal of Asian and African Studies* 59, no. 6 (2024): 1892–1907.

Giannecchini, Philip, and Ian Taylor. "The Eastern Industrial Zone in Ethiopia: Catalyst for Development?" *Geoforum* 88 (2018): 28–35.

Giese, Karsten, and Alena Thiel. "The Vulnerable Other: Distorted Equity in Chinese-Ghanaian Employment Relations." *Ethnic and Racial Studies* 37, no. 6 (2014): 1101–20.

Gillman, Howard. "What's Law Got to Do with It? Judicial Behavioralists Test the 'Legal Model' of Judicial Decision Making." *Law and Social Inquiry* 26, no. 2 (2001): 465–504.

Glynn, Adam N., and Maya Sen. "Identifying Judicial Empathy: Does Having Daughters Cause Judges to Rule for Women's Issues?" *American Journal of Political Science* 59, no. 1 (2015): 37–54.

Gonzalez-Vicente, Ruben. "The Limits to China's Non-Interference Foreign Policy: Pro-State Interventionism and the Rescaling of Economic Governance." *Australian Journal of International Affairs* 69, no. 2 (2015): 205–23.

———. "Make Development Great Again? Accumulation Regimes, Spaces of Sovereign Exception and the Elite Development Paradigm of China's Belt and Road Initiative." *Business and Politics* 21, no. 4 (2019): 487–513.

———. "Varieties of Capital and Predistribution: The Foundations of Chinese Infrastructural Investment in the Caribbean." *Made in China Journal* 5, no. 1 (2020): 164–68.

Goodfellow, Tom, and Zhengli Huang. "Contingent Infrastructure and the Dilution of 'Chineseness': Reframing Roads and Rail in Kampala and Addis Ababa." *Environment and Planning A: Economy and Space* 53, no. 4 (2021): 655–74.

Graeber, David. *Toward an Anthropological Theory of Value.* London: Macmillan, 2001.

Grossman, Katrin, and Elena Trubina. "Dignity in Urban Geography: Starting a Conversation." *Dialogues in Human Geography* 12, no. 3 (2022): 406–26.

Guesh, Abel. *Inakhedkha M'tsbay* [You came to see me]. Mekelle: Fareast Trading, 2017.

Gukurume, Simbarashe. "Chinese Migrants and the Politics of Everyday Life in Zimbabwe." *Asian Ethnicity* 20, no. 1 (2019): 85–102.

Gupta, Akhil. *Red Tape: Bureaucracy, Structural Violence, and Poverty in India.* Durham, NC: Duke University Press, 2012.

Hagmann, Tobias, and Benedikt Korf. "Agamben in the Ogaden: Violence and Sovereignty in the Ethiopian-Somali Frontier." *Political Geography* 31, no. 4 (2012): 205–14.

Hailu, Tesfaye. "Foreign Direct Investment (FDI) Outlook in Ethiopia: An Evidence from Oromia Region Selected Special Zones." *International Journal of African and Asian Studies* 35 (2017): 31–39.

Halegua, Aaron, and Xiaohui Ban. "Labour Protections for Overseas Chinese Workers: Legal Framework and Judicial Practice." *The Chinese Journal of Comparative Law* 8, no. 2 (2020): 304–30.

Hanisch, Sarah. *Searching for Sweetness: Women's Mobile Lives in China and Lesotho*. Hong Kong: Hong Kong University Press, 2022.

Hansen, Thomas Blom. "Sovereignty in a Minor Key." *Public Culture* 33, no. 1 (2021): 41–61.

Hansen, Thomas Blom, and Finn Stepputat. "Sovereignty Revisited." *Annual Review of Anthropology* 35 (2006): 295–315.

Hardy, Vincent, and Jostein Hauge. "Labour Challenges in Ethiopia's Textile and Leather Industries: No Voice, No Loyalty, No Exit?" *African Affairs* 184/473 (2019): 712–36.

Haruyama, Justin Lee. "Shortcut English: Pidgin Language, Racialization, and Symbolic Economies at a Chinese-Operated Mine in Zambia." *African Studies Review* 66, no. (2023): 18–44.

Haugen, Heidi Østbø, and Jørgen Carling. "On the Edge of the Chinese Diaspora: The Surge of Baihuo Business in an African City." *Ethnic and Racial Studies* 28, no. 4 (2005): 639–62.

He, Xin and Jing Feng. "Unfamiliarity and Procedural Justice: Litigants' Attitudes Toward Civil Justice in Southern China." *Law & Society Review* 55, no. 1 (2021): 104–38.

Heinonen, Paula. *Youth Gangs and Street Children: Culture, Nurture and Masculinity in Ethiopia*. Oxford: Berghahn, 2013.

Henderson, Lynne. "The Dialogue of Heart and Head." *Cardozo Law Review* 10, no. 1–2 (1988): 123–48.

Hendriks, Thomas. *Rainforest Capitalism: Power and Masculinity in a Congolese Timber Concession*. Durham, NC: Duke University Press, 2022.

Hill, Kathrin, and David Pilling. "China Applies Brakes to Africa Lending." *Financial Times*, January 11, 2022.

Hobbes, Thomas. *Leviathan*. London: Penguin, 2017.

Hoben, Allan. "Social Stratification in Traditional Amhara Society." In *Social Stratification in Africa*, edited by Arthur Tuden and Leonard Plotnicov, 187–224. New York: Free Press, 1970.

Hodzi, Obert. "African Political Elites and the Making(s) of the China Model in Africa." *Politics & Policy* 48, no. 5 (2020): 887–907.

———. *The End of China's Non-Intervention Policy in Africa*. London: Macmillan, 2019.

Howard, Sarah. "Stable Jobs, Precarious Lives: Rural Public Servants in Ethiopia." PhD diss., Goldsmiths, University of London, 2020.

Hoyle, Mark. *Mixed Courts of Egypt*. Leiden: Brill, 1991.

Hsu, Carolyn L. "Capitalism Without Contracts Versus Capitalists Without Capitalism: Comparing the Influence of Chinese *Guanxi* and Russian *Blat* on Marketization." *Communist and Post-Communist Studies* 38 (2005): 309–27.

Huang, Chuling, Yan Huang, and Jingyi Mai. "China-Africa Encounter and Worker Resistance: A Case Study of Wildcat Strikes Against a Chinese-Owned Company in Ethiopia." *Journal of Contemporary China* 33, no. 147 (2024): 448–64.

Huang, Mingwei. *Reconfiguring Racial Capitalism: South Africa in the Chinese Century*. Durham, NC: Duke University Press, 2024.

Huang, Zhengli. "Rwanda Market in Addis Ababa: Between Chinese Migrants and a Local Food Network." *China Perspectives* 4 (2019): 17–25.

Humphrey, Caroline. "Sovereignty." In *A Companion to the Anthropology of Politics*, edited by David Nugent and Joan Vincent, 418–36. Malden, MA: Blackwell, 2007.

Ishiyama, John, and Post Basnet. "Ethnic Versus National Identity in Ethiopia: Is Ethnic Identity Growing and Among Whom?" *African Security Review* 31, no. 1 (2022): 82–98.

Jalata, Gedion G. "Development Assistance from the South: Comparative Analysis of Chinese and Indian to Ethiopia." *Chinese Studies* 3, no. 1 (2014): 24–39.

Jembere, Aberra. *An Introduction to the Legal History of Ethiopia, 1434–1974*. Münster: LIT Verlag, 2000.

Johnson, Alix. "The Mechanics of Sovereignty: Autonomy and Interdependence Across Three Cables to Iceland." *American Anthropologist* 123, no. 3 (2021): 578–89.

Jonas, Raymond. *The Battle of Adwa: African Victory in the Age of Empire*. Cambridge, MA: Harvard University Press, 2011.

Kahn, S. Jeffrey. *Islands of Sovereignty: Haitian Migration and the Borders of Empire*. Chicago: University of Chicago Press, 2018.

Kanokanga, Prince. "The China-Africa Joint Arbitration Centre (CAJAC)." *Pretoria Student Law Review* 16 (2022): 144–63.

Kant, Immanuel. *Groundwork for the Metaphysics of Morals*. Translated by Christopher Bennett. Oxford: Oxford University Press, 2019.

Kapiszewski, Diana. "Tactical Balancing: High Court Decision Making on Politically Crucial Cases." *Law & Society Review* 45, no. 2 (2011): 471–506.

Kaushal, Asha. "The Politics of Jurisdiction." *Modern Law Review* 78, no. 5 (2015): 759–92.

Ke-Schutte, Jay. *Angloscene: Compromised Personhood in Afro-Chinese Translations*. Oakland: University of California Press, 2023.

Kefale, Asnake. *Federalism and Ethnic Conflict in Ethiopia: A Comparative Regional Study*. London: Routledge, 2013.

Kenaw, Setargew. "The Rite of 'Footwashing' at *Abinet* Schools and Its Ethics of Humility." In *Ethnic Diversity, National Unity: Moral Pedagogies of Togetherness for Ethiopians*, edited by Theodrow A. Teklu, 182–200. Eugene, OR: Wipf and Stock, 2020.

Kidane, Won L. "The Legal Framework for the Protection of Foreign Direct Investment in China." In *The Oxford Handbook of the Ethiopian Economy*, edited by Fantu Cheru, Christopher Cramer, and Arkebe Oqubay, 742–62. Oxford: Oxford University Press, 2019.

———. "China's Bilateral Investment Treaties with African States in Comparative Context." *Cornell International Law Journal* 49, no. 1 (2016): 141–78.

———. *China-Africa Dispute Settlement: The Law, Economics and Culture of Arbitration*, Alphen aan de Rijn: Wolters Kluwer, 2011.

Kimari, Wangui. "'Under Construction': Everyday Anxieties and the Proliferating Social Meanings of China in Kenya." *Africa* 91, no. 1 (2021): 135–52.

Kimari, Wangui, and Henrik Ernstson. "Imperial Remains and Imperial Invitations: Centering Race Within the Contemporary Large-Scale Infrastructures of East Africa." *Antipode* 52, no. 3 (2020): 825–46.

Kipnis, Andrew. "The Language of Gifts: Managing *Guanxi* in a North China Village." *Modern China* 22, no. 3 (1996): 285–314.

Kirsch, Stuart. *Mining Capitalism: The Relationship Between Corporations and Their Critics*. Berkeley: University of California Press, 2014.

Krasner, Stephen. *Sovereignty: Organized Hypocrisy*. Princeton, NJ: Princeton University Press, 1999.

Łągiewska, Magdalena. "International Dispute Resolution of BRI-Related Cases: Changes and Challenges." *Journal of Contemporary China* 33, no. 149 (2024): 809–22.

Lam, Katy N. "Chinese Adaptations: African Agency, Fragmented Community and Social Capital Creation in Ghana." *Journal of Current Chinese Affairs* 44, no. 1 (2015): 9–41.

———. *Chinese State–Owned Enterprises in West Africa: Triple-Embedded Globalization.* London: Routledge, 2017.

Large, Daniel. *China and Africa: The New Era.* Cambridge: Polity, 2021.

Lauria, Valeria. "Chinese Financing in Ethiopia's Infrastructure Sector: Agency Distribution Within and Outside the State." *Third World Quarterly* 44, no. 3 (2023): 594–611.

Lavers, Tom. "Agricultural Investment in Ethiopia: Undermining National Sovereignty or Tool for State Building?" *Development and Change* 47, no. 5 (2016): 1078–1101.

———. *Dams, Power, and the Politics of Ethiopia's Renaissance.* Oxford: Oxford University Press, 2024.

———. *Ethiopia's "Developmental State": Political Order and Distributive Crisis.* Cambridge: Cambridge University Press, 2023.

Lazarus-Black, Mindie. "Why Women Take Men to Magistrate's Court: Caribbean Kinship Ideology and Law." *Ethnology* 30, no. 2 (1991): 119–33.

Lee, Ching Kwan. "Raw Encounters: Chinese Managers, African Workers and the Politics of Casualization in Africa's Chinese Enclaves." *The China Quarterly* 199 (2009): 647–66.

———. *The Specter of Global China: Politics, Labor, and Foreign Investment in Africa.* Chicago: Chicago University Press, 2017.

Lee, Ching Kwan, and Yonghong Zhang. "The Power of Instability: Unraveling the Microfoundations of Bargained Authoritarianism in China." *American Journal of Sociology* 118, no. 6 (2013): 1475–1508.

Leutert, Wendy. *China's State-Owned Enterprises: Leadership, Reform, and Internationalization.* Cambridge: Cambridge University Press, 2024.

Levenson, Laurie. "Courtroom Demeanor: The Theater of the Courtroom." *Minnesota Law Review* 92, no. 3 (2008): 573–633.

Levine, Donald N. *Wax and Gold: Tradition and Innovation in Ethiopian Culture.* Chicago: University of Chicago Press, 1972.

Levinson, Justin D., and Danielle Young. "Different Shades of Bias: Skin Tone, Implicit Racial Bias, and Judgments of Ambiguous Evidence." *West Virginia Law Review* 112, no. 2 (2010): 307–50.

Li, Hak Yin. *China's New World Order: Changes in the Non-Intervention Policy.* Cheltenham: Edward Elgar, 2021.

Li, Hangwei, and Xuefei Shi. "Home Away from Home: The Social and Political Roles of Contemporary Chinese Associations in Zambia." *Journal of Current Chinese Affairs* 48, no. 2 (2020): 148–70.

Li, Ji. "'Going Out' and Going In-House: Chinese Multinationals' Internal Legal Capacity in the United States." *Law & Social Inquiry* 46, no. 2 (2021): 487–517.

Li, Lianjiang, Mingxing Liu, and Kevin J. O'Brien. "Petitioning Beijing: The High Tide of 2003–2006." *The China Quarterly* 210 (2012): 313–34.

Liu, Haifang. "Africa and China: Winding into a Community of Common Destiny." In *Africa and the World: Bilateral and Multilateral International Diplomacy*, edited by Dawn Nagar and Charles Mutasa, 71–93. London: Macmillan, 2018.

Liu, Sida. "Lawyers, State Officials and Significant Others: Symbiotic Exchanges in the Chinese Legal Services Market." *The China Quarterly* 206 (2011): 276–93.

Liu, Ying-Ying Tiffany. "(Mis)communicating Through Conflicts: Chinese Restaurant Owners and Zimbabwean Employees in Johannesburg." *Africa Journal of Management* 4, no. 4 (2018): 426–46.

Lonsdale, John. "Agency in Tight Corners: Narrative and Initiative in African History." *Journal of African Cultural Studies* 13, no. 1 (2000): 5–16.

Lu, Vivian Chenxue. "Emplacing Capital: Securing Commerce and Citizenship in the Nigerian Megacity." *American Ethnologist* 49, no. 4 (2022): 491–507.

Lubman, Stanley B. *Bird in a Cage: Legal Reform in China after Mao.* Stanford, CA: Stanford University Press, 1999.

Lund, Christian. *Nine-Tenths of the Law: Enduring Dispossession in Indonesia.* New Haven, CT: Yale University Press, 2021.

Lyons, Terrence. "Closing the Transition: The May 1995 Elections in Ethiopia." *The Journal of Modern African Studies* 34, no. 1 (1996): 121–42.

Macaulay, Stewart. "Non-Contractual Relations in Business: A Preliminary Study." *American Sociological Review* 28, no. 1 (1963): 55–67.

Mains, Daniel. "Blackouts and Progress: Privatization, Infrastructure, and a Developmentalist State in Jimma, Ethiopia." *Cultural Anthropology* 27, no. 1 (2012): 3–27.

———. *Hope Is Cut: Youth, Unemployment, and the Future in Urban Ethiopia.* Philadelphia: Temple University Press, 2012.

———. *Under Construction: Technologies of Development in Urban Ethiopia.* Durham, NC: Duke University Press, 2019.

Mains, Daniel, and Robel Mulat. "The Ethiopian Developmental State and Struggles over the Reproduction of Young Migrant Women's Labor at the Hawassa Industrial Park." *Journal of Eastern African Studies* 15, no. 3 (2021): 359–77.

Makahamadze, Tompson, and Muluken Fikade. "Popular Protests in the Amhara Region and Political Reforms in Ethiopia, 2016–2018." *Journal of Eastern African Studies* 16, no. 1 (2022): 115–37.

Malara, Diego Maria, and Tom Boylston. "Vertical Love: Forms of Submission and Top-Down Power in Orthodox Ethiopia." *Social Analysis* 60, no. 4 (2016): 40–57.

Marsden, Philip. *The Barefoot Emperor: An Ethiopian Tragedy.* New York: Harper Perennial, 2008.

Massoud, Mark Fathi. *Law's Fragile State: Colonial, Authoritarian, and Humanitarian Legacies in Sudan.* Cambridge: Cambridge University Press, 2013.

Mathur, Nayanika. *Paper Tiger: Law, Bureaucracy and the Developmental State in Himalayan India.* Cambridge: Cambridge University Press, 2015.

Maurer, Bill. "Cyberspatial Sovereignties: Offshore Finance, Digital Cash, and the Limits of Liberalism." *Indiana Journal of Global Legal Studies* 5, no. 2 (1998): 493–520.

———. "Due Diligence and 'Reasonable Man,' Offshore." *Cultural Anthropology* 20, no. 4 (2008): 474–505.

———. "Re-Regulating Offshore Finance?" *Geography Compass* 2, no. 1 (2008): 155–75.

Mauss, Marcel. *The Gift: The Form and Reason for Exchange in Archaic Societies.* London: Routledge, 2002.

Mbembe, Achille. *Out of the Dark Night: Essays on Decolonization.* New York: Columbia University Press, 2021.

McCann, Michael W. *Rights at Work: Pay Equity and the Politics of Legal Mobilization.* Chicago: Chicago University Press, 1994.

Merry, Sally E. *Getting Justice and Getting Even: Legal Consciousness Among Working-Class Americans.* Chicago: Chicago University Press, 1990.

Merry, Sally E., and Susan S. Silbey. "What Do Plaintiffs Want? Reexamining the Concept of Dispute." *The Justice System Journal* 9, no. (1984): 151–78.

Michelson, Ethan. "Lawyers, Political Embeddedness, and Institutional Continuity in China's Transition from Socialism." *American Journal of Sociology* 113, no. 2 (2007): 352–414.

Miller, Sarah Clark. "Reconsidering Dignity Relationally." *Ethics and Social Welfare* 11, no. 2 (2017): 108–21.

Minzner, Carl F. "Xinfang: An Alternative to Formal Chinese Legal Institutions." *Stanford Journal of International Law* 42, no. 1 (2006): 103–80.

Mitta, Gifawosen Markos. "Labor Rights, Working Conditions, and Workers' Power in the Emerging Textile and Apparel Industries in Ethiopia: The Case of Hawassa Industrial Park." *New Research in Global Political Economy*, Working Paper No. 01/2019, 2019.

Moges, Mulatu Alemayehu. "Ethiopian Journalism from Self-Censoring to Silence: A Case of Reporting on Internal Conflict." *Journal for Communication Studies* 10, no. 1 (2017): 111–28.

Moges, Zola. "Shaping Amhara Nationalism for a Better Ethiopia." *Ethiopia Insight*, September 1, 2020.

Mohan, Giles. "Beyond the Enclave: Towards a Critical Political Economy of China and Africa." *Development and Change* 44, no. 6 (2013): 1255–72.

Moreda, Tsegaye. "Large-Scale Land Acquisitions, State Authority and Indigenous Local Communities: Insights from Ethiopia." *Third World Quarterly* 38, no. 3 (2017): 698–716.

Moyer, Laura P., and Susan B. Haire. "Trailblazers and Those That Followed: Personal Experiences, Gender, and Judicial Empathy." *Law & Society Review* 49, no. 3 (2015): 665–89.

Mulualem, Melaku. *Africa–China Relations: Ethiopia as a Case Study.* Published by the author, 2023.

Mulugeta, Daniel. "Everyday Conceptions of the State in Ethiopia: Corruption Discourses, Moral Idioms and the Ideals of *Mengist.*" *Critical African Studies* 11, no. 3 (2019): 285–300.

———. *The Everyday State in Africa: Governance Practices and State Ideas in Ethiopia.* London: Routledge, 2020.

Mumuni, Sigli M. "China's Non-Intervention Policy in Africa: Principle Versus Pragmatism." *African Journal of Political Science and International Relations* 2, no. 9 (2017): 258–73.

Nader, Laura, and Harry F. Todd (eds.). *The Disputing Process—Law in Ten Societies.* New York: Columbia University Press, 1978.

Ng, Kwai Hang, and Xin He. *Embedded Courts: Judicial Decision-Making in China.* Cambridge: Cambridge University Press, 2017.

———. "The Institutional and Cultural Logics of Legal Commensuration: Blood Money and Negotiated Justice in China." *American Journal of Sociology* 122, no. 4 (2017): 1104–43.

Nielsen, Morten. "Roadside Inventions: Making Time and Money Work at a Road Construction Site in Mozambique." *Mobilities* 7, no. 4 (2012): 467–80.

Nyíri, Pál. "Enclaves of Improvement: Sovereignty and Developmentalism in the Special Zones of the China-Lao Borderlands." *Comparative Studies in Society and History* 54, no. 3: 533–62.

O'Brien, Kevin, and Lianjiang Li. *Rightful Resistance in Rural China.* Cambridge: Cambridge University Press, 2006.

Okoth, Edwin. "SGR Pact with China a Risk to Kenyan Sovereignty, Assets." *Nation*, January 12, 2019 (updated on June 28, 2020).

Ong, Aihwa. "Graduated Sovereignty in South-East Asia." *Theory, Culture & Society* 17, no. 4 (2000): 55–75.

———. *Neoliberalism as Exception: Mutations in Citizenship and Sovereignty*. Durham, NC: Duke University Press, 2006.

Oqubay, Arkebe. *Made in Africa: Industrial Policy in Ethiopia*. Oxford: Oxford University Press, 2015.

Oya, Carlos and Florian Schaefer. "Do Chinese Firms in Africa Pay Lower Wages? A Comparative Analysis of Manufacturing and Construction Firms in Angola and Ethiopia." *World Development* 168 (2023): 106266.

———. "The Politics of Labour Relations in Global Production Networks: Collective Action, Industrial Parks, and Local Conflict in the Ethiopian Apparel Sector." *World Development* 146 (2021): 105564.

Pang, Laikwan. *One and All: The Logic of Chinese Sovereignty*. Redwood City, CA: Stanford University Press, 2024.

Pankhurst, Alula. "Introduction: Dimensions and Conceptions of Marginalisation." In *Peripheral People: The Excluded Minorities of Ethiopia*, edited by Dena Freeman and Alula Pankhurst, 1–26. Lawrenceville, NJ: The Red Sea Press, 2003.

Pankhurst, Richard. "Menilek and the Utilisation of Foreign Skills in Ethiopia." *Journal of Ethiopian Studies* 5, no. 1 (1967): 29–86.

Papagianneas, Straton. "Towards Smarter and Fairer Justice? A Review of the Chinese Scholarship on Building Smart Courts and Automating Justice." *Journal of Current Chinese Affairs* 51, no. 2 (2022): 327–47.

Pavel, Carmen. *Divided Sovereignty: International Institutions and the Limits of State Authority*. Oxford: Oxford University Press, 2014.

Pérez, Miguel. "Toward a Life with Dignity: Housing Struggles and New Political Horizons in Urban Chile." *American Ethnologist* 45, no. 4 (2018): 508–20.

———. *The Right to Dignity: Housing Struggles, City Making, and Citizenship in Urban Chile*. Redwood City, CA: Stanford University Press, 2022.

Perham, Margery. *The Government of Ethiopia*. London: Faber and Faber, 1969.

Peters, Julie Stone. "Legal Performance Good and Bad." *Law, Culture and the Humanities* 4 (2008): 179–200.

Philips, Susan U. *Ideology in the Language of Judges: How Judges Practice Law, Politics, and Courtroom Control*. Oxford: Oxford University Press, 1998.

Plaut, Martin, and Sarah Vaughan. *Understanding Ethiopia's Tigray War*. London: Hurst, 2023.

Plumm, Karyn M., and Cheryl A. Terrance. "Battered Women Who Kill: The Impact of Expert Testimony and Empathy Induction in the Courtroom." *Violence Against Women* 15, no. 2 (2009): 186–205.

Posner, Richard A. *How Judges Think*. Cambridge, MA: Harvard University Press, 2009.

———. *The Problems of Jurisprudence*. Cambridge, MA: Harvard University Press, 1990.

Potts, Shaina. *Judicial Territory: Law, Capital, and the Expansion of American Empire*. Durham, NC: Duke University Press, 2024.

Repnikova, Maria. *Competing for Soft Power: China's Uneven Image-Making in Africa*. Cambridge: Cambridge University Press, in press.

Richland, Justin. "Dignity as (Self-)Determination: Hopi Sovereignty in the Face of US Dispossessions." *Law & Social Inquiry* 41, no. 4 (2016): 917–38.

———. "Hopi Tradition as Jurisdiction: On the Potentializing Limits of Hopi Sovereignty." *Law & Social Inquiry* 36, no. 1 (2011): 201–34.

———. "Jurisdiction: Grounding Law in Language." *Annual Review of Anthropology* 42 (2013): 209–26.

Robinson, Cedric J. *Black Marxism: The Making of the Black Radical Tradition*. London: Penguin, 2021.

Rogelja, Igor. "Concrete and Coal: China's Infrastructural Assemblages in the Balkans." *Political Geography* 81 (2020), 102220.

Roitman, Janet. *Fiscal Disobedience: An Anthropology of Economic Regulation in Central Africa*. Princeton, NJ: Princeton University Pres, 2005.

Rosen, Lawrence. 1989. *The Anthropology of Justice: Law as Culture in Islamic Society*. Cambridge: Cambridge University Press.

Ross, Mitchell S. "Rethinking Diplomatic Immunity: A Review of Remedial Approaches to Address the Abuses of Diplomatic Privileges and Immunities." *American University Journal of International Law and Policy* 4, no. 1 (1989): 173–206.

Ruskola, Teemu. *Legal Orientalism: China, the United States, and Modern Law*. Cambridge, MA: Harvard University Press, 2013.

Rutherford, Danilyn. *Laughing at Leviathan: Sovereignty and Audience in West Papua*. Chicago: University of Chicago Press, 2012.

Saksena, Priyasha. "Jousting over Jurisdiction: Sovereignty and International Law in Late Nineteenth-Century South Asia." *Law and History Review* 38, no. 2 (2020): 409–57.

Sawyer, Suzana. "Disabling Corporate Sovereignty in a Transnational Lawsuit." *Political and Legal Anthropology Review* 29, no. 1 (2006): 23–43.

———. *The Small Matter of Suing Chevron*. Durham, NC: Duke University Press, 2022.

Schmitt, Carl. *Political Theology: Four Chapters on the Concept of Sovereignty*. Translated by George Schwab. Chicago: University of Chicago Press, 1985.

Schmitz, Cheryl Mei-ting. "Kufala! Translating witchcraft in an Angolan-Chinese Labor Dispute." *Hau: Journal of Ethnographic Theory* 10, no. 2 (2020): 473–86.

———. "Making Friends, Building Roads: Chinese Entrepreneurship and the Search for Reliability in Angola." *American Anthropologist* 123, no. 2 (2021): 343–54.

———. "Significant Others: Security and Suspicion in Chinese-Angolan Encounters." *Journal of Current Chinese Affairs* 43, no. 1 (2014): 41–69.

Scholler, Heinrich. *The Special Court of Ethiopia, 1920–1935*. Stuttgart: Franz Steiner Verlag, 1985.

Sedler, Robert Allen. "The Chilot Jurisdiction of the Emperor of Ethiopia: A Legal Analysis in Historical and Comparative Perspective." *Journal of African Law* 8, no. 2 (1964): 59–76.

Segal, Jeffrey A., and Harold J. Speath. *The Supreme Court and the Attitudinal Model*. New York: Cambridge University Press, 1993.

Seppänen, Samuli. "Chinese Legal Development Assistance: Which Rule of Law? Whose Pragmatism?" *Vanderbilt Journal of Transnational Law* 51, no. 1 (2018): 101–58.

Setegn, Mekuria Tsegaye. "Legislative Inaction and Judicial Legislation Under the Ethiopian Private International Law Regime: An Analysis of Selected Decisions of the Federal Supreme Court's Cassation Division." *Journal of Private International Law* 16, no. 1 (2020): 112–37.

Seymour, Lee J. M. "Sovereignty, Territory and Authority: Boundary Maintenance in Contemporary Africa." *Critical African Studies* 5, no. 1 (2013): 17–31.

Shapiro, Martin. *Courts: A Comparative and Political Analysis*. Chicago: Chicago University Press, 1981.

Sheridan, Derek. "'If You Greet Them, They Ignore You': Chinese Migrants, (Refused) Greetings, and the Inter-Personal Ethics of Global Inequality." *Anthropological Quarterly* 91, no. 1 (2018): 237–65.

———. "The Semiotics of Heiren (黑人): Race, Everyday Language, and Discursive Complicities in a Chinese Migrant Community." *Journal of Ethnic and Migration Studies* 49, no. 13 (2023): 3308–26.

———. "Weak Passports and Bad Behavior: Chinese Migrants and the Moral Politics of Petty Corruption in Tanzania." *American Ethnologist* 46, no. 2 (2009): 137–49.

Shever, Elana. "Engendering the Company: Corporate Personhood and the 'Face' of an Oil Company in Metropolitan Buenos Aires." *Political and Legal Anthropology Review* 33, no. 1 (2010): 26–46.

———. "Neoliberal Associations: Property, Company, and Family in the Argentine Oil Fields." *American Ethnologist* 35, no. 4 (2008): 701–16.

Shi, Xuefei, and Paul Hoebink. "From Chengdu to Kampala: The Role of Subnational Actors in China's Foreign Aid." *Journal of Contemporary China* 29, no. 121 (2020): 125–40.

Simpson, Audra. *Mohawk Interruptus: Political Life Across the Borders of Settler States*. Durham, NC: Duke University Press, 2014.

Singh, Ajit. "The Myth of 'Debt-Trap Diplomacy' and Realities of Chinese Development Finance." *Third World Quarterly* 42, no. 1 (2021): 239–53.

Smart, Alan. "Gifts, Bribes, and Guanxi: A Reconsideration of Bourdieu's Social Capital." *Cultural Anthropology* 8, no. 3 (1993): 388–408.

Soulé, Folashadé. "'Africa+1' Summit Diplomacy and the 'New Scramble' Narrative: Recentering African Agency." *African Affairs* 199/477 (2020): 633–46.

Spencer, John H. *Ethiopia at Bay: A Personal Account of the Haile Selassie Years*. Addis Ababa: Tsehai, 1984.

Statz, Michele. "On Shared Suffering: Judicial Intimacy in the Rural Northland." *Law & Society Review* 55, no. 1 (2021): 5–37.

Steinmüller, Hans. "Sovereignty as Care: Acquaintances, Mutuality, and Scale in the Wa State of Myanmar." *Comparative Studies in Society and History* 64, no. 4 (2022): 910–33.

Stern, Rachel E., Benjamin L. Liebman, Margaret E. Roberts, and Alice Z. Wang. "Automating Fairness? Artificial Intelligence in the Chinese Courts." *Columbia Journal of Transnational Law* 59, no. 3 (2021): 515–53.

Stiglitz, Joseph E. *Globalization and Its Discontents Revisited: Anti-Globalization in the Era of Trump*. London: Penguin, 2017.

Strauss, Julia C. "The Past in the Present: Historical and Rhetorical Lineages in China's Relations with Africa." *The China Quarterly* 199 (2009): 777–95.

Tadiar, Neferti. *Remaindered Life*. Durham, NC: Duke University Press, 2022.

Tamanaha, Brian Z. *Beyond the Formalist-Realist Divide: The Role of Politics in Judging*. Princeton, NJ: Princeton University Press, 2009.

Tang, Keyi. "Lessons from East Asia: Comparing Ethiopia and Vietnam's Early-Stage Special Economic Zone Development." China Africa Research Initiative working paper, no. 26, 2019.

Tang, Xiaoyang. *Coevolutionary Pragmatism: Approaches and Impacts of China-Africa Economic Cooperation.* Cambridge: Cambridge University Press, 2020.

Tarrósy, István. "China's Belt and Road Initiative in Africa, Debt Risk and New Dependency: The Case of Ethiopia." *African Studies Quarterly* 19, no. 3–4 (2020): 8–28.

Taylor, Ian. *Africa Rising? BRICS—Diversifying Dependency.* Martlesham: Boydell & Brewer, 2014.

———. "Kenya's New Lunatic Express: The Standard Gauge Railway 1." In *Africa's Railway Renaissance,* edited by Tim Zajontz, Pádraig Carmody, Mandira Bagwandeen, Anthony Leysens, 179–200. Milton Park: Taylor & Francis, 2023.

Taylor, Ian, and Tim Zajontz. "In a Fix: Africa's Place in the Belt and Road Initiative and the Reproduction of Dependency." *South African Journal of International Affairs* 27, no. 3 (2020): 277–95.

Tazebew, Tezera. "Amhara Nationalism: The Empire Strikes Back." *African Affairs* 120, no. 479 (2021): 297–313.

———. "Infrastructures of Renaissance: Tangible Discourses in the EPRDF's Ethiopia." *Critical African Studies* 14, no. 3 (2022): 250–73.

Terrefe, Biruk. "Urban Layers of Political Rupture: The 'New' Politics of Addis Ababa's Megaprojects." *Journal of Eastern African Studies* 14, no. 3 (2020): 375–95.

Terrefe, Biruk, and Harry Verhoeven. "The Road (Not) Taken: The Contingencies of Infrastructure and Sovereignty in the Horn of Africa." *Political Geography* 110 (2024), 103070.

Tesema, Yonas. "Despotism on the Shop Floor: Foreign Company Labour Governance in Ethiopia's Industrial Park." *Anthropology Today* 40, no. 4 (2024): 1–31.

———. "Unjust Manufacturing: Industrial Workers' Struggle against Exploitation in Ethiopia." *Journal of Anthropological Research* 80, no. 1 (2024): 57–75.

Tesfaye, Aaron. *China in Ethiopia: The Long-Term Perspective.* Albany, NY: SUNY Press, 2020.

Tian, Xin. "Private Security Companies: Emerging Protectors of China's Overseas Interests." *China Quarterly of International Strategic Studies* 6, no. 2 (2020): 205–21.

Tirfesa, Kurabachew. "The Right of Access to Justice and Diplomatic Immunity in Ethiopia: The Need for Revisiting the Existing Remedial Approach." LLM thesis, Addis Ababa University, 2020.

Tura, Hussein Ahmed. "Uniform Application of Law in Ethiopia: Effects of Cassation Decisions of the Federal Supreme Court." *African Journal of Legal Studies* 7 (2014): 203–31.

Turton, David, ed. *Ethnic Federalism: The Ethiopian Experience in Comparative Perspective.* Athens, OH: Ohio University Press, 2006.

Valverde, Mariana. "Jurisdiction and Scale: Legal 'Technicalities' as Resources for Theory." *Social & Legal Studies* 18, no. 2 (2009): 139–57.

Van Boekel, Titus, Veronique Schutjens, and Annelies Zoomers. "Can the Dragon Make the Lion Breathe Fire? The Links of Chinese Entrepreneurs in the Addis Ababa Economy." *The European Journal of Development Research* 35 (2023): 1127–48.

Vanderlinden, Jacques. "Civil Law and Common Law Influences on the Developing Law of Ethiopia." *Buffalo Law Review* 16, no. 1 (1966): 250–66.

Vark, Rene. "Personal Inviolability and Diplomatic Immunity in Respect of Serious Crimes." *Juridica International* 8 (2003): 110–19.

Vaughan, Sarah. "Revolutionary Democratic State-Building: Party, State and People in the EPRDF's Ethiopia." *Journal of Eastern African Studies* 5, no. 4 (2011): 619–40.

Verheul, Susanne. *Performing Power in Zimbabwe: Politics, Law, and the Courts Since 2000*. Cambridge: Cambridge University Press, 2021.

Verhoeven, Harry. "The Grand Ethiopian Renaissance Dam: Africa's Water Tower, Environmental Justice and Infrastructural Power." *Daedalus* 150, no. 4 (2021): 159–80.

Vestal, Theodore M. "Consequences of the British Occupation of Ethiopia During World War II." In *Rediscovering the British Empire*, edited by Barry J. Ward, 43–57. Malabar, FL: Krieger, 2002.

Von Pezold, Johanna, and Miriam Driessen. "Made in China, Fashioned in Africa: Ethnic Dress in Ethiopia and Mozambique." *Africa* 91, no. 2 (2021): 317–36.

Wagaw, Teshome G. "Emerging Issues of Ethiopian Nationalities: Cohesion and Disintegration." *Northeast African Studies* 2/3, no. 3 (1980–81): 69–75.

Waldron, Jeremy. "How Law Protects Dignity." *Cambridge Law Journal* 71, no. 1 (2012): 200–22.

Wang, Jie, and Josh Stenberg. "Localizing Chinese Migrants in Africa: A Study of the Chinese in Libya before the Civil War." *China Information* 28, no. 1 (2014): 69–91.

Wang, Jinpu. "'Hurdles and 'Lubricants': Petty Corruption and Chinese Migrants in Africa." *Sociological Forum* 39, no. 1 (2024): 66–78.

Wang, Lusheng. "*Sifa dashuju yu rengongzheneng jishu yingyong de fengxian ji lunli guizhi* [The dangers and ethical regulation of using judicial big data and artificial intelligence technology]." *Fashang Yanjiu [Law and Business Research]* 2 (2019): 101–12.

Wang, Yuan. *The Railpolitik: Leadership and Agency in Sino-African Infrastructure Development*. Oxford: Oxford University Press, 2024.

Wang, Yuan, and Hong Zhang. "Individual Agency in South-South Policy Transfer: China and Ethiopia's Industrial Park Development." *Review of International Political Economy* 31, no. 5 (2024): 1544–68.

Weill, Sharon. "Transnational Jihadism and the Role of Criminal Judges: An Ethnography of French Courts." *Journal of Law and Society* 47, no. 1 (2020): 30–53.

Weldemichel, Teklehaymanot G. "Tigray War: Modern Geographies of Mass Violence and the Invisibilization of Populations." *Political Geography* 118 (2025), 103298.

Weldesellassie, Isaac. "The Prosecution of the Derg Criminals in Ethiopia." *Uluslararası Suçlar ve Tarih* 9/10 (2010): 135–60.

Welker, Marina. *Enacting the Corporation: An American Mining Firm in Post-Authoritarian Indonesia*. Berkeley: University of California Press, 2014.

Whitfield, Lindsay, Cornelia Staritz, and Mike Morris. "Global Value Chains, Industrial Policy and Economic Upgrading in Ethiopia's Apparel Sector." *Development and Change* 51, no. 4 (2020): 1018–43.

Workneh, Téwodros W. "Chinese Multinationals in the Ethiopian Telecommunications Sector." *Communication, Culture & Critique* 9, no. 1 (2016): 126–47.

———. "From State Repression to Fear of Non-State Actors: Examining Emerging Threats of Journalism Practice in Ethiopia." In *Journalism and Safety*, edited by Oscar Westlund, Roy Krøvel, Kristin Skare Orgeret, 267–84. London: Routledge, 2024.

Wu, Di. *Affective Encounters: Everyday Life Among Chinese Migrants in Zambia*. London: Routledge, 2020.

Wu, Tao, and Man Chen. "*Lun zhihui fayuan de jianyi* [On the construction of smart courts: Value orientation and system design]." *Shehui Kexue [Journal of Social Sciences]* 5 (2019): 105–13.

Wyrod, Robert, and Kimberlee Chang. "Tensions in Sino-African Labour Relations: The View from the Karuma Hydroelectric Dam in Uganda." *Journal of Modern African Studies* 61, no. 4 (2023): 583–604.

Xiao, Allen Hai. "In the Shadow of the States: The Informalities of Chinese Petty Entrepreneurship in Nigeria." *Journal of Current Chinese Affairs* 44, no. 1 (2015): 75–105.

Xu, Yi-Chong. "Chinese State-Owned Enterprises in Africa: Ambassadors or Freebooters?" *Journal of Contemporary China* 23, no. 89 (2014): 822–40.

Yalew, Mesafint Tarekegn, and Changgang Guo. "China's 'Belt and Road Initiative': Implication for Land Locked Ethiopia." *Insights on Africa* 12, no. 2 (2020): 175–93.

Yan, Hairong, and Barry Sautman. "China, Ethiopia and the Significance of the Belt and Road Initiative." *The China Quarterly* 257 (2024): 222–47.

Yan, Xunxiang. *The Flow of Gifts: Reciprocity and Social Networks in a Chinese Village*. Palo Alto, CA: Stanford University Press, 1996.

Yang, Beibei. "Following the State-Owned Enterprises: Chinese Expatriate Construction Workers in Zambia." *Asian and Pacific Migration Journal* 30, no. 4 (2021): 428–49.

Yang, Mayfair Mei-hui. *Gifts, Favors, and Banquets: The Art of Social Relationships in China*. Ithaca, NY: Cornell University Press.

Yang, Yuezhou. "Varieties of Chinese Capital in African Agriculture: A Bounded Improvisation Analysis." *World Development* 195 (2025): 107091.

Ye, Min. *The Belt Road and Beyond: State-Mobilized Globalization in China: 1998–2018*. Cambridge: Cambridge University Press.

Yeh, Emily T. *Taming Tibet: Landscape Transformation and the Gift of Development*. Ithaca, NY: Cornell University Press, 2013.

Yeh, Emily T., and Elizabeth Wharton. "Going West and Going Out: Discourses, Migrants, and Models in Chinese Development." *Eurasian Geography and Economics* 57, no. 3 (2016): 286–315.

Yoon, Kate. "When the Sovereign Contracts: Troubling the Public/Private Distinction in International Law." *Yale Law Journal* 133, no. 6 (2024): 2101–64.

Zeleke, Elleni Centime. *Ethiopia in Theory: Revolution and Knowledge Production, 1964–2016*. Chicago: Haymarket Books, 2020.

Zewde, Bahru. "Concessions and Concession-Hunters in Post-Adwa Ethiopia: The Case of Arnold Holz." *Africa: Rivista trimestrale di studi e documentazione dell'Istituto italiano per l'Africa e l'Oriente* 45, no. 3 (1990): 365–83.

———. *History of Modern Ethiopia, 1855–1991*. Woodbridge: James Currey, 2001.

Zhang, Denghua, and Graeme Smith. "China's Foreign Aid System: Structure, Agencies, and Identities." *Third World Quarterly* 38, no. 10 (2017): 2330–46.

Zhang, Hong. "The Aid-Contracting Nexus: The Role of the International Contracting Industry in China's Overseas Development Engagements." *China Perspectives* 4 (2020): 17–27.

Zhang, Mingyuan. "Burn to Harvest, Burn to Sabotage: Between Fire and Water on a Sugar Planation in Madagascar." *American Anthropologist* 125, no. 1 (2023): 100–11.

Zhang, Taisu. "*Zhongguoren zai xingzheng jiefen zhong weihe pianhao xinfang?* [Why do Chinese prefer to settle disputes through petitioning?]" *Shehuixue Yanjiu* [*Social Research*] 3, no. 3 (2009): 139–62.

Zheng, George G. "China's Grand Design of People's Smart Courts." *Asian Journal of Law and Society* 7 (2020): 561–82.

Zhu, Weidong. "Arbitration as the Best Option for the Settlement of China-African Trade and Investment Disputes." *Journal of African Law* 57, no. 1 (2013): 149–63.

Zi, Yanyin. *Iron Sharpens Iron: Social Interactions at China Shops in Botswana*. Bamenda: Langaa RPCIG, 2017.

Ziso, Edson. "The Political Economy of the Chinese Model in Ethiopia." *Politics & Policy* 48, no. 5 (2020): 908–31.

Founded in 1893,
UNIVERSITY OF CALIFORNIA PRESS
publishes bold, progressive books and journals
on topics in the arts, humanities, social sciences,
and natural sciences—with a focus on social
justice issues—that inspire thought and action
among readers worldwide.

The UC PRESS FOUNDATION
raises funds to uphold the press's vital role
as an independent, nonprofit publisher, and
receives philanthropic support from a wide
range of individuals and institutions—and from
committed readers like you. To learn more, visit
ucpress.edu/supportus.

www.ingramcontent.com/pod-product-compliance
Lightning Source LLC
Chambersburg PA
CBHW030329270326
41926CB00010B/1559